From Mandeville
to Marx

Louis Dumont

From Mandeville to Marx

The Genesis and Triumph of Economic Ideology

The University of Chicago Press
Chicago and London

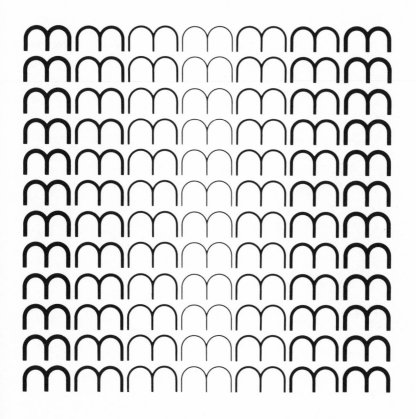

The University of Chicago Press,
Chicago 60637
The University of Chicago Press,
Ltd., London
© 1977 by Louis Dumont
All rights reserved.
Published 1977
Printed in the United States of
America
82 81 80 79 78 77   987654321

Louis Dumont is Director of
Studies at the Ecole des Hautes
Etudes en Sciences Sociales in
Paris. His previous publications
include Homo Hierarchicus,
published by The University of
Chicago Press in 1970.

A French version of this work,
entitled Homo aequalis: Genèse
et épanouissement de l'idéo-
logie économique, is being published by Gallimard.

Library of Congress Cataloging in Publication Data

Dumont, Louis, 1911–
  From Mandeville to Marx.

  Based on a series of lectures delivered at Princeton
University in 1973.
  Bibliography: p.
  Includes index.
  1. Economics—History. I. Title.
HB75.D87   330'.09   76-8087
ISBN 0-226-16981-2

Contents

Preface

> We are craftsmen ... and we are
> building Thee, O high central
> nave.
>
> Rainer Maria Rilke
> *The Book of Hours*

At the end of my book on India, *Homo Hierarchicus,* I outlined what was to be my next task. It was to consist in reversing the perspective and throwing light on our modern, equalitarian type of society by contrasting it with the hierarchical society. I added, somewhat lightheartedly, that this might be done in a book called *Homo aequalis.*

I have now come to a soberer assessment of the situation. I contemplate, not a single book, but several separate studies— slimmer volumes or, in some cases, even articles. Each of these will deal with one aspect of modern ideology, as I shall explain later on. This plan is more in keeping with what I can hope to realize single-handedly in such a vast field—more in keeping with the necessarily incomplete and preliminary character of the work, and also with the need to go into detail here and there. The aim is less to present a finished picture, a more or less acrobatic magnum opus, than to test the approach on a variety of problems.

Here then is the first installment, as it were, of *Homo aequalis,* with an Introduction designed to locate it within the general endeavor. The incentive to write it has come largely from an invitation of the Christian Gauss Seminars in Criticism, of Princeton University, to deliver a series of six lectures in the fall of 1973. I am very grateful to the seminars and to their director, Professor Joseph Frank, for this invitation, and for the hospitality of Princeton University, all the more so because such an enlightened audience is probably the main need of a writer in my present position. I am particularly thankful to the members of the seminars and of the university who cared to extend the discussion and to provide information and whose convergent interests led to very heartening and fruitful exchanges, and to all those who made my stay in Princeton as pleasant and encouraging as it was.

I take this occasion to thank all the persons who helped me in these last years with their friendship, confidence, and kindly help to effect the shift in the subject matter of my research. Most particularly I want to express my abiding indebtedness and gratitude to David M. Schneider in Chicago and Clemens Heller in Paris. The logic and finality of research is one thing; the relation of the researcher to his environment is another. To leave the relatively sheltered waters of a particular branch of social anthropology, in principle a well-defined specialized community where one writes in the first place for one's fellow-specialists—to leave these sheltered waters for the high seas of general intellectual history is not an altogether unproblematic transition, and I wish to add a few words on the point.

For some, an interest in ideas is indicative of, if not equivalent to, a disregard of facts, of hard facts. Unlikely as it may seem, a hostile critic suggested that my most recent book was a piece of apriori theorizing or philosophizing, with occasional factual illustrations. Well, this work in its turn will take care of itself regarding the evidential aspect. But there is more to it. Any general statement or thoroughgoing analysis is liable to be called meta-anthropological or metascientific. As if we were to bend our bodies and lower our heads to the task without ever straightening up again and raising our gaze to the skyline. The relative weakness of the scientific community (or communities) in the social sciences and the current inflation of personality make it all too easy to mistake the craftsman for a "thinker." I fear that, seeing this author hurdling well-established academic boundaries in pursuit of a few strange ideas, the reader might attribute to him a strong belief in his own originality. I hope that what follows will dispel this misrepresentation. The craftsman works for others: if not for a well-defined community, then for a vaguer, more complex audience—and this fact, by the way, determines the level of truth he may possibly reach. He builds no system and raises only limited questions; he wants his product to be usable and therefore feels responsible for each statement he makes. He may fail for having attempted too much, but he should not be trapped in rhetoric or sloppiness. He may thus use a foreign language on occasion, it being a matter of clarity rather than elegance (and with due apology to the readers!). The more ambitious the outlook, the more meticulous the detail must be, and the humbler the craftsman. What is attempted in the following pages—inevitably through a particular agent and at his own risk—is the pursuit, in some of its aspects, of the encounter between two civilizations.

Yet, all in all, this book is inevitably very different from what I have written hitherto. Whatever efforts are made and precautions taken in the detail, the endeavor is disproportionate to the means, in terms of anthropological certainty. It is therefore not only incomplete, but tentative to a degree, and offered as such.

The writing was completed in mid-1974. I have now revised the text by taking advantage of the corrections proposed by an anonymous reviewer and by incorporating some amendments and details that came up in the meantime during the preparation of a French version.

To conclude, I wish to express my thanks to all the persons who have taken an interest in this book and helped at the various stages of preparation for it to come out.

Paris
December 1975

Introduction

Here lies the tragedy of the modern mind, which "solved the enigma of the Universe," but only to replace it by the enigma of itself.

Alexandre Koyré,
Etudes Newtoniennes

A Comparative Approach
to Modern Ideology
and to the Place within It
of Economic Thought

This study is a part of a wider endeavor that determines its orientation. The idea of a study of modern ideology in general has grown out of my work as a social anthropologist. In terms of academic pursuits, the distance is wide between anthropology and an inquiry that would come under the history of ideas, or intellectual history. I must therefore in the first place describe—if not justify—the transition, in order to characterize more precisely the enterprise of which this book represents, so to speak, one installment.

The transition will appear at once less unlikely if one considers that ideas and values constitute an important aspect of social life and that social anthropology is comparative at heart even when it is not explicitly so (see, for example, Dumont 1964, pp. 15–16). For some twenty years I was busy applying social anthropology to the study of a complex type of society, which is historically linked with one of the world's great civilizations: the society of India. This society can be called, from its most prominent morphological aspect, "the caste society." It so happens that this society appears in stark contrast, regarding its values, to the modern type of society. The study reached its conclusion in a book in which I tried to lay bare those values. I called the book *Homo Hierarchicus*, to mean, first, that the real varieties of men that can be distinguished are *social* varieties and, second, that the variety corresponding to the caste society is characterized essentially by its adherence to *hierarchy* as the paramount value, exactly opposite to the *equalitarianism* that is one of the main values in our own, modern type of society.

Actually, the hierarchy/equality contrast, if it is very apparent, is only an aspect of the matter. Underlying this contrast, there is another that is more general in its application. On the one hand, most societies value, in the first place, order: the conformity of every element to its role in the society—in a word, the society as a whole; this is what I call "holism." On the other hand, other societies—at any rate ours—value, in the first place, the individual human being: for us, every man is, in principle, an embodiment of humanity at large, and as such he is equal to every other man, and free. This is what I call "individualism." We may immediately remark that in the holistic type the requirements of man as such are ignored or subordinated, just as are the requirements of society in the individualistic type. Now, it so happens that, among the great civilizations the world has known, the holistic type of society has been overwhelmingly predominant; indeed, it looks as if it had been the rule, the only exception being our modern civilization and its individualistic type of society. This is a central point, to which I shall return. But first to clarify the relation between the holism/individualism contrast and the hierarchy/equalitarianism contrast. There is a logical relation, in the sense that holism entails hierarchy while individualism entails equality; but in fact it is by no means the case that all holistic societies stress hierarchy to the same degree, nor do all individualistic societies stress equality to the same degree. On the one hand, individualism entails not only equality but also liberty; equality and liberty are by no means always convergent, and the combination of them varies from one society of the individualistic type to another. On the other hand, and somewhat similarly, hierarchy appears most of the time intimately combined with other elements. Indian culture, in my view, is characterized by the probably unique phenomenon of a thoroughgoing distinction between hierarchy and power, and it is due to this circumstance that hierarchy appears there in its pure form, exclusive and undiluted. We may say that India stays at the extreme end of holistic societies, while France at the time of her Revolution was, according to Tocqueville, distinguished from England and the United States by an extreme ideological stress on equality at the expense of liberty.

I am sketching only a general perspective, and there is no room here for all the distinctions, qualifications, or methodological precautions that are called for. Yet one point must be made: what I have in view here are wholesale, all-embracing, or encompassing social valuations, not the mere occurrence of a feature or an idea at one level or another of the society or of the ideology. For instance, equality and hierarchy must combine in some manner in any social system, as the ranking of social groups entails equality within each of them (Talcott Parsons 1953, p. 3 n. 1; cf. my *H.H.*, 1967, App. A, § G at end). Thus, it is possible for equality to be valued, even to a great extent, without its being an entailment of individualism. In such cases, however, it will not attain the status of an overall valuation. Thus, in ancient Greece the citizens were equal while the main value stress fell on the polis, and Aristotle did not find slavery contrary to reason. The same is probably true, *mutatis mutandis*, of Islamic civilization. It is so, at any rate, according to a perceptive critic, for the societies of Islamic allegiance of the Middle East (Yalman 1969, p. 125).[1]

Individualism, in its present definition as an overall valuation, goes together with one or two features of great import that will come forth in the following study but that it is perhaps as well to introduce immediately. In most societies, and in the first place in the higher civilizations, which I shall designate henceforth as the "traditional societies," the relations between men are more important, more highly valued, than the relations between men and things. This primacy is reversed in the modern type of society, in which relations between men are subordinated to relations between men and things. This is a point Marx has stressed in his own manner, as will be recalled later on. Closely combined with this reversal of primacy, we find in modern society a new conception of wealth. In the traditional type of society, immovable wealth (estates) is sharply distinguished from movable wealth (money, chattels) by the fact that rights in land are enmeshed in the social organization in such a manner that superior rights accompany power over men. Such rights or "wealth," appearing essentially as a matter of relations between men, are intrinsically superior to movable wealth, which is disparaged, as is natural in such a system for a mere relation between men and things. Again, I find that Marx perceived clearly the exceptional character of those small commercial societies in which movable wealth had attained an autonomous status:

> Wealth appears as an end in itself only among the few merchant peoples ... who live in the pores of the ancient world

like the Jews in medieval society. (*Grundisse*, p. 387, on pre-capitalist formations; similarly, in *Capital*, I, chap. iv, on commodity fetishism)

With the moderns, a revolution occurred in this respect: the link between immovable wealth and power over men was broken, and movable wealth became fully autonomous in itself, as the superior aspect of wealth in general, while immovable wealth became an inferior, less perfect, aspect; in short, there emerged an autonomous and relatively unified category of wealth. It should be noted that it is only at this point that a clear distinction can be drawn between what we call "political" and what we call "economic." This is a distinction that traditional societies do not admit. As an economic historian recently recalled, it happened in the modern West that "the ruler abandoned, voluntarily or involuntarily, the right or practice of arbitrary or indefinite disposition of the wealth of his subjects" (Landes 1969, p. 16). This is a factual precondition for our familiar distinction.

We verge here on the forceful demonstration by Karl Polanyi in *The Great Transformation* (1957a) of how exceptional the modern era is in the history of mankind with regard to the segregation of the economic aspects and the sacrosanct role of the market and its concomitants in the "liberalism" that dominated the nineteenth century and the opening decades of the twentieth. I am only proposing a somewhat wider view, while at the same time building on an old sociological tradition. The holism/individualism contrast as it has developed from my study without any direct or conscious imitation[2] is in line with Maine's Status and Contract and with Tönnies's *Gemeinschaft* and *Gesellschaft*. I am only putting the hierarchy of values in the foreground, which makes the contrast more pointed and useful—or so it is hoped. In fact, it is not difficult to trace the parentage further back. Tönnies himself expressed his distinction in terms of essential or spontaneous will (*Wesenwille*) and explicit will (*Kürwille*) (1971, p. 6 and passim). The expression has a strong Hegelian flavor, not only in the emphasis on the will, which has closer parallels and is, after all, largely German, but in its general tenor. One recalls the young Hegel, preoccupied by the contrast between the spontaneous participation in

the life of the city by the ancient Greek citizen and the isolation
that results for the Christian individual from his conquest of
subjectivity and freedom. One thinks of Rousseau's saying in
the *Contrat* that the Christian is a bad citizen and advocating,
consequently, "civil religion." We shall find here that if the distinction is not used analytically by Marx, it is because he chose to
take it as a pathological feature to which the proletarian revolution would put an end. In other words, he himself offers an
acknowledgment of the contradiction.

We are separated from traditional societies by what I call the
modern revolution, a *revolution in values,* which has taken place,
I believe, through the centuries in the Christian Occident. This
fact determines the axis of comparison. More often than not,
comparison until now has centered on the modern case: why
did not one or the other of the higher civilizations develop
natural science, or technology, or capitalism, as we know them?
The question should be reversed: how and why has this unique
development that we call "modern" occurred at all? The main
task of comparison is to account for the modern type in terms of
the traditional type. For this reason, most of our modern vocabulary is inadequate for comparative purposes: the basic comparative model has to be nonmodern. (On a different level, is it
not a reason why his *Formes élémentaires* is relatively so seminal
in Durkheim's work?) This view of comparison will be objected
to; but before defending and illustrating it, a minimum of precision is needed.

As previously (1967, index), I define *ideology* as the totality of
ideas and values common to a society or to a group of people in
general. This is only a broad initial definition, sufficient for the
moment. Since there is, in the modern world, a set of ideas and
values that is common to many societies, countries, or nations,
we may speak of a "modern ideology" in contrast to the ideology of one or another traditional society—corresponding, be it
recalled, to a higher civilization. Modern ideology is thus a case
of several societies partaking of a common "civilization," as
Mauss called this international or intersocietal social phenomenon (Mauss 1930, pp. 86 ff.; cf. Dumont 1970, p. 6). Yet ideology is not quite the same thing as civilization in Mauss's sense.
Nor is it the same as culture in the American usage, which

opposes it to society, especially because a crucial importance attaches, for the comparative meaning of the ideology, to nonideological social features (see 1967, §§ 22, 118).

For clarity, two meanings of the expression "the individual man" should be distinguished (1965, p. 15; 1967, § 3):

1. the *empirical* subject of speech, thought, and will, the indivisible sample of mankind, as found in all societies

2. the independent, autonomous, and thus (essentially) nonsocial *moral* being, as found primarily in our modern ideology of man and society

What is called here "individualism" is embodied in the second usage. I shall make an effort to distinguish these two senses of the term, sometimes by writing "the Individual" to indicate the moral sense, sometimes by using another expression for the empirical sense, like "the particular man," "the particular human agent," etc. Yet, precisely because it is necessary, the distinction is often very difficult to express briefly in ordinary language. Similarly, the word "individualism" should here designate only the global valuation defined above as corresponding to the Individual, but I am not sure that I have always avoided using it more loosely and thus lapsing into the vague current usage.

To return to the opposition between modern ideology and traditional ideology. What will be disputed in the first place is the level of contrast. Is there not as much distance between, say, French and German modern ideologies as between Indian and Chinese traditional ideologies? There is a difference between the two cases. It should be obvious that England, France, and Germany, among others, have held, from, say, the seventeenth century, a common ideology. This does not mean that national differences—or for that matter class differences, regional differences, and so forth—are not found within each country. On the contrary, the very attempt to delineate what they have in common immediately brings forth discrepancies. Nevertheless, each national pattern can be taken as a variant of the common ideology. (For a condensed statement of the Franco-German difference re the conception of the nation, see 1971a, pp. 33–35.)

Regarding India and China—and leaving aside the question of internal diversity, which is quite irrelevant on the present level—

I am not asserting that India and China are not profoundly dissimilar. They are similar only in comparison to us. There is no doubt that traditional Chinese, Japanese, and Indian ideologies are holistic while ours is individualistic. That they are holistic in different ways does not alter an important consequence: the task of describing comparatively those societies would be made easier if our own fundamentally individualistic frame of reference could be substituted by another that would be developed from those societies themselves. Whenever we lay bare an idiosyncrasy of the modern mind, we make a little less impossible the task of universal comparison. (This point lies beyond our present concern; for a few more remarks, see 1975). Yet it should be borne in mind that the present comparative attempt is and remains limited and represents only a beginning insofar as only one traditional ideology, the Indian, lies at its basis, notwithstanding the generalization I tentatively propose (from hierarchy to holism, etc.). In other words, it is more than likely that similar comparative attempts, starting with China, or Islam, or ancient Greece, can in their turn throw light on some aspects of our ideology that the India-based attempt, even if supposed complete and perfect, would leave in the dark.

To sum up, the modern revolution in values represents the central problem in the comparison of societies—insofar as ideas and values are not blocked out of such a comparison—especially of the societies called here traditional, whether we propose to describe and understand such societies and cultures (the usual task of anthropology), or whether we propose to locate our own society and culture in relation to others. This latter task also belongs to anthropology; actually, the two tasks are but one, for it should be evident that if only we could evolve an anthropological view of our own society, the understanding of other societies would be made much easier. We could then refer them to a set of coordinates that would no longer be our own coordinates but truly universal ones.

So much for the anthropological angle. There is also a native angle. Our inquiry can be shown to be not quite untimely from a point of view internal to modern ideology itself. I shall be brief, for I mean only to hint at a general or remote fit. There was much talk some years ago about an "end of ideology." Borrowing loosely, after many others, from Thomas Kuhn (1962, but see 1970, pp. 174 ff.), one should rather say that we are witnessing a crisis of the modern ideological paradigm. It is true that the tendency to see crises everywhere is strong in modern ideology and that, if crisis there be, it was not born yesterday but has been there for quite some time; in a wider sense, the crisis is more or less congenial, to the extent that some of us take pride in it. Yet, we may perhaps say that the twentieth-century crisis of the paradigm has recently gone through an intensification, deepening, or generalization.

On the level of scholarly pursuits, one gets the general impression that modern man, closed in upon himself and perhaps misled by his sense of superiority, has some difficulty in grasping his own problems. The fact is perhaps particularly glaring in the reflection on politics. It comes as a shock, for instance, to discover that the need has not been felt to define the nation comparatively. The modern nation is generally defined only within modern conditions, taken implicitly as obvious or universal. No effort is made to define it specifically by comparison with analogous nonmodern political societies or groupings, of which so many in our day are in the process of becoming nations or are so regarded (see my essay on nationalism and communalism in India, Dumont 1970, pp. 89–110). More generally, political theory stubbornly persists in identifying itself with a theory of power, that is, mistaking a minor problem for the basic one, which lies in the relation between power and values, or ideology. The moment hierarchy is eliminated, subordination has to be explained as the mechanical result of interaction between individuals, and authority degrades itself into power, power into influence, and so on. It is forgotten that this sort of question appears only on a definite ideological basis, namely, individualism: political speculation has enclosed itself unawares within the walls of modern ideology. Yet recent history has afforded us an imposing demonstration of the vacuity of mere power—I mean the vain, if devastating, attempt of the Nazis to base power on itself alone. The parallelism may be disputed; I hold it neither far-fetched nor gratuitous.

While political thought thus lavishes sophistication on a dead end, the problems that burden the history of the past two centuries are rarely made the object of serious reflection. Are wars, more and more total and universal wars, dictatorships, and to-

talitarianisms the necessary implications, the inevitable accom-
paniments, of modern democracy? Was Tocqueville right in
assigning determined conditions and precise limits to the realization of the democratic principle? Or again, has the European
workers' internationalist movement been unable to draw the
lesson from its reduplicated defeat in 1914 and 1933? Does the
Marxist socialist theory, to renew or salvage which so much
effort is made here or there, belong to the past from that point of
view? If so, why? Comparative social science can throw light on
those questions which the philosophers neglect. On the whole,
the thorough reflection on the modern world that was so intense
in the first half of the nineteenth century appears to have gone
to sleep in the arms of partisan conformisms or inarticulate protests. Even the racking and ominous experience we endured
with Hitler has not yet, after thirty years, been mastered in
thought.

Perhaps one reason why all this is true is that one cannot
move a mass from within; one needs an external fulcrum. Modern civilization has the unique advantage of commanding a relatively good knowledge of many other civilizations and cultures;
comparison is the fulcrum. To "see ourselves in perspective," as
the late Sir Edward Evans-Pritchard put it, is a way to understand ourselves better.

To begin, I present an idea of the sort of renewal that comparison affords. If there is beyond or, rather, within all their differences, a certain constancy in human societies, if at the same time
modern ideology is as exceptional as I have said, then the accession of such an unprecedented ideology must have produced
equally unprecedented consequences. The surmise is substantiated in fact by phenomena that run counter to the admitted
values and that, for this very reason, are not properly recognized in the native modern view and call for a comparative
grasp.

After we have found holism and hierarchy in India, we may
ask what becomes of them in a set of societies that, on the
contrary, valorize the individual and equality (cf. 1967 § 118).
We find, for example, in modern societies a residue of hierarchy
in the form of social inequalities, but, as hierarchy as such is
here condemned and unthinkable, we find that this residue is
currently designated by an expression that evokes inanimate

nature and thus presents the phenomenon as devoid of human meaning, incomprehensible: we call it "social *stratification.*" This is not all, for we also find that, in one of the societies in question, the abolition of slavery gave rise after a short time to racism. Here is a spectacular example of the involuntary consequences of equalitarianism. I mention the fact only in passing, as I have dealt with it elsewhere (1967, App. A). To add only one observation: I never said, as some seemed to believe, that hierarchy is better than equality, or in the present instance that slavery is preferable to racism. I say only that facts of this kind show that ideology has the power to transform social reality only between certain limits and that when we ignore those limits we produce the contrary of what was desired.

Let us take a second example of a phenomenon that is both undesirable and yet present in our modern universe, that of totalitarianism. I shall argue from the case of Nazism and leave open the question of generalization. A major difficulty in the effort to grasp totalitarianism comes from the spontaneous tendency to consider it a form of holism. The word itself refers us at first sight to the social "totality"; and the regime, in its contrast to democracy, is first thought of as "reaction," a return to the past. These are vulgar notions, which serious studies reject. They acknowledge that totalitarianism is no holism, that it is quite different from the traditional naive conception of the society as a whole. Yet, as the totalitarian regime constrains its subjects most radically, it appears to oppose individualism in the current meaning of the term, so the analyst is faced with a contradiction. To solve it, one should remember that the phenomenon is internal to the modern world, that the totalitarian ideology is contained *within* modern ideology. The hypothesis is that totalitarianism results from *the attempt, in a society where individualism is deeply rooted and predominant, to subordinate it to the primacy of the society as a whole.* It combines, *unknowingly,* conflicting values. The contradiction that we encounter is internal to it. Hence its inordinate, ferocious stress on the social whole; hence its violence and its worship of violence. It is not solely a matter of obtaining submission where the consensus on values as a basis for normal subordination cannot be reached, for violence abides in the very promoters of the movement, torn apart as they are by conflicting forces and thus doomed to desperate attempts to substitute violence for value.

One might ask, seeing the contagion of violence at present,
whether those people have not, after all, succeeded in some
measure. Apparently, totalitarianism managed to inoculate the
world with its virus. It is clear that the contemporary
development—the presumed, but spectacular, development—
of violence in the world is linked in many ways with modern
ideology, yet I can in this place allude to it only briefly. I submit
the following statement as likely. Whatever reprobation *one particular act* of violence receives from public opinion, the contemporary development is not independent from a weakening of
the condemnation of private violence *in general,* in the same
opinion. That the condemnation has weakened is perhaps not
immediately seen, but it results from a confusion that is very
apparent. A confusion has arisen in the minds of people—and is
multiplied by the mass media—between actions and domains
that the progress of our civilization had consisted in distinguishing, in particular between domains from which violence had
been banished as the illegitimate exercise of force and other domains where men had not succeeded in their efforts to make it
unlawful—essentially, the domain of international relations.

Precisely on this point we have witnessed how totalitarianism
has blurred the boundary between war and peace by extending
to the time of peace, and to relations within the State, modes of
conduct, techniques, and strategies (notice the present usages of
this word!) taken from the practice of war. Today, at least in
continental Europe, examples abound of confusions of this
sort—between war (recently, the United States in Vietnam) and
the camps or psychiatric asylums in the Soviet Union, between
war and political terrorism, between political terrorism and pure
gangsterism. The expression "taking hostages," which has
spread from specific military usage to the two other levels in
succession, is highly characteristic. Its current use in the media
to designate the threat to human lives in a ruthless form of
blackmail shows how public opinion can, through the confusion
I denounce, acknowledge in some manner, or acclimatize, new,
unspeakable practices. I do not pretend that totalitarianism is
here a cause. On a deeper level, there is a homology or a reso-
nance between these two diseases of our times. First of all, the
widespread tendency to increase one's power without regard to
other than practical limitations is at work here, a tendency obviously connected with modern individualism and artificialism. I

mean only that the predominant contemporary ideology represents a favorable condition for terrorism and that the widespread confusion between norm and fact, between institutionalized law and morality, between justice and tyranny, between public and private is a harbinger of barbarity.

The promises that such a comparison seemed to hold lured me, ten years ago, to embark on this timely but perhaps presumptuous journey. I was well aware of the toil and perils ahead and of the necessary safeguards and precautions (1965, p. 18). In Tocqueville's phrase, I would turn back the mirror—the Indian mirror in this case—on ourselves, in order to look from a new angle at the fundamental conceptions of our modern mind. The historical dimension being indispensable, it would be a literary inquiry, a study of texts. The history of ideas in the modern Occident would be considered as a whole, along its main lines of development, in the fundamental unity it could not fail to disclose when viewed against the background of a different civilization. As I now see it, the subject may be approached along three relatively concrete lines: one historical, one that I would call configurational, and one national or "subcultural." The historical line is the most obvious: a deep transformation has taken place in western Europe through the centuries, signaled from our point of view most spectacularly by the emergence of new categories of thought or special points of view such as politics and economics, and of corresponding institutions, the genesis of which can be studied. But these points of view are always given as part of a configuration sui generis for each author, school, tendency, or period. These configurations are the real objects of our study, and nothing less than their sum integral, so to speak, is what is here called modern ideology. Among these configurations one encounters almost immediately (at least, say, from the seventeenth century on) national differences. It would not be enough to say that modern ideology is diversely accommodated in different countries or (in the first approximation, linguistic) cultures. There are in fact more or less national—for example, British, French, German—subcultures that should be taken as equivalent variants of the general ideology.

So far, only one long essay has been published: "The Modern Conception of the Individual: Notes on Its Genesis and That of

Concomitant Institutions" (1965). It is an attempt to delineate
the genesis of modern ideology regarding the individual and
politics, together with the State, from the Middle Ages up to and
beyond the French Revolution. This is done by isolating a few
stages or aspects with the help, on the one hand, of general
works by recognized authors from different special fields (Fig-
gis, Gierke, Elie Halévy) and, on the other, of condensed
monographic pictures of classic works (*Leviathan* and others).
This paper did not aim at completeness, and it suffers from
some shortcomings, the main one of which is the assumption
that the ideology was holistic at the point of departure (Thomas
Aquinas), which is true only if one looks narrowly at the terrestrial community of Christians; it is not true of the ideology as a
whole. A later, unpublished study of the first centuries of the
Church led to a general formula of the Church's ideology
through the centuries (until Calvin), which accommodates the
changes and accounts for their general direction. In summary,
individualism was a characteristic of Christian thought from the
start; the evolution was from otherworldly individualism to
more and more this-worldly individualism, in which process the
holistic terrestrial community almost disappeared as such. Fortunately, this initial flaw in the published paper does not distort
its description of the progress of individualism, of the birth of
the State, and of the political category.

In the first stages (§§ 1–4) the paper is more descriptive than analytical. The most striking feature to emerge is the complexity of
the process of schizogenesis by which the all-embracing realm of
religion gave birth (with the help of law) to the new special
category, politics; and, regarding institutions, how the State
inherited its essential features from the Church, which it
superseded as the global society. Through the centuries, down
to the French Revolution, religion exercised its action in ever-
renewed forms: the Conciliar movement, the Reformation, the
wars of religion, the Protestant sects—all contributed willy-
nilly to the new political world. In sum, politics and the State
resulted from a differentiation, the effect of which was to
detach from the central reservoir a modicum of absolute values.
The reader will ask why the social background is absent from that
study. It seems especially odd that feudalism and the communes
are not mentioned. A general question is involved, which will

be considered below. Along the historical line, the present study follows that of 1965: just as religion gave birth to politics, politics in turn will be shown to give birth to economics.

As to the configurational aspect, it represents, as I have stated, the basic unit of the study, as each configuration is the elementary concrete whole from which all developments should be derived. For that reason, configuration is present in some measure everywhere in the study. I say "in some measure" because what is actually considered is, most of the time, the relation, in one particular work or author, between the concepts, categories, etc., on which consideration is focused. Here, for instance, chapter 4 on Locke focuses on the relations among politics, economics (or its germ), morality, and religion. The changes in these relations are for our purpose the basic historical events.

The third, a subcultural or national approach, is actually a particular case of comparing configurations. Struck by the deep difference between the French and German representations of the individual and the nation, but having started spontaneously from the French variant, the most clear-cut (1965, 1967, introd.), I found it necessary at an early stage to characterize the German one. This need gave rise to a study of the German ideology of the individual, the State, and the *Volk* in the literature of the formative period, from 1770 to 1830. I hope to publish that study shortly; for the present, it is briefly summed up in a lecture (1971*a*, pp. 33–35). I intend to make a similar study of the British variant, in which the accent will be on the place and function of empiricism in relation to the individualistic valuation; as to utilitarianism—which is, let us recall, an essentially Anglo-Saxon phenomenon—it will be characterized here in its beginning (see chapter 5 on Mandeville; empiricism is of course not wholly absent). The study of the German ideology was followed by a study of Nazism and particularly of Hitler's own *Weltanschauung* and anti-Semitism, already mentioned. This is a configurational study, but it takes great advantage of its predecessor. Not that German philosophy explains the Nazi phenomenon: the phenomenon is essentially European, modern—a crisis of modern ideology. Yet it is not understandable apart from the form it takes, and the form it takes is determined by the German variant of modern ideology.

*

I do not intend to dwell at length on problems of method in the abstract and thus delay the beginning of the concrete inquiry. Nevertheless, some preliminary remarks are called for regarding the ideology in general and what I called, for brevity in the subtitle, "economic ideology," meaning the relation of the economic category to the ideology, its place within it. My remarks will cluster around two questions which the reader probably has in mind at this point: How do we go about constructing the object that is here called *ideology*? and Is it legitimate—and apposite—to separate the ideology from the rest of social reality for a separate study? I define ideology as the totality of ideas and values—or "representations"—common to a society or current in a given social group.

It is probably expected at this stage that I should distinguish more or less substantially between ideology, on the one hand, and science, or rationality, or truth, or philosophy, on the other. To make such a distinction is the last thing I would do. The only aspect common to the present view and a widespread, more or less Marxist, usage is the social relativity: any ideology is a *social set of representations*—certainly a very complex affair. The fact that one particular representation in that set is judged as true or false, rational or traditional, scientific or not, is irrelevant to the social nature of the idea or value. For example: that the earth revolves around the sun is, I take it, a scientific statement, but it is admitted by most of our contemporaries without their being able to demonstrate it. Moreover, even for those who are able to do so, this statement is part of their world view, together with many other statements they cannot demonstrate. As such, it may legitimately be taken as an integral part of the ideology as a whole, that is, as entertaining certain relations with other components of it.

Here we certainly must guard against a widely prevalent tendency that is in the last analysis scientistic and that blurs the problems arising from the relations between the specialized scientific pursuits that are so highly developed around us and the general forms of consciousness. No ideology in its entirety can be said to be true or false, as no form of consciousness is ever complete, definitive, or absolute. Marx characterized religion as a form of consciousness working "through a detour" (*auf einem*

Umweg) ("The Jewish Question," *Werke*, I:353). We know better: all forms of consciousness are similar, in the sense that none operates without a grid, through which we take cognizance of the given and at the same time leave out a part of it. There is no direct and exhaustive consciousness *of* anything. Thus, in everyday life it is through the ideology of our society in the first place that we become conscious of everything around us. The only thing we can affirm about the relation between what is represented and what "actually happens" is that such a relation is necessary and that it is not an identity. This point is essential, for it leads to the recognition of a duality between the ideological and the nonideological, which makes it possible to avoid both idealism and materialism, at the cost, it is true, of endless toil (1967, n. 1a, etc.). This duality also helps guard us against relativism, which would conclude from diversity to unreality. I have mentioned "the social relativity" of the ideology as given. This relativity is not final, for comparison transcends it. Our task is to make possible the intellectual transition from one ideology to the other, and this we can do through the inclusion in our comparison of the nonideological residue, which is itself revealed through comparison, and through comparison only (1967, § 118). This is the reason for some reserve about the expression "world view," or *Weltanschauung*—so highly charged with relativism that it was adopted with some predilection by the Nazis. Their creed, let us recall, furiously denied the intercommunicability of cultures, as part and parcel of their racism.

Thus, the ideology of a given country at a given time can be taken as embracing its whole intellectual patrimony, provided that only social, and not exceptional or unique representations, are included. Here we encounter a difficulty: our material is made up of particular texts of particular authors. How shall we recognize in each text what is social and what is not? The answer lies, first, in the relation between these different texts. They may either merely copy each other or, at the other extreme, have nothing in common. On the whole, there are basic representations and configurations that are common to many of them. Or they may be implied in discussions between contemporaries. I touch here on a more delicate point: the relative importance of these representations in the society at large. As usual in the study of cultures in general, it is important to isolate the main

lines of force, most often the one predominant trend, which, as
Marx says of economic features in a remarkable passage, is like
the ether that tinges the whole scene (quoted below, p. 162),
what I call "the all-embracing aspect."

I do not want to minimize the problem posed by the attempt
to recognize the ideology of a school or group from the thought
of a philosopher like Locke (below, chapter 4) or the representations of a political leader (say, Hitler, with the initial difficulty of
distinguishing the representations he really held from those he
paraded). The two examples are as different as possible in themselves and in the use to which I put them. Yet in both examples,
what I fasten on—punctually in the first, more globally in the
second—is the emergence or manifestation of a "collective representation," in the sense of a relation or a set of relations that
are found recurrently or that throw light on other current relations and representations—that is, they constitute a particular
form (perhaps the initial one) of an ideological phenomenon.

A basic paradox confronts us here: the fundamental tenets of
the ideology are likely to remain implicit. Fundamental ideas are
so obvious, so omnipresent, that they do not need expression:
that phenomenon is called "tradition" (1970, p. 7). On this point
I used to cite Mauss quoting a missionary in his inaugural lecture in 1902. Here it is in the words of David Hume: "The views
the most familiar to us are apt, for that very reason, to escape
us" (1875, 4:196); yet it would probably be too much to speak of
these views as "unconscious," given the special sense of that
term. It is not difficult to descry behind "liberty" and "equality"
their substratum, the valuation of the individual, yet most of the
time only the predicates are expressed while the subject is not.
We come to isolate it through a double movement: on the one
hand, we find it again and again in other parts of the ideological
realm; on the other, we contrast this global orientation with
another, namely, holism, which, similarly, most holistic
societies do not carry on their banners. (It takes the acumen of
the author of the *Republic* to isolate it.) Similarly again, when a
wide-ranging analysis emboldened me to propose hierarchy as
the fundamental principle of caste society, I was not translating
an Indian word, although the notion is in some manner and in
one or another aspect ubiquitous in Indian ideology. (It is
perhaps characteristic that the fiercest critics have impugned

this way of looking at society and the construction of the concept, not, however, the frequency and the importance of its diverse manifestations in the society.) It is a matter, then, of bringing to light the implicit subject of many manifest predicates, of adding their necessary but unexpressed relation to representations that are conscious. This is, by the way, a much more modest procedure than replacing the native model by an assumedly quite different one.

It is at the level of those unstated "views" that the different parts of the ideology hang together. Therefore, the wider our consideration, the more clearly will they reveal themselves. They constitute the basic categories, the distinctive operative principles of what I called the "grid" of consciousness, the implicit coordinates of common thought. The impact of this recognition for the present purpose lies in the fact that in the modern world each of our particular viewpoints or specialized pursuits does not know very well—or does not know at all—what it is about and the reason for its existence or distinctness, which is more often a matter of fact than of consensus or rationality. Just as our rationality is mostly a matter of the relation between means and ends, while the hierarchy of ends is left out, so also our rationality manifests itself within each of our neatly distinct compartments but not in their distribution, definition, and arrangement. If we want to take a view of our culture as a whole, we must dive to the level of the unexpressed as we would for any less "rational" society.

Thus, the definition of politics or economics, not to speak of the natural sciences, is by no means beyond discussion. After all, it is natural that this should be so, for the part cannot define itself but through its place in the whole, and the sciences find no whole above them any more than do the nations: there is no society of nations, no science of sciences. (It was sometimes the ambition of philosophy to be this science of sciences, but, wherever the ambition is maintained, it remains a particular, not a social, construction.) If there is no science of sciences, there is in actual fact a social unity of them, a society of specialized viewpoints. It has to be unearthed from the ideology, conjured up from the silences of common sense.

Thus, for instance, politics and the State can be and are variously defined: through subordination, through the monopoly of

legitimate force within a given territory, through the friend-foe
pair, etc. Except perhaps the first one, these are definitions of
the part by itself. In a particular case, that of Hegel, I showed
elsewhere that there is more to the State than these definitions
indicate (1965, pp. 57–59). The State in Hegel is more than the
political institution we call by that name; it is at the same time
the sociologist's global society. More precisely, with Hegel it is
at the level of the State that the modern individual merges into
the holism of the society. The paradox is hardly surprising, as
the reconciliation of opposites is Hegel's stock-in-trade; its point
is that, for Hegel, once the individual (of civil society) is given,
the merging is possible only through consciousness, explicit
will, and consensus—in other words, on the political level. Only
as State is the society as a whole accessible to individual consciousness. Hegel obscured the point in his *Philosophy of Right,*
but his continuity with Hobbes and Rousseau on the basic thesis
makes it unmistakable (ibid.). It is what Marx, and many others
with him, did not understand or could not accept (see below,
chapter 7), and this fact alone is enough to make the point historically important. It is strange for us to see the assertion of
individual will, which was the instrument of revolution, be
made the only tool of social unity—yet, Hegel offers fleetingly
the recognition of the social nature of man that underlay Rousseau's contract (cf. the quotation on p. 122). The lesson for us is
that we should miss the essence if we considered Hegel's theory
from within our contemporary "political" viewpoint, and that,
on the contrary, we can renew the understanding of this text
(with the help of our individualism/holism distinction) by concentrating on the whole configuration of ideas and on the actual
place and role there of politics or of the State. Hereafter, the
example of Locke will stress this point regarding the relation
between politics and economics (chapter 4).

One can now perceive the reason why I refused to make a
sharp distinction between ideology and science, philosophy,
etc.; there is already too much of a dovecote here. The intention
of this research is quite the opposite: it is to reveal the links and
relations between the familiar pigeonholes of our mental and
occupational inventory, to recover, with the unsuspected determination of each of them, the unity of the whole and the
major lines of force of our culture in its vital but neglected

interconnectedness. To me, this is not only a programmatic statement; it has already become in some measure an effective conclusion. I thus suggested, again regarding our general
categories, that, each taken in its stronger sense, politics and
economics on the one hand, religion and society on the other,
stand opposed, the first two concepts representing the modern
innovation and the second two "the continuity with the traditional universe that remains in the modern universe" (1971, p.
33). This is only a preliminary or at any rate a very general
statement.

Our definition of ideology thus rests on a distinction that is not
a distinction of matter but one of point of view. We do not take
as ideological what is left out when everything true, rational, or
scientific has been preempted. We take everything that is socially thought, believed, acted upon, on the assumption that it is
a living whole, the interrelatedness and interdependence of
whose parts would be blocked out by the a priori introduction of
our current dichotomies. The ideology is not a residue; it is the
unity of it all—a unity that does not exclude contradiction or
conflict.

With the global level thus firmly located, it should be acknowledged at once that the distinction I have just rejected is actually
used by me in the process of constructing the ideology. If a
ubiquitous statement presented as rational or scientific shows
itself unjustified as such, there is a strong chance that it was
imposed by another type of consistency and can be identified as
one outcrop, as it were, of the underlying ideological network.
To blandly call it traditional, that is, largely "nonrational,"
would be begging the question. We shall soon have some examples of this heuristic device, which is probably indispensable in
order to identify ideological elements—to fill in the details of the
ideological map. It does not prejudice the global image; in particular, it leaves open the question of the development of the
"scientific" out of the general ideology, a question so basic that
it should be reserved as a final test of our inquiry.

There is another sense of ideology that I am sorry to neglect,
as it is of interest to the historian. It bears on the modern condition: ideology supersedes religion when the world is *entzaubert*,
that is, when it is believed that everything is knowable (or that
there can be a consciousness without detour). (I am drawing

from a remark of François Furet, who was thinking of the men of
the French Revolution.) Important as this is, our present viewpoint is broader. What we need here, in the first place, is a
general label under which we can compare the exceptional modern case, in which the general configuration of values is not
coterminous with religion, with the general traditional case, in
which it is, and I have found no better word than the one I am
using (cf. 1971, pp. 32–33).

I can now apply these general remarks to the economic viewpoint. I begin by observing that to define economics is not easy.
In his monumental *History of Economic Analysis*, Schumpeter
does not give any definition; he defines such terms as
"economic analysis," etc., but from the start he takes "economic
phenomena" for granted (1954, introd.). It is difficult to propose
a definition that would be universally accepted, particularly if it
was to be a definition which the economists of the past as well as
those of the present could approve. This difficulty might be one
reason for Schumpeter's silence, for certainly Ricardo did not
deal with "scarce resources." This difficulty to achieve a definition is probably a general modern phenomenon: not only is it
true of the sciences in general, but it can also be said of modern
man that he knows what he is doing ("analysis") but not what it
is "really about" ("economic").[3] Schumpeter writes of Adam
Smith and others: "They failed to see that their ethical
philosophies and political doctrines were logically irrelevant for
the explanation of economic reality as it is . . . . They had not yet
a clear conception of the distinctive purposes of analysis—have
we?" (1954, pp. 448–49).

The difficulty of definition is still greater from a comparative
point of view, namely, in anthropology. Anthropologists are
strongly motivated to identify an economic aspect in any society, but where does it begin and where does it end? In recent
years, two antithetic viewpoints have been expressed. The
proponents of the formal one insist with good reason that
economics is identical with its concept, and they propose as a
consequence *their* conceptions of the alternate uses of scarce
means, of methods to maximize gain, etc. The supporters of the
substantive view argue that this attitude would be destructive of
what is really the economy "out there" as an objective and universal datum—briefly, the ways and means of the subsistence of

men. If a point of view that issues in such a divorce between the concept and the thing clearly shows itself to be inapplicable, then we have here a significant situation: what is meaningful in one world is simply not meaningful in another. Thus Karl Polanyi, taking the latter position, threw overboard "economics" in their contemporary version ("economizing") to retain "the economy." This is not only an inconvenient language, but it represents also a regrettable step backward on the part of a scholar to whom we owe so much. True, Polanyi hastens to add, in conformity with the fundamental thesis of his previous book, *The Great Transformation*, that, in contradistinction to us, other societies have not segregated economic aspects—that they are found everywhere "embedded" in the social fabric (Polanyi 1957b, pp. 243 ff.). If there is any consensus in the matter, it is this: that to isolate economic phenomena the anthropologist has to dis-embed them—on the face of it a hazardous and probably destructive procedure, a Procrustean operation. It is particularly difficult—and, I would add, unrewarding—to separate political and economic aspects. This is no wonder, as we shall witness in our own culture the birth of the economic viewpoint from within the political; but when it is proposed to distinguish more and more sharply a "political anthropology," an "economic anthropology," this does not make sense regarding the progress of knowledge. Quite the reverse; it is indicative of a renunciation of the anthropological inspiration ("only connect!") in favor of our modern tendency to increase compartmentalization and specialization.

It should be obvious that there is nothing like an economy out there, unless and until men construct such an object. Once it has been built, we are able to descry everywhere in some measure more or less corresponding aspects that we should in all rigor call "quasi-economic" or "would-be economic." Of course they should be studied, but the proviso ("quasi-") is operative. In other terms, the place of such aspects in the whole is not the same here and there, and this is essential to their nature.

Now, if the object—"the economy"—is a construct, and if the particular discipline that constructs it cannot tell us how it does it— if it cannot, that is, give us the essence of economics, the basic *presupposition(s)* on which it was built up—then we should find it in the *relation between economic thought and the global ideol-*

ogy, that is, in its place in the general ideological configuration. This supposes of course that we are equipped to identify this relation; and, as our comparative equipment is, as I said before, incomplete and tentative, it may be that we shall find this relation only incompletely. In that sense, the question will have to remain open. But such is our initial hypothesis.

We shall find that the construction of the reputedly external objective reality called "the economy" was governed by internal constraints—I mean constraints internal to the general ideology. An application of this finding that would indirectly verify it would be to throw light on the extraordinarily checkered course of development of economics as a science in its beginnings, as it becomes manifest in Schumpeter's monumental masterpiece, the *History of Economic Analysis.* This is a book in the absence of which the present inquiry could probably not have been contemplated. As his title indicates, and as he points out in detail and repeatedly, Schumpeter is concerned not with economic thought at large, but exclusively with what can be considered scientific within it. His *History* sifts the scientific grain from the chaff. From that angle it will be used as the mainstay of this study. Now perhaps the most striking result of Schumpeter's painstaking inquiry, based on lifelong study and immense erudition, is not so much that there is plenty of chaff but that the historical sequence shows, not a regular growth, but a great disorder and the most astounding discontinuities on decisive points. Schumpeter is never tired of underlining these irregularities: how early acquisitions and discoveries remained long unheeded or were bypassed by the mainstream and had to be rediscovered much later (as regarding marginal utility, etc., in Galiani and Daniel Bernoulli and others; see 1954, pp. 300–305, 1054, etc); how the works that have been most influential were not the most seminal or scientific (Adam Smith); how fruitful avenues and sound developments had inexplicably to be willfully abandoned or canceled for a time; how strange in retrospect the "Ricardian detour" looks—that distinct approach which dominated the classical period (even if, according to Schumpeter, it was less influential among British specialists than is frequently admitted).

Schumpeter expresses his astonishment and dismay at all this; he does not explain it, and at bottom he cannot because his inquiry takes the economic point of view for granted and locates itself *within* it. Only someone standing outside it can possibly try to show how the particular viewpoint has come into existence. In this sense, Schumpeter's *History* calls for a complement of the kind here attempted, whatever may be the disproportion in knowledge, coverage, and merit between the two.

When we look at the economic view as part of the ideology, we do not ask to start with whether a given economic statement is true or false but only *how* it is thought—I mean, in which relation to other statements, whether internal or external to the economic discourse, and, quite particularly, in which covert relation with noneconomic statements. It may then happen that a given statement appears strongly founded in its intraideological relations while weakly founded in its objective reference. After all, this should be expected, since economics as a science did not develop in a vacuum but in a field where unscientific, common-sense representations were already in existence. But we shall find that there is more to it than that, for the economic consideration developed from an ideological pull that powerfully inflected its course, at least in the initial stages. In other words, the scientific object was not easy to construct, and the vagaries of its constructors show that it was not merely a matter of registering an externally given datum.

Conversely, to learn something about the place of economics enriches the ideological map. To anticipate: the economic category rests on a value judgment, an implicit hierarchy. It supposes that something else is excluded or subordinated. In other words, we learn what kind of detour (Marx's *Umweg*) we are actually taking. Are these high claims? I felt impelled to articulate them; the reader will judge how far they will be substantiated. Given the primacy of the economic view in the modern world, the hypothesis is that this view must be deeply rooted in the mental constitution of modern man, that it must have for him particular and not insignificant implications that, as Hume makes us expect, are apt to escape him.

At this point, the most patient reader, who has subdued his impatience until now, may be expected to shrug his shoulders: "Nonsense," says he, "the primary fact is the tremendous economic development that surrounds us and is paramount in our lives; the primacy of the economic view is nothing but the

expression of this fact in our common thought." Things are not
that simple, but certainly there is a correspondence between the
two planes. Yet this reader poses the most redoubtable question, which I cannot avoid any longer: how far is it legitimate,
and apposite, to single out the ideology for separate consideration without taking into account its social background, that is,
primarily, in the present instance, what would most commonly
be called the economic development that actually accompanied
the genesis and development of economic thought? To do so is
to go against not only current practice but also an exceptionally
wide consensus about what social science and history itself
should do. More: to thus isolate a part of social reality is, on the
face of it, in direct contradiction to the anthropological inspiration and to my own insistent plea for a holistic approach, so that
it may seem that I should be the last person to engage in such an
exercise. On this last point, though, I may rejoin that my criticism bore in the first place on the uncritical or definitive division
of social phenomena into our own familiar rubrics, like political,
economic, etc. (DeReuck and Knight 1967, pp. 28–38), and that,
on the methodological level, I have admitted and have advocated the distinction between ideological and nonideological features (1967, §§ 22, 118; 1970, pp. 154–56) both in anthropological
practice and—which is not very different—in a comparative approach. Yet this is not a sufficient justification for what I shall do
here, and as a matter of fact I do not take very seriously some
recent anthropological attempts to unravel a foreign ideology
without maintaining a demonstrably close connection with observed behavior, for we are too much exposed in that case to
gross misunderstanding if we do not give full weight to the
control through "what actually happens." But the case is quite
different in our own intellectual universe.

   Here, to isolate our ideology is a sine qua non for transcending it, simply because otherwise we remain caught within it as
the very medium of our thought. This observation is enough to
cut short what would otherwise develop into a tedious, fruitless
debate around the conundrum of the relative priority of the hen
and the egg. To illustrate: the general tendency among us is to accept, be it only as a familiar and useful schema, something like the
Marxist infrastructure/superstructure construct: at one end, material life and subsistence relationships; at the other, everything

else (the rest of social relationships, including the political ones, religion, art, and ideology in general)—the former pole being endowed, at least hypothetically, with a preeminent causal efficiency. I need not labor the point, I suppose, to establish that this view is part and parcel of a contemporary ideological trend. It is how most of our contemporaries like, in the first approximation, to fancy that things are and how they happen. By saying this, I remain uncommitted to the truth or untruth of any of the statements belonging to the class. Nevertheless, it is fair to say—and I suppose a social scientist may be allowed to state—that such statements are often false and may even be recognized as such without causing a sizable impact on the vitality of the general belief. To give a single but massive example, I take it that the Industrial Revolution in its diverse phases and aspects on the continent of Europe, and particularly in France, is currently antedated (implicitly, of course) by some thirty to fifty years by the proponents of a materialistic explanation of the French Revolution (in the general literature, as distinguished from the technical but not always the historical). In my view, we have here an example of wishful thinking, the trace of a hard belief, which makes it especially interesting as indicative of its situation at the core of modern ideology. As such, it is part of the object of our study, not part of our investigative tools. Moreover, this general bias makes more difficult the ascertainment of extraideological facts, which is already very difficult in itself and requires the skills of a trained historian. The discussion goes on among specialists on too many crucial questions of fact, and the outsider rarely feels that a lasting consensus has been reached on which he could build. Strange as it may seem, it is easier to form a relatively certain idea of the *Wealth of Nations* than of the state of England in 1776.

Therefore, while the analyst suffers from any insufficiency in his knowledge of the context, it is safer for him to avoid in his writing what does not strictly belong to his object: the relation of economic thought to the general ideology. The resulting picture will not be a complete sociological picture but will present a partial whole whose final sociological meaning will thus remain out of reach. Such will be our detour or *Umweg*. Moreover, I would point out that, for the inquiry itself, the loss is less than it at first appears, because the nonideological dimension that is left out is substituted in some measure by the comparative dimen-

sion, that is to say, by the small set of simple tools already
mentioned.

These comments anticipate the conclusion of the study. I present only the approach, with the hope that the reader will not
reject it out of hand. If, in the end, this essay throws some light
on the history of economic thought, if it reveals meaningful
interrelations in the disjointed puzzle or seemingly atomized
heap of our own culture, if it brings this exceptional development into some intelligible relation to the more common run of
higher civilizations, then the approach will have justified itself.

*

Coming now to my discussion, I shall give an outline that states
the limitations of the study and the technical precautions or
safeguards that flow from them. My study was originally limited
to the genesis of economic thought, from the seventeenth century through the Physiocrats to Adam Smith (and Ricardo), that
is to say to the emergence, by disentanglement or disembedding,
of the new viewpoint. Then I noticed that Marx's approach had
been precisely the reverse: he had reintegrated the same viewpoint, this time in a dominant position, within the general configuration. This was not only his contribution as seen by us; it
had also been, all along, his stated intention and the aim he had
pursued regarding economics: to remodel "bourgeois" political
economy in accordance with his global image of man's destiny.
Thus, the circle closed itself neatly: I could follow the growth of
the phenomenon from the seed to the mighty tree, from its birth
to its blossoming, climax, or triumph. More commonly,
perhaps, it is economic liberalism (see Polanyi 1957a) that will be
considered the acme of economic ideology. Yet there remains in
it an element of limitation: *Homo oeconomicus* is not exclusive of
other aspects of man, nor has he all the ambition of the *homo* of
Marx. The view will be more precisely justified later on.

There is, of course, no technical counterindication to going
from Smith and Ricardo to Marx. Now and then I shall designate
this line, for sheer convenience, as "the early classics"—an arbitrary label. My study cannot claim to cover even a limited
chronological span in the history of economic thought; it concentrates on the relation to the global ideology, and it is highly
selective as to the themes as well as the authors.

This concentration is what makes this book, as I stated in the

Preface, so different from an anthropological work, and it has required severe control. But after all, what matters on this level is what passes into the common pool, and the real subject of knowledge—or ideology—is a collective being. Therefore, regarding the form, the views I propose should be carefully presented so as to allow the reader to form his own opinion. Furthermore, I am not an economist, and I should probably be unable to cover more advanced stages of economics. Such an author must be wary of possible mistakes on this account and make all the more or less technical statements easy to check by specialists; thus the origin or derivation of the statements will be explicit.

All the main general works used, apart from Schumpeter's *Analysis*, deal with economics in its intellectual context. They have shaped my understanding or confirmed my approach. They are: Gunnar Myrdal's *The Political Element in the Development of Economic Theory* (published in Swedish in 1929); Thorstein Veblen's long essay "The Preconceptions of Economic Science," originally published in 1899–1900 and found in his book *The Place of Science in Modern Civilization* (1919); and James Bonar's *Philosophy and Political Economy in Some of Their Historical Relations* (1927). Only recently have I had access to some of Jacob Viner's works, which will be referred to in the notes, as will generally be the case for recent accessions or accretions. Elie Halévy's *The Formation of Philosophical Radicalism* (1901–4) touches significantly on the subject, though it does not center on it. It is the type of book that I found could be heavily relied upon in my inquiry in general.

Some general exposition or summary seemed necessary, but I have reduced it to a minimum, preferring for methodological and other reasons to anchor the development on a few monographic moorings—where, I hope, the anthropologist comes into his own again. A few texts were chosen for their interest and relevance and are studied with relative thoroughness. These monographs vary much in breadth and extent. They are devoted in turn to Locke's *Two Treatises,* to Mandeville's *Fable of the Bees,* to Adam Smith's theory of value, and, finally, to some of the early texts of Marx. Ricardo is hardly mentioned at all. I have now completed a study of his theories of value and of rent in relation to those of Marx, but it is not included here.

Genesis

The Conditions of Emergence of the Economic Category

The modern era has witnessed the emergence of a new mode of consideration of human phenomena and the carving out of a separate domain, which are currently evoked for us by the words *economics, the economy.* How has this new category appeared, a category that constitutes at one and the same time a separate compartment in the modern mind and a continent delivered to a scientific discipline and that, moreover, embodies a more or less paramount value of the modern world? It is convenient, and not too arbitrary, to take the publication by Adam Smith in 1776 of the book entitled *An Inquiry into the Nature and Causes of the Wealth of Nations* as the birth registration of the new category. What is it, then, that has happened in the *Wealth of Nations,* and in what relation does the book stand to what was there before?

Stressing the continuity between the Scholastics and subsequent writers down to the eighteenth century and the contributions of theologians and canonists from the fourteenth to the seventeenth century, Schumpeter wrote that, in the latter's works, "economics gained definite if not separate existence" (1954, p. 97). Our problem focuses precisely on the "separate existence," on the separation from existing viewpoints and disciplines through which economics began to exist as such, whether it was designated as "political economy" or otherwise.

For such a separation to occur, the subject matter had to be seen or felt as a system, as constituting in some manner a whole apart from other matters. This condition can be analyzed into two aspects: the recognition of some raw material, and a specific way of looking at it. The first aspect was present early, the second only later. This is what Schumpeter tells us when he speaks for the intermediate stage of a "definite but not separate" existence of economics. The canonists dealt with an array of questions relating to the public good that bore on what we call economic matters; however, those questions appeared in their works unconnected or only loosely connected among themselves, and they were treated, not from a specific, but from a more general point of view. Similarly, the writers called "mercantilists," of the seventeenth and eighteenth centuries, mingled the phenomena we classify into *economic* and *political*. They considered economic phenomena from the point of view of the polity. With them, more often than not, the end is the prosperity and power of the State. "Political economy" appears in that period as an expression designating the study of particular means—"economical" means—to that end, that is to say, a particular branch of policy (Heckscher 1955). Actually, the general subservience of wealth to power in that period has been challenged (Viner 1958),[1] yet I think it is safe to assume that, while the two were thought of as closely interdependent, wealth remained on the whole subordinated to or encompassed in power.

To make a brief comparative remark, I note that in the Indian civilization, while the political had been distinguished from and subordinated to the religious, the economic was never conceptually detached from the political. "Interest" remained an attribute of the king (Dumont 1970, pp. 78 and 80–81). Moreover, it is clear that this feature is linked with the fact that immovable wealth remained, as associated to power over men, the only recognized form of wealth, as in the configuration I noticed above. Therefore, the preoccupation of our mercantilists with trade and money appears comparatively pertinent.

True, there never was a "commercial or mercantile system" as Adam Smith later presented it. In particular, we have it on Schumpeter's authority that no serious writer ever believed that the wealth of a state or nation consisted in the accumulation of treasure (1954, pp. 361–62). What seems to be the case is that, once it had attained its independence, economics began to look down upon its humble beginnings and disparaged everything that had gone before, to the point of disregarding many valuable insights. Schumpeter regrets this discontinuity (ibid., p. 376), but there are reasons for it. In particular, it is natural that the champions of what was popularly, at any rate, known as Free Trade became impatient with those who had started, at any rate, from the point of view of State intervention. But then another question comes up: if the writings of those whom we shall go on calling, for convenience, the mercantilists are not entirely devoid of merit, how far is it true that they presented only disconnected statements and no system? All considered, we may at the most speak of partial systems in the making (Schumpeter 1954; see also the plan of Heckscher 1955 and his remark in Coleman 1969, p. 34). To be brief, we shall concentrate on one aspect that is crucial regarding the lack of unification of the field: the close relation to the State has this consequence, that *international transactions are considered in one manner and transactions within the State or country in another.*

Thus, what Schumpeter singles out as perhaps the foremost achievement of the period, Malynes's "automatic mechanism," is a partial theory of equilibrium in international trade which was to receive its definitive formulation from Cantillon and Hume (Schumpeter 1954, p. 365). To see the point more clearly, we may refer to a basic ideological change that occurred in the period. The primitive idea is that, in trade, the gain of one party is the loss of the other. This idea was popular, and it came spontaneously even to acute minds like Montaigne. I am tempted to call it a basic ideological element, an "ideologeme," and to see it in relation to the general disparagement of trade and money that is characteristic of traditional societies in general. To think of exchange as advantageous to both parties represented a basic change and signaled the advent of economics. Now this change occurs precisely in the mercantilist period, not suddenly, but progressively (Barbon). The ideologeme lingers on; while it recedes from the domain of internal trade—be it only because, considered globally, the gains and losses of particular agents cancel each other out—it is found in full force in the domain of international trade. It lies at the root of what Heckscher calls the "statism" of the economy as opposed to the dynamism of the State: the sum of wealth present in the world is taken as constant, and the aim of the policy is for one particular State to get the greatest possible share of that total and constant sum of wealth. Thus, with Colbert (Heckscher 1955, 2:24 ff.).

On a different level, it is striking to find in a thinker of Locke's caliber a clear trace of the heterogeneous conception of internal and external transactions and of the inability to unify the field across national boundaries. Reasoning about the optimum amount of money a country ought to possess, Locke sees the price of the goods in international trade as determined solely by internal conditions, namely, by the internal price in the exporting country. External trade, that is, is not conceived as a sort of trade existing in its own right but only as an adjunct to internal trade, not as an economic phenomenon per se but as a set of transactions in which the price is determined by economic (internal) phenomena (ibid., 2:239–42).

Thus, mercantilist literature clearly shows that, if a separate domain was to be recognized as economic, it must be carved out of the political domain: the economic point of view demanded to be emancipated from the political. Subsequent history tells us that there was another side to this "emancipation": economics had to emancipate itself from morality. (This is an inexact formula, but let it serve for the time being.)

This point may seem strange at first glance, but the necessity can be understood—or, at any rate, we can familiarize ourselves with the climate in which it appears—by a brief reflection. One may well ask, in a quite general manner, whether there can be a social or human science that would not be normative. We social scientists mostly contend or suppose not only that such can be, but also that such should be the case; in imitation of the natural sciences, we hold that science is value-free. But the philosopher can argue a priori that a science *of man* is by definition normative, and he will support this statement by denying either that our social science is really a science, or that it is devoid of value judgments. We may perhaps leave the question open regarding a hypothetically global science of man in society, but the philosopher's doubt is strongly reinforced if we consider the case of a *particular* social science—of a social science, that is, that studies only some aspects and not others of social life, as is the case with economics.

Here the philosopher will ask whether the initial postulate by which such a science ideally separates, that is, constitutes itself, can possibly be free of value judgment. Rather than discussing the question in the abstract, I observe that the history of the genesis of economics and of its first or "classical" phase fully confirms the philosopher's surmise. Gunnar Myrdal has shown that a normative aspect clings all along to economics. As to the genesis itself, we shall see in some detail that the distinctness of

the economic domain rests on the postulate of an inner consistency *oriented to the good* of man. This is easy to grasp, in the
circumstances: the emancipation from politics required the surmise of inner consistency, for otherwise order should be introduced from the outside. But that was not quite enough, for
supposing it was shown that the inner consistency worked for
evil, then again it would have required the politician and
statesman to intervene. We may observe, en passant, that the
assumption of consistency itself may be viewed as the residue,
within an avowedly purely descriptive social science, of its normative or teleological foundation. In the eagerness with which
the founders of economics took hold, in the most uncritical
manner, of any correlations that presented themselves immediately to their minds, we see a reflection of this sine qua non
condition. When Schumpeter wonders at such arbitrary assumptions as, for instance, the ubiquitous notion that
foodstuffs, by their very existence, create the population that
will consume them,[2] he simply forgets the paramount need that
engendered such beliefs, the need for immanent laws to guaran-
tee the independence of the domain and of the consideration
applied to it. Thus James Mill:

> The production of commodities ... is the one and uni-
> versal cause which creates a market for the commodities
> produced ... [and further,] the quantity of any one com-
> modity [produced] may easily be carried beyond its due
> proportion; but by this very circumstance is implied that
> some other commodity is not provided in sufficient pro-
> portion. (Mill 1807, pp. 65–68)

That the independence of economics from politics was not
given immediately and without struggle or contradiction is seen
indirectly as well, when one finds that it is not only in our times
or in political circles that pleas for reintegration or subordination
were made, but that all along, in economic circles, the question
was present in some minds.

As to the second aspect: that the internal consistency of the
economic domain is such that it is beneficent if left to itself is
transparently expressed in the axiom of "the natural harmony of
interests," as Elie Halévy called it. Not only are the interests of
two parties in a transaction not opposed, as it was originally

believed, but individual interest is also congruent with the general interest. We shall have to inquire into the genesis of this remarkable notion and its place on the global ideological map. That it was most of the time accompanied by the notably different notion of "the artificial harmony of interests" illustrates my preceding point.

The immediate impression is that it was not a simple matter to fulfill these conditions. We shall admit that they are all assembled for the first time in the *Wealth of Nations*. This fact accounts for the success of Adam Smith's book in subsequent times, its unique historical importance, even for those who would admit with Schumpeter that there is little in it that is original and that in some respects the compilation could have been more complete or better (1954, pp. 184–86 etc.). Regarding internal consistency, it is generally recognized that the decisive step was made by Docteur Quesnay and the Physiocrats, and there are good reasons to believe that without them the *Wealth* would not have seen the light of day or would have been a very different book. At the same time, Smith's divergence from Quesnay is at least as marked as his dependence on him.

The point can be related to our external conditions: with Quesnay, economics is not made radically independent from politics, nor is it severed from morality. Characteristically, with him it cannot be said that all economic interests harmonize by themselves, while in Adam Smith they do so, in principle if not always in fact. To account for this aspect of the *Wealth*, we must turn to works that are not generally recognized as landmarks in the history of economic thought. It is indeed only natural that we do so, for we then deal with the relations between the economic and the noneconomic. I found Locke's *Two Treatises of Government* enlightening as regards the relation with politics and, similarly, Mandeville's famous/infamous *Fable of the Bees*, as regards morality. The link with Adam Smith, admitted in the case of Mandeville, is to my mind no less clear, *pace* Schumpeter, in the case of Locke, whether it is direct or indirect.

To prevent misunderstanding, I should perhaps at this point insist that my basic concern is not with individual writers, their original merits, and the affiliation between them, but with, in each case, a configuration of ideas. That a particular configuration, as studied in one particular writer, is not special to him or, let us suppose, was borrowed by him from another source, only secondarily affects the argument insofar as the argument rests, in the first place, on the inner consistency of the configuration. In relation to our theme, certain configurations appear significant. Our touchstone will lie, first, in their presence in the *Wealth of Nations* and, second, in the interrelations they will bring to light. That they are common to several or many authors is important; less so is their particular pedigree.

I shall now consider in succession Quesnay, Locke's *Two Treatises*, and Mandeville's *Fable*.

Quesnay, or the Economy
as a Whole

The *Docteur* Quesnay confronts us with a paradox. By common consent, economic thought made a great step forward, thanks to the genius of this man. Yet he lived, not in the economically most progressive country of the age, England, but in France, then relatively less advanced. This can be partially explained if one thinks of the intense interchange between the two countries and insists, as Schumpeter does, on the continuity from Petty through Cantillon to Quesnay. But the paradox is found again in the content of the doctrine: industry and trade are disparaged and agriculture is extolled. The emphasis is on capitalist agriculture, and the farming entrepreneur is the central figure. As Marx remarked as early as the 1844 "Manuscripts," there is in Quesnay (and in the Physiocrats in general: I shall not make the distinction) a combination of feudal survivals and of modern or bourgeois features:

> Physiocracy is in a direct sense the *economic* decomposition of feudal property, but for this reason it is equally directly the *economic transformation*, the reestablishment, of this same feudal property, with the difference that its language is no longer feudal but economic. All wealth is reduced to *land* and *cultivation* [agriculture]. ("Manuscripts," 2d Ms.; trans., p. 121)

Is this a matter of chance? Quite to the contrary. I shall argue that there is a necessary relation between the "traditional" elements in Quesnay and his basic contribution. Marx and Schumpeter are in almost complete agreement in identifying the central merit of Quesnay. Marx stresses and extols the *Tableau Economique*. Here is an extract from his notes for book 4 of *Capital* ("Theorien über den Mehrwert"):

> ... this attempt: to represent the whole process of production of capital as process of reproduction, and circulation as

the mere form of this process of reproduction, the circulation
of money only as an element [*Moment*] of the circulation of
capital; to encompass within this process of reproduction the
origin of revenue, the exchange between capital and revenue,
the relation between reproductive consumption and definitive consumption; to encompass within the circulation of capital
the circulation between consumers and producers [actually
between capital and revenue]; finally to represent the circulation between the two great divisions of productive labor,
production of raw materials and industry, as moments in the
process of reproduction; to group all that, in the second
third [Marx: "first third"] of the eighteenth century, in the
infancy of political economy, in a table of five lines with six
points of departure or arrival, this was an extremely genial idea, no doubt the most genial idea that economics has put
to its account until now. (Translated from *Werke*, 26.1:319)[1]

As to Schumpeter, he distinctly separates Quesnay's general
theory from the *Tableau* itself (1954, p. 239). But after all, from
the present point of view, this is only a minor difference, for
both authors agree that Quesnay has given the first idea of the
economic domain as a consistent whole, as a whole made up of
interrelated parts. With him, for the first time, the economic
viewpoint brought forth, not a series of more or less disconnected observations, correlations, or aspects (like the "equilibrium mechanism," above), but the idea of an ordered whole, of
a system of logical interrelations extending to the whole domain.
Schumpeter expresses this precisely when he credits Quesnay
with the first "explicit formulation of interdependence." He
adds that Quesnay gave of the "fundamental problem" of
economics—(static) equilibrium between interdependent
quantities—a "picture" (the *Tableau*) where only much later Wal-
ras was to give a set of equations (Schumpeter 1954, pp. 242–43).

Now, my contention is that such a holistic idea could not be
reached initially from within the economic point of view itself—
insofar as the latter can be said to have existed before Quesnay's
invention—but had to be derived from outside it, had to result,
so to speak, from the *projection on the economic plane of the general
conception of the universe as an ordered whole*. This is what happened with Quesnay, and it accounts for the presence in his
thought of a very marked traditional component, which I shall
stress briefly.[2]

What Quesnay explicitly presents is a particular development of "natural law" theory, a general social-cum-political theory *with strong emphasis on the economical aspects,* which are constructed into a logical system. One could almost say that Quesnay describes the old society from a new viewpoint: his sociology-and-politics theory is quite traditional in many important respects, and within it he fits a properly economic system that is almost modern.

The traditional aspect is obvious, barefaced, when the stability of China is given as a model and as an argument against the historical relativism of a Montesquieu: there are eternal, metaphysical principles; they need only to be recognized. And, first of all, as in traditional systems in general, real wealth consists in land as distinguished from movables, and is inseparable from power over men.[3] More properly, land is the only source of real wealth, and Quesnay's landowners, *les propriétaires,* are at the same time in charge of political functions, including the administration of justice, with all the responsibilities and liabilities that this entails: the taxes should fall exclusively upon their income. Only agriculture is "national"; trade in particular is conceived as an international, that is to say, antinational, interest. The monarch is something like the first among the landowners, having a right of co-ownership (an eminent right) in the land; the taxes he levies are a revenue attached to that right. He is properly a sovereign (priest together with ruler), and the Physiocrats are not afraid of calling the political regime they support a "legal despotism." It is true that natural law rules supreme over all. The State should not interfere with it, and it should make natural law the object of compulsory public education (Quesnay 1958, 2:741; Weulersse, 2:65–66).

Within this polity, wealth circulates in a regular and harmonious fashion. The only source of it is nature, or rather the soil, aided by human activity and initiative. The basic condition of this economic order within the political order is private property, the corollary of which is freedom as the absence of any interference or regulation, whether direct or indirect, on the part of the State. We find combined here holism and individualism: holism in its traditional religious-and-political form, individualism on the economic level. As a distant but striking parallel, one would think of Leibniz's metaphysics. But my present

concern is to insist on the fact that the economy reaches the
status of a consistent system precisely in a place where it is
associated with and propped by a strictly traditional social
theory or put in the framework of a holistic view.

Two aspects of this relation may be distinguished: on the one
hand, the State, the kingdom, affords the physical as well as
moral boundaries of the system. The circulation of the annual
produce that is represented in Quesnay's famous *Tableau* is, in
its utmost extension, a picture of the circulation of nourishment
through the whole kingdom, as blood circulates in a human
body. On the other hand, the natural law, moral as well as
physical, which Quesnay thinks he is expounding, is that of the
order of the world as preordained by God. Thus, the economic
order, or system, depends both upon the body politic and upon
a general teleological orientation bearing on all aspects of human
life.

The present point of view differs from that of Schumpeter
(1954, p. 233): Schumpeter insists that Quesnay's theological
beliefs do not enter into his analysis, which is thus, according to
him, scientific. I am not disputing this; I am only observing that
the analysis does not produce its own framework, and I am
tracing the origin of this framework in Quesnay..

It is clear under the circumstances that, on the one hand, the
domain can be thought of as a whole, while, on the other hand,
it is not autonomous. This is in conformity with Quesnay's conception of order, as expressed in his definition of natural law:

> Natural laws are either physical or moral. We understand
> here by physical law *the regular course* [cours réglé] *of any
> physical event of the natural order obviously the most advantageous
> to the human genus.* We understand here by moral law *the rule*
> [la règle] *of any human action of the moral order in conformity
> with* [conforme à] *the physical order obviously the most advanta-
> geous to the human genus.* These laws together form what is
> called *the natural law.* (Trans. from *Droit Naturel,* chap. 5, Ques-
> nay 1958, 2:740)

As Schumpeter observes, we are here in line with the Scholastics: within the teleological order man as free agent is not separated from nature, and his assent is necessary for the order to
extend to his affairs. Only if men act in accordance with natural

law will the order be realized. The *Tableau* is an ideal picture, and Quesnay traces the deplorable consequences of any departure from its requirements. The right policy on the part of the State is a necessary condition of the economic order. This is a point that Adam Smith could not leave unnoticed: he argued, in substance, that the economic order is more independent of human decisions than Quesnay had made it (1904, 2:172). It must be added, though, that according to Quesnay, the right policy of the State is by and large one of abstention. The State has few positive duties: external protection, the maintenance of a network of communications, the care of the poor, the levy of its income exclusively from land, and education of the people in natural law. Yet again, as Schumpeter observes, Quesnay was concerned with reforming the bad practices of the State, and reform meant that the State had to act upon itself in order to become nonactive in economic matters.

On the whole, here is our paradox: the consistency of the domain is "explicitly formulated" for the first time, not by someone who separates it from politics, morality, and religion, but by a man who argues from the overall consistency of the world, including human, or moral, affairs, to the *conditional* consistency of the particular domain. And I might add: not by starting from the individual agent and arguing in terms of cause and effect, but by starting from a teleological order including and warranting the freedom of the individual agent. No doubt Adam Smith went further than that. We shall have to see how.

There is perhaps one more fundamental feature that classical economics owes to Quesnay, which Marx underlines and Schumpeter does not ignore. To paraphrase Marx very briefly: it was essential to separate production from circulation, etc., for no progress was possible as long as "surplus value" could be searched for in the sphere of circulation and was not considered independently from circulation. To begin with, it was possible to do so only in agriculture, where surplus value is clearly visible apart from circulation, and this is one reason why agriculture is prominent in the place where this separation is made for the first time ("Mehrwert," French trans., 1:44 ff.).

It is a fact that Quesnay neatly separates two processes: the *production* (or reproduction) of the "annual produce," which includes, over and above the equivalent of the total investment,

the "net produce," which in Marx's view can be roughly
equated with what he calls "surplus value." Then in a second
stage Quesnay studies, in his *Tableau*, the circulation, or *distribution*, of the produce among his three classes of economic agents.
A similar dichotomy, it is well known, rules in Smith, Ricardo,
and Marx and in the classics in general. (I say "similar"; cf.
Myrdal 1953, p. 113.) Schumpeter at bottom deplores it—and
this is a valuable indication for us—but he does not explain its
prevalence, even if we may gather hints from him for gaining
some understanding of it.

In this regard, Quesnay represents a step in a process that will
be easier to grasp when we reach Adam Smith. Let me for the
moment try to characterize Quesnay's step. Opposing the mercantilist spirit, it was essential for him to stress what "real
wealth" consisted in, or rather (Schumpeter has the word) the
creation of real wealth. He saw it in agriculture, called it "production," and therefore called all other pursuits unproductive. In
doing so he was making a value judgment in accordance with
his world view (the means of human subsistence, the objects of
human consumption, are the essential goods). He was also mod-
ifying a tenet of Cantillon, and of Petty before him, who had
isolated land and labor as the twin sources of wealth. Instead of
thinking of a "par" or rate of correspondence between the two
factors, making it possible to express both in terms of one of
them—land—Quesnay hierarchized them: land was the productive factor—the natural fertility of the soil alone accounted for
the increase in real wealth from seed to harvest—and human
labor and initiative were merely necessary adjuvants in the process, in keeping with the idea of natural law as physical-cum-
moral law.[4] On the whole, the economic process was essentially
a process of increase in wealth, that is, *production*, and the secret
of this increase lay in land (or the set of natural powers): a
single, self-sufficient entity enshrined the rationale of the
economic process. Economy was production, and production
was land. Through a quite traditional hierarchization—nature
commands morality, land commands labor—we have here the
first step in the identification of the economy with a single essential factor, a *causa sui*, a substance. The subsequent development leaves no doubt on the point. To anticipate, I can adduce
one of the passages in Marx where the word *substance* is used

and which shows that for him, at any rate, the process was of the kind I suggest. He says that, with the Physiocrats, surplus value does not yet take its proper form because "they have not yet reduced *value* itself to its simple substance [*einfache Substanz*]," that is, labor ("Mehrwert," *Werke*, 26.1:14).

If, as I shall insist later on, this mode of thinking is individualist at one remove—the individual, as a self-sufficient entity, thinking of his world in terms of self-sufficient entities or substances—then we have here one more individualist feature in Quesnay. But just as this feature is still half-decided, so are his economic conceptions and his moderate version of natural-law theory encompassed in a holistic framework. If this framework gives Quesnay the rare privilege of seeing the economy as a whole, it is at the same time relatively unmodern as compared to what is to come. We can thus understand that Quesnay's "innovation" came from France, and not from England: the line of thought of Cumberland, for instance, whose influence on Quesnay was stressed by Hasbach (1893), is largely submerged in England in Quesnay's time.

All in all, with Quesnay order commands property, and property commands freedom; that is, order commands property and freedom. This configuration appears the more remarkable if, together with the time interval between the two authors, Locke's undoubted influence on Quesnay is borne in mind, for in Locke property has pride of place, as we shall see presently.

4

Locke's *Two Treatises:* Emancipation from Politics

From a trend of thought in which individualism remains contained, as in fetters, within holism, we pass now to a trend of thought in which holism is superseded and individualism reigns supreme. This is my reason for discussing Quesnay prior to Locke, which does not mean that Quesnay was uninfluenced by Locke in other regards or on other levels. As I stated earlier, this second trend of thought, which will be represented here by Locke and Mandeville only, enters as a basic component into the *Wealth of Nations*.

If, as we found from mercantilism, the full assertion of the economic dimension demanded its emancipation from politics, then it will be hard to find a text more important for our consideration than Locke's *Two Treatises of Government*. [1] Economics as such is not present there; it is only a matter of the dimension, which we know in retrospect to be the economic dimension *in statu nascendi*, powerfully asserting itself against the political. If such is our main concern, this relation is only an aspect of a wider configuration of ideas; and, just as it would be dangerous to isolate entirely the *Two Treatises* from Locke's philosophy in general, so it is impossible to leave the relations with morality and religion out of the picture, even if the study is very delicate and threatens to wreck the student's course. This is the more important, as the relation with morality is also implicated in the birth of economics and will come to the foreground with Mandeville.

I recalled above how the political dimension had developed from within religion (see Introd., p. 15). We reach here a further stage in this process of differentiation, a stage that, needless to say, occurs in its turn within the general religious and philosophical ideology.

The Christian religion has directly contributed to the initial

and sometimes the lasting assumptions of many disciplines or
trends of thought. This kind of general osmosis has been the
object of some study concerning "natural philosophy." In the
human sciences this osmosis is sometimes obvious, as it is in
the philosophy of history, but more often it is unknown or
unheeded, as it is in economics. As to the relation between
politics and economics, it would seem that either predominates
over the other in any given trend of thought: thus politics in
what is often called mercantilism, economics in the Marxist
philosophy of history (cf. below, pp. 134 ff.).

Nothing is clearer than Locke's polemics against Filmer in the
first of the *Two Treatises of Government*. When Filmer states that
Adam was the first patriarchal monarch, he is postulating a
continuity between the authority of the father in the family and
that of the king in society. He is implying as well a whole view of
social order in which we can isolate the following components:
(1) the stress is on society or the group, as a whole built on
subordination: the king or father rules by a delegation from the
ultimate Ruler, the Creator; (2) this idea of subordination
applies not only to men but also to all earthly beings, which God
has explicitly committed to man's rule (Adam's and, more definitely, we are told, Noah's). To put it in another light, Adam's
prescribed rulership over creatures is interpreted by Filmer as
extending to human and nonhuman alike, and this is one of the
points on which Locke takes Filmer sternly to task for his interpretation of the Bible. The word *rulership* perhaps lacks clarity, but what I mean is that man's relation to animals and things
is thought of on the model of the king's relation to inferior men
or subjects. This represents, I submit, a traditional view, where
economics is not distinguished for its own sake within the political (or politicoeconomic) sphere characterized by subordination.
In other words, subordination is here acknowledged as natural
and necessary, as a cardinal principle that transcends the distinction between human and nonhuman and encompasses relationships between which we would distinguish.

In contradistinction to Filmer's traditionalism, Locke's innovation stands crystal-clear before our eyes: subordination goes
overboard and with it the link it maintained between relationships among men and relations between men and inferior creatures. A split between the two is established, one could say

institutionalized. Between men and beasts it is a matter of property or ownership: God has given the earth to the human
species for appropriation—and homologously, man is, in the
second Treatise, God's work and property. As for men, there is
among them no inherent difference, no hierarchy: they are all
free and equal in God's eyes, the more so since any difference in
status would, in this system, tend to be coterminous with ownership.

> . . . there cannot be supposed to be any such *Subordination*
> among us, that may Authorize us to destroy one another, as if
> we were made for another's uses, as the inferior ranks of
> Creatures are for ours. (Locke 1963, II, § 6, ll. 16–19).

Let me add that, as some kind of subordination is empirically
necessary in political society, such subordination can be built
only on the unanimous consent of the constituting members.
Locke's law of nature pictures essentially a three-tiered world
order—God, mankind, and inferior creatures—in which
equality characterizes the human tier, and the relation between
one superior and one inferior tier tends to be thought of as
"property." This order is of course much simplified or im-
poverished as compared to the celestial and terrestrial hierar-
chies of yore; it centers in the solidification and unification of the
human species as against the rest of nature or terrestrial beings,
that is, in a man-versus-nature dualism that is warranted by the
ultimate reference to the Creator.

To insist on the wholesale aspect of the transformation
(whether the transformation was or was not entirely Locke's
invention is immaterial) concerning social and political life in
general, a holistic view centering on subordination and encompassing what we call economic phenomena has been replaced
by a view centering on property—that is, on the individual and
on economics—and reducing politics to an ontologically marginal adjunct to be constructed by men according to their lights.
This is an incomplete, unilateral formula. The converse formulation would be that politics has been raised from the status of the
merely given to the status of the freely devised and willed. The
latter modern formula is itself, of course, grievously insufficient
unless we complement it with the former.

On the historical importance of the event there is no need to insist, but a comment on vocabulary is apposite: the exact nature of the event remains hidden as long as we persist in merely comparing Filmer's and Locke's "political theories," for the event embodies a sea change in the very essence of "the political." If we define it through subordination, we must then recognize that subordination is ontologically present in Filmer while it is ontologically denied and only *empirically* present in Locke, whose main motive was to destroy absolutism, the "French disease" (see Laslett, in Locke 1963, pp. 62 ff., 99). We cannot call "political" in this sense either Locke's general theory or even the restricted part of it that concerns "government": it is clear that the scope and meaning of it are totally different from what it aims to replace. Should we take the opposite view and define politics from the individualistic angle—and, as we start from ourselves, this is what is done most frequently in our time—then it should be clear that we cannot consider in the same light representations of Filmer's sort without forcing on them a sociocentric reduction. (What applies to Filmer applies a fortiori to traditional or "primitive" societies.) Comparatively, the modern theory appears to be rather an attempt to avoid the recognition of subordination as a basic principle, while producing synthetically a makeshift, an *ersatz*, of it for empirical purposes—what Locke calls a "Magistrate." To speak of "politics" generally and unwarily is to throw an imaginary bridge over an abyss. To survey the abyss we need to map out the entire configuration of ideas and values. For the moment, it is only a matter of the relation between what we loosely call "politics" and "economics": while subordination encompasses what we call economic phenomena, property commands the artificial construction of a polity from individual atoms. If these statements sound strange, it is only a measure of the falling apart of everything in our atomized universe.[2]

An objection can be raised against the conclusion I have just reached. I took "property" to be an economic category, and yet it would not be difficult to find a number of passages where property is something different or, in any case, something much wider than my interpretation warrants. The opportunity to look into Locke's concept of property is welcome.

No one will dispute that property is crucial in Locke's political theory or that he innovated by putting it back, so to speak, into the state of nature and by basing it, in principle at least, on labor. The later developments of the latter innovation in economic theory favor my interpretation.[3] In recent years, Macpherson has happily affixed to Locke's theory the label *possessive individualism* and has rightly insisted on the importance of Locke's second stage in the development of property, when, in the state of nature itself, the invention of money removes the initial limitations on property rights and allows for unlimited accumulation not only of money but of land as well (Macpherson 1962).

Macpherson argues that Locke read back into the state of nature conceptions of his own time and mixed with them older, essentially medieval, conceptions. A glance at the transition proves to be revealing. When Locke introduces property as deriving from the necessary appropriation by the individual of whatever he removes from nature, as given to mankind in common for its immediate use, we are reminded of the Pope explaining to the Franciscan monks in the fourteenth century that the soup or cheese they eat are thus their property and that they should therefore own themselves as proprietors of the riches they dispose of for their maintenance. We are further reminded of Locke's nominalist ancestor, Ockham, rejoining on this occasion that use is one thing and that ownership, as sanctioned by positive law, is another (Dumont 1965, pp. 20–21, nn. 7, 11). Similarly, the limitations that Locke recognizes to the primitive right of appropriation seem to be in line with medieval, holistic justice and wisdom. In essence, this right should be oriented to the social needs as a whole or—what here amounts in practice to the same thing—to the preservation of all individuals equally. This is not the case when, in his second stage, Locke justifies unlimited accumulation, which was later to be guaranteed by the political order. But, as yet in the first stage, we observe that to base property on the individual's *labor* and not on his *needs* is typically modern,[4] and that whatever is consonant with medieval ideas appears here only in the guise of *limitations* (to be removed later without remnant) to that individualistic definition.

Along the same lines, and whatever precise meaning is attached to the word *property,* when justice is derived from property, we are obviously at the antipodes of medieval thought. The conception of justice as arising, not from the idea of the whole and of ordered relationships within it, but rather from the individual in whatever aspect, is strikingly modern. This innovation stems from Hobbes and was to be accepted by Hume, so it deserves to be called British. By what stretch of the imagination can such a system be supposed collectivist instead of individualist (Kendall 1965)? The misconception can arise only from having concentrated on the formal political aspects while losing sight of what is undoubtedly their basis.

But let us return to our difficulty. The word *property* has most often in Locke a very broad meaning: "Life, liberty, and estate." Thus, men enter into society for the "mutual *Preservation* of their Lives, Liberties and Estates, which I call by the general Name, *Property*" (II, § 123). Or again (II, § 173): "By *Property* I must be understood here, as in other places, to mean that Property which Men have in their Persons as well as Goods." Peter Laslett aptly discusses this usage, which seems to have been widespread or "normal" in the seventeenth century, and which at the same time is clearly important or functional in Locke himself (Laslett, in Locke 1963, introd., pp. 100–102; notes to I, § 90, II, §§ 27, 87). For to base property in goods on labor is precisely to derive a title to extraneous things from what most evidently and actually belongs to the individual, his body and effort—in other words, to take advantage of the widest meaning of "property" (or "propriety") in order to establish the restricted meaning (property in goods), which in turn is equivalent to deriving a juridical relation between man and things, not from the necessities of the social order, but from an intrinsic property of man as an individual. This is only one aspect of the concept, but I believe it to be an important one. To borrow from Laslett's formulation: what man *can* alienate seemingly belongs to him more surely when it is lumped together with what he *cannot* alienate.

Macpherson has discussed in detail, not only Locke's theory of property right, but also the Levellers' views on franchise and freedom, and I find the parallel enlightening. He says, in a footnote,

> The Levellers spoke of having a property *in* a thing, meaning a right to use, enjoy, exclude others from, or dispose of, that thing. Thus they could speak of a property in land, in estate,

in right to trade, in the franchise, or in one's person. (Macpherson 1962, p. 143, n. 3)[5]

Two points are worth noticing: wage-earners and beggars are excluded from the franchise on the ground that they are not independent, that they are "included in their masters" (ibid., p. 145); moreover, men are free as proprietors of themselves, that is, in particular, of their body and their labor (the difference with the Independents on this point is certainly important, but it need not detain us here). To paraphrase: to be independent, not to be "included" in anyone, and to be guaranteed against the attacks or encroachments of anyone, is to be able to dispose of oneself without interference from the outside, that is to say, indifferently, to be free or to be the proprietor of oneself, body, labor, and all. In Macpherson's words, the Levellers conceived of freedom as "proprietorship of one's own person and capacities."

We are close to Locke, but what I should like to single out is one particular aspect of the parallelism: the Levellers' conception of franchise gives one clue regarding what it is that their conception of freedom and property is opposed to: wage-earners are not independent; they are "included in their masters." Whatever the practical impact of the expression, I surmise that "included" means here essentially what I call "encompassed": such people are not independent because they are caught in a hierarchical relationship, and it is in contradistinction to this situation that freedom-proprietorship emerges. We have thus in the notion of inclusion in one's master the equivalent, in relation to property or freedom, of subordination in Locke.[6]

To return to Locke, I think that this discussion of property does not invalidate the view I proposed, but leads to a more precise expression of it: property here is not an economic category, pure and simple, but an economic category *in statu nascendi,* before the umbilical cord has been cut. What is essential is that, with property, something that is exclusively of the individual is made central to a realm of consideration and facts that was governed by holistic, hierarchical considerations.

This is the point where we part company with Macpherson: possession is not a historically transient accident of a permanent phenomenon called individualism; on the contrary, it is in the guise of possession or property that individualism raises its head, knocks down any remnant of social submission and ideal hierarchy in society, and installs itself on the throne thus made vacant. I need not here labor the point: economics as a "philosophical category" represents the acme of individualism and as such tends to be paramount in our universe.

*

Polin has pointed out that Locke realized an original synthesis of morality and politics (Polin 1960); this partial truth is best combined with our recognition of the relation between economics and politics, and I think we shall not be far off the mark if we say that, in Locke, politics as such is *reduced to an adjunct of morality and economics*. Morality and economics provide, in the "law of nature," the basis on which political society should be constructed. Of course, the view can be reversed by saying that, while morality and economics are merely given (in nature), society is freely contrived by man. But man's freedom consists here in obeying the law of nature.

I have noted the disappearance of subordination as a social principle; it is largely replaced by moral obligation. I mean that both have the same function as regards the empirical individual, for, obviously, it is moral obligation that prevents liberty from degenerating into mere license. This statement affords an insight into the mechanism of the transformation of which Locke is the exponent, or at least a sociological approach to it. When we say that subordination is functionally replaced by moral obligation, we hint at a procedure for comparing holistic and individualistic values; in some way, morality must provide an equivalent of social order: it may be considered from one angle as an internalization of directly social values. A process of this kind has been—and still is—at work all through the transformation: and, regarding Locke, I think the view is confirmed by the whole of his philosophy, general as well as political. Thus the "true and solid happiness" that should be preferred by the free and rational creature is finally human order (or what remains of cosmic order) *as it appears to the individual, who is bound to think in terms of hedonism.* [7]

Let us look at the act of constituting civil or political society: individuals living in the state of nature congregate and agree to

unite and constitute a power, a "judge on earth," by laying
down and uniting the powers they had over each other in the
state of nature. Clearly, this is only the obverse of the coin, the
face of rights, and there is a reverse—that of duties—whereby
the obligation to the "common judge" is derived from a previous obligation. In other terms, there can be a factual subordination only because there had already been obligation. (A previous
obligation to whom? To each other or to God?)

If it is easy to see how Locke's view of morality underlies and
makes possible his politics, it is difficult to grasp the full articulation between religion in general and politics. I must here make
do without a good deal of preliminary discussion.[8]

One point can be singled out: the question of the relation
between God and the law of nature, also called "rule of morals."

Regarding the law of nature, Peter Laslett has insisted on the
peculiar relation between the political work (the *Two Treatises*)
and the philosophical, or epistemological, *Essay on Understanding.* In the *Two Treatises* we find the existence of the law of nature
"suavely asserted" and taken for granted. But if we turn to the
Essay for demonstration, we are greatly disappointed, as it is
practically absent from that work. Laslett concludes that Locke
has purposely left the question in the air, which thus creates a
gulf between his political theory and his metaphysics—a gulf
that may have been very profitable to the former—and was content to take, in the matter of natural law, a stance that was
sufficient—if I understand rightly—to procure the benevolent
attention of his contemporaries (Laslett, in Locke 1963, pp. 83–
87).

Leo Strauss has been more radical in his criticism. According
to him, Locke could not fulfill his promise of a deductive theory
of ethics, nor could he demonstrate the existence of a law of
nature, because of the lack, in Polin's phrase, of "a sufficient
theological ... support" (Strauss 1953, chap. 5b; Polin 1960, p.
113 n.). The "prudent" Locke did not dare to assail his contemporaries' belief in God, which he found of some practical value,
and yet he was unable to endorse it and thus give a solid basis to
his "rule of morals." Strauss is certainly not sympathetic to
Locke. He does not reconstruct Locke's preoccupations, nor
does he allow for differences in point of view or even in thought
between his different writings, and yet we cannot deny that

something of Strauss's criticism sticks in the mind of the reader. Subsequent to Strauss's criticism, Von Leyden published the Latin text and a translation of the eight *Essays on the Law of Nature*, dating from Locke's early period in Christ Church (1660–64), which afford precisely the demonstration of which Strauss had judged Locke incapable. Yet, as Laslett has observed, this does not solve the problem posed by later texts and attitudes. Other writers have maintained (for example, Gough, Polin) that Locke truly and deeply believed in God while being as latitudinarian as could be wished and maintaining in a Socinian fashion that revelation contained nothing contrary to reason. Polin vindicated against all critics the consistency of Locke's political philosophy, centering it largely on the link between liberty and moral obligation, the existence of God being the warrant of it all insofar as it guaranteed the coincidence between the rational and the natural orders.[9]

What is the problem for us? It is not so much to know whether Locke sincerely believed in God or merely pretended to in order to speak with the desired effect to his contemporaries, for in both cases a link is supposed between religion and Locke's ideas, whether this link is at the level of the individual Locke or at that of the reading public in England or Europe at the time. Moreover, if we bear in mind our inquiry into Locke's view of property, we shall better understand that only a religion reduced to deism could possibly support such a possessive individualism as his. The question is, rather, of the degree of necessity in the association of religion and the rest or of what religion affords in the matter, of which exchange takes place between religion and the special consideration of civil or political society. There are close Stoic parallels to much of Locke's moral utterances (Polin), and one might think that the Christian religion is not here a necessary ingredient. Nevertheless, the Stoics did not engineer political societies. Maybe there are two clues to the solution of our problem. The first is found in the general history of political and other speculation: here as elsewhere the special consideration, politics, was emancipated gradually from the general and normative consideration, religion. In this regard, the role afforded in Locke by morality marks a transition, as there is scarcely any doubt that his notion of the individual as a

moral being is closely bound up with his religion, at least at the
outset (in the Essays of the 1660s).

The second clue is found in Locke's own evolution, as
documented by Von Leyden from comparison between the early
essays and the subsequent writings, up to those of 1690. The
development of hedonism, negated at the start, stands out
clearly. It helps to reinforce the importance of rewards and
punishments in the afterlife, for otherwise the coincidence between pleasure and good, pain and evil, would be impaired. No
wonder that later on, in the "Reasonableness of Christianity,"
Locke confessed that reason had failed in its major business
(Laslett, in Locke 1963, p. 88): he had been caught in a circle; he
had not been able to offer the deductive theory of abstract ethics
that he had promised—nor, about 1690, had he consented to
publish his early essays on natural law, although he kept using
materials for them (Von Leyden, in Locke 1954, p. 60 ff.; Laslett,
in Locke 1963, pp. 81 ff.). This evolution that ended in failure—
a failure, by the way, that is more to the credit of the
philosopher than many a success—seems to testify that for him
the backing of religion was still indispensable to his individualistic politics. The same conclusion can be reached in another way.
As Von Leyden rightly insists, Locke maintains an easy transition from factual to corresponding normative statements. Now,
this point can be understood only if we bear in mind that the
individual is given, together with the species, within a teleology
based on God's will: the *individual is given in relation to God*. In
other words, the link of morality with religion ensures moral
obligation.

The latter corresponds to a feature of Locke's politics.
Willmoore Kendall has dared to reverse the more common view
of Locke by asserting that he was more of a collectivist than
an individualist in politics or, more precisely, that he deserves to
be taken as the father of the "metaphysical theory of the State"
(1965).

What seems more likely is that Locke supplemented his individualistic ideology with a good deal of empiricism. The argument as to majority rule is exemplary in this sense: in practice the
system cannot effectively work without majority rule; hence it is
supposed that the original contract of society implied majority

rule. No attempt is made to show that the rule of the majority is compatible and consonant with the individualistic basis. It is assumed that there must be a workable system answering the ideological conditions that have been posited. In other terms, the ideology is supplemented by an arbitrary assertion, an act of faith that can be taken as well as a statement from experience. That there lurks in the background some trace of holism is seen from the (rare) assertion of the common will as "one Will" (II, § 212; see also §§ 214, 222). It will be left to Rousseau to attempt to justify the device ideologically in his doctrine of the general will. Now my point is that such a simple procedure, or such an assertion as that of the workability of the system, rests on teleology, that is, in the last analysis, on faith.

Locke was content to introduce his basic ideological or normative principle in order to destroy subordination and to base the political order on consent. To complete or correct the picture, he could here or there rely on the empirical, that is, he could open the door surreptitiously to holism or to religion.

Similarly, but more directly, morality takes support from faith to offer a substitute for holism in the human species as a carrier of moral obligation. This will be my last point. Kendall again observes that, in the state of nature, the rights inhere, not in the individual as such, but in the individual-in-relation-to-others, and he concludes that some kind of community (which in my own terms means some form of holism) is thus presupposed (1965, p. 69).[10] This is only partially true. Kendall does well to insist on the reciprocity of rights and duties in the state of nature. But to say *relation* is not to say *community*. Among the different meanings of *society* in Locke, there is one that comes from the Stoics and designates the human species as the ideal society of all men, taken abstractly:

> ... he and ... *Mankind are one Community* .... And were it not for the corruption and vitiousness of degenerate Men, there would be no need ... that Men should separate from this great and natural Community and ... combine into smaller and divided associations. (Locke, II, § 128)

To be sure, this is not a society for us, but it is within this so-called society and not, by any means, within a concrete community that the reciprocal structure of rights and duties is conceived. What Kendall no longer understands—and many others with him—is that the individual is a moral being and as such is characterized by *outward relations as well as inward qualities.* He is given *in relation* to God and his fellow men, and, thanks to the relation to God, the abstract relation between members of the human species can be substituted for the links within a community. In subsequent history, at least on the commonsense level, the individual has emancipated himself— once more—from this still-compelling structure, but that is another story. I submit that, for Locke, to conceive a society as the juxtaposition of abstract individuals was possible only because for the concrete bonds of society he could substitute morality as uniting those individuals into the human species under the eye of God.

In other terms, I submit that in this case the substitution of man as an individual for man as a social being was possible because Christianity warranted the individual as a *moral* being. The transition was thus made possible from a holistic social order to a political system raised by consent as a superstructure on an ontologically given economic basis.

It can be objected that in this condensed formulation of the configuration of ideas found in the *Two Treatises* the configuration is unduly dynamized and historicized. I take, in effect, the polemics against Filmer as marking a transition, a watershed between holism in the past and individualism in the future. Of course, this is schematic. More precisely, the view is that Locke's exposition is highly symbolic of a clash between two ideologies that were predominant, the one in the past, the other in the future. It is not necessary to suppose either that the transition appeared here for the first time or that Locke expressed a notion that was present in some manner in the minds of his contemporaries. Locke's configuration appears meaningful in the context of the development of ideas as it is for the moment still largely assumed and will be, I think, to some extent confirmed subsequently. In other words, its significance in modern ideology in general will be clearer later on, especially in relation to Adam Smith. Yet I am confident that a thoughtful reader has already some feeling of its relevance, from what we said above, on the one hand, and from his general knowledge of more recent views, on the other. Thus, perhaps the most revealing

aspect in this configuration is that economics is not simply juxtaposed to politics but is hierarchically superior to it, a parallel to
the Marxist infrastructure/superstructure that is not inferred
from observation but proceeds from the internal consistency of
the ideology. In our formulation—which is largely hypothetical
at this stage—the parallel is commanded by the ideological constraint of the transition from holism (primacy of the relations
between men) to individualism (primacy of the relations of man
to things; in this case, property). In other terms, it looks as if the
emancipation of the economic dimension from politics corre-
sponded to that change in primacy, a change that is equivalent,
in later terms, to seeing the infrastructure as more important
than the superstructure.

5 Mandeville's *Fable of the Bees*: Economics and Morality

That the economic dimension could not assert itself without emancipating itself from politics was obvious from the starting point, where it is found embedded in politics. On the contrary it becomes clear that something of the same kind had to happen in relation to morality only once after the process had been completed—in the end product, the *Wealth of Nations* (insofar as it may be taken at any rate as a "first" end product). But, to speak simply of an emancipation from morality would be at once excessive and insufficient: in this case the relation is more subtle. There is actually an emancipation *from the general or common run of morality,* but it is accompanied by the recognition that economic action is by itself oriented to the good, that it has a *special moral character of its own.* It is by virtue of this special characteristic that it is allowed to escape the general form of moral judgment. In other words, there is only a specialization of morals; or again, economics escapes the fetters of general morality only at the price of assuming a normative character of its own.

This general statement can be illustrated by a view that I shall try to substantiate in what follows: Adam Smith is not only the author of the *Wealth* but also of the *Theory of Moral Sentiments.* For him, in opposition to the general sphere of moral sentiments based on *sympathy,* economic activity is the one activity of man in which there is no need for anything but *self-love:* by pursuing only their particular interests, men unwittingly work for the common good, and this is where the famous "Invisible Hand" comes into play. In this doctrine of the *natural harmony of interests,* as Elie Halévy called it, morality is superseded for the particular sphere. For morality, if anything, teaches that self-love should be subordinated to higher ends. Adam Smith's Invisible Hand performs here a little-noticed function. It is as if God told us,

"Don't be afraid, my child, of apparently trespassing against my commands. I have so arranged everything that you are justified in neglecting morality in this particular case."

In my Introduction, I related the feature under consideration to the ideological constraints that must bear on any attempt to isolate a special view of social phenomena in general and to the value judgment that must implicitly, at least, ground it; perhaps the study of Locke's *Treatises* has revealed such a judgment, but it is only a part of the story. When turning from Hobbes and Locke to Adam Smith and beyond, one is struck by a remarkable difference between political and economic speculation. In political speculation, from Hobbes onward, the great motive force is artificialism, the idea that we can properly know only what we make or, with Locke, only the ideas of our own mind. In such an approach, norms are present in one form or the other from the start, and the same is true of any speculation based on natural law. Economics will constitute itself much more as a natural science; it will study what happens "out there" as a natural phenomenon. It will thus represent an appeal from the norms to the facts; and since such an appeal is impossible, it is clear that economics will have to bring in its own special norms in one guise or another (perhaps from its own version of natural law or, as springing immediately from the facts, "natural harmony"). Both deduction and induction are present in Adam Smith, as in Hume, but the growth of empiricism as against artificialism is characteristic. As artificialism is no doubt one of the major axes of modern ideology, the contrast is interesting.

After all, the same appeal from norms to facts was present at the birth of politics, when Machiavelli detached it from religion and morality with his "reason of state." This can be raised in objection to the contrast made above, but in Hobbes the Machiavellian fact has become a norm. Or again, Montesquieu was no artificialist either, but he played no leading role in political speculation in the epoch and milieu here referred to. His influence is more on the level of a kind of general sociology, like that of Ferguson.

Such features as I have tried to sketch certainly do not exhaust the question of the particular relation between economics and morality. If a secret remains, then no witness is in a better position to reveal it than Mandeville, who subtitled his *Fable of the Bees:* "Private Vices, Publick Benefits." [1]

It is widely admitted that the central theme of Adam Smith, the idea that self-love works for the common good, comes from Mandeville. In the introduction to his edition of the *Wealth* (Smith 1904), Edwin Cannan has elaborated the point and has given good reasons for supposing that Adam Smith had been drawn to Mandeville while still a student of Hutcheson in Glasgow. Now, Mandeville traced back to self-love all the motives of human action and equated self-love with vice. Hutcheson was much concerned with refuting Mandeville and must have lectured repeatedly about him. When Adam Smith, in his turn, in *The Theory of Moral Sentiments,* discards Mandeville's "licentious system," he adds a revealing statement: "But how destructive soever this system may appear, it could never have imposed upon so great a number of persons ... had it not in some respects bordered on the truth" (Smith 1963, p. 555). In what respects, Adam Smith does not say in this passage, but the whole *Wealth* is an answer to the question: Mandeville was right as regards the place of self-love in economic phenomena. Indeed, if one remembers that "benevolence" loomed large in Hutcheson's theory of morals, a famous passage of the *Wealth,* quoted by Cannan, sounds like a rebuttal directed at Hutcheson in the name of Mandeville: "It is not from the benevolence of the butcher, the brewer, or the baker that we expect our dinner, but from their regard to their own interest" (I, ii; 1904, p. 16).

We are thus sent back from Adam Smith to Mandeville for the origin of the key assumption of the *Wealth of Nations,* and this is more than a minute point of literary history, for, as we are going to see, the problem of the relation between economics and morality was acutely—indeed, explosively—posed by Mandeville at the beginning of the century.

Bernard de Mandeville, born in the Netherlands, had settled in London as a physician. In 1705 he published a sixpenny satire in verse called *The Grumbling Hive; or, Knaves Turn'd Honest.* This poem in doggerel verse grew into a book by the addition of "Remarks" and other pieces in two successive editions (1714, 1723), under the title: *The Fable of the Bees; or, Private Vices, Publick Benefits* (Kaye's critical edition: Mandeville 1924). The subtitle summarizes the argument of the poem: a hive, presented as a mirror of human society, lives in corruption and prosperity. Harboring some nostalgia for virtue, it prays to recover it. When the prayer is granted, an extraordinary transformation takes place: with vice gone, activity and prosperity disappear and are replaced by sloth, poverty, and boredom in a much reduced population.

The 1723 edition started a scandal, which Mandeville attributed to the inclusion in that edition of "An Essay on Charity, and Charity-Schools," detrimental to the good conscience and cheap humanitarianism of their patrons. Be that as it may, the refutations followed each other, the book became an object of execration, and it became known to everybody in educated Europe, as is evidenced by the fact that every moralist referred to it (see Kaye's appendixes, ibid.). Apart from the "Remarks" and the essay already mentioned, the book contains a short "Enquiry into the Origin of Moral Virtue" (immediately following the poem) and, at the end, "A Search into the Nature of Society," in which Mandeville expounded his views in opposition to those of Shaftesbury. "A Vindication of the Book" was added after it had been "presented as a nuisance" by the Grand Jury of Middlesex and made the object of "an abusive letter." In 1729 there appeared separately a "second part" to the book, which contains six dialogues that are ingeniously contrived as a defense and a development of the thesis and that present, partly, perhaps, for this reason, a distinct shift of emphasis.

The first volume, the *Fable* proper, presents already a distinct shift as compared with the initial poem, the *Grumbling Hive*. As a recent editor has noticed (Phillip Harth, in his introduction to the Penguin edition, Mandeville 1970, pp. 19 ff.), not only are new themes introduced, but the "Remarks," which ostensibly refer, as extended notes, to passages in the poem, at the same time supplement the "Enquiry into the Origin of Moral Virtue," which precedes them. Moreover, of the trio of vices that are given in the poem as the causes of prosperity and greatness— "Fraud, Luxury, and Pride" ("The Moral"; 1924, p. 23, vs. 7)—the first, Fraud, is finally retained only as one of the "inconveniences" that accompany a brisk trade, like the dirt in the streets of London. Only Luxury and, more fundamentally, Pride maintain their status as causal factors. The place of Pride is vindicated in the "Enquiry" on Virtue, which does two things worth noting from our point of view: first, it absolutely separates morality from religion. Mandeville justifies this step by remarking that a fairly constant morality—as he defines it—is

found in different societies, together with the most diverse or
aberrant religions; actually, he takes the example of ancient
Rome. Second, the "Enquiry" presents the thesis that
morality—that is, the definition of Virtue and Vice—was in-
vented by "the Moralists and Philosophers of all Ages" or by
"wary Politicians" in order to make men sociable by submitting
their other passions to the most inveterate and powerful among
them: Pride, which makes men eager to receive praise ("the
Breath of Man, the Aerial Coin of Praise") and to avoid shame.

I think we may read here, expressed in the language of the
times, a recognition of the social nature or function of morality,
provided we do not, at the same time, forget that for
Mandeville—as for Hobbes—man is given in the presocial state
as an Individual, and as an Individual endowed with all the
mechanism of passions that Mandeville could observe among
Londoners of his day, including presumably a high development of pride. Only later was Rousseau to take the development
of pride—l'amour-propre—as a consequence of the development of civilization.[2] I insist on the proviso (that man is given
fundamentally as an Individual) because it seems to me to have
been left out by an author to whom we are otherwise deeply
indebted for his insights and for his sensitive treatment of a
theme very close to my own. I mean J. H. Tufts, in his small but
important book, *The Individual in Relation to Society as Reflected in
British Ethics of the Eighteenth Century* (Part II, 1904). Tufts traces
in the literature the progress in the recognition of the social
nature—or the social aspects—of man. He sees in Mandeville
"the Moral resolved into the merely Social" and, more widely,
"the individual as a product of social and economic forces"
(1904, pp. 14 ff.), which is true, I think, only in a limited sense,
as we shall see more and more clearly as we proceed.

We find a first indication in the last piece in the *Fable*, the
anti-Shaftesbury pamphlet on the nature of society. Its argument shows that, for Mandeville, the individual is logically prior
to society: where Shaftesbury starts from the whole, Mandeville
starts from the element. As a distinct clue to Mandeville's often
ambiguous personal stand, it is worth noting that Shaftesbury is
the only author toward whom he professes downright hostility:
the optimist, the platonizing rationalist—not to say the rigorist
Churchman—is his archenemy. (It is true that Shaftesbury had

been dead for twelve years when Mandeville added this pamphlet to the *Fable* in 1723.) At the start Mandeville writes: "The attentive Reader ... will soon perceive that two Systems cannot be more opposite than his Lordship's and mine" (1924, 1:324). And again:

> This Noble Writer ... Fancies, that as Man is made for Society, so he ought to be born with a kind Affection to the whole, of which he is a part, and a Propensity to seek the Welfare of it.... His Notions I confess are generous and refined: They are a high Compliment to Human-kind.... What Pity it is that they are not true: I would not advance thus much if I had not already demonstrated in almost every Page of this Treatise, that the Solidity of them is inconsistent with our daily Experience. (Ibid., pp. 323–24)

And to quote from the conclusion:

> I flatter myself to have demonstrated that, neither the Friendly Qualities and kind Affections that are natural to Man, nor the real Virtues he is capable of acquiring by Reason and Self-Denial, are the Foundation of Society; but that what we call Evil in this World, Moral as well as Natural, is the grand Principle that makes us sociable Creatures, the solid Basis, the Life and Support of all Trades and Employments without exception. (Ibid., p. 369)

To prevent misunderstanding, it must be added that not all vices are public benefits, nor is vice automatically beneficial: it needs the "dextrous Management of a skilful Politician" (last line; also, cf. the Moral of the poem), and the idea is rather that "all benefits are based on actions ... fundamentally vicious" (Kaye, in Mandeville 1924, 1:lxxv–lxxvi). It will be observed that Mandeville here purposely widens the thesis of the poem: evil is basic, not only to social prosperity, but also to social existence altogether. How is this so? "I demonstrate that the Sociableness of Man arises only from these two things, *viz.* The Multiplicity of his Desires, and the continual Opposition he meets with in his Endeavours to gratify them," that is to say, moral evil (men's imperfections, wants, and passions) and natural evil (the obstacles presented by an intractable natural world). In other words, on the one hand man is sociable through those of his qualities that are judged to be negative, either from a strict moral view,

which judges them to be vices, or from an extended moral view,
which judges them to be wants, imperfections, or "uneasi-
nesses" (to borrow from Locke). On the other hand, man is compelled to live in society by the external world, which accumulates
obstacles to "the Business of Self-Preservation." All in all, a very
wide connotation of evil is used here to effect a transition from
the thesis of the poem—that pride and luxury are economically
useful—to a new thesis. "Diving into the very rise" of society,
Mandeville has found that the satisfaction of the individual's
material needs is the only reason why men live in society. The
point deserves to be remembered, for the notion plays, if I am
not mistaken, a key role in modern ideology: the relations between men and things—material needs—are primary, the relations between men—society—secondary.

The point is confirmed in the second volume of the *Fable*, in
which the origin and the gradual development of society constitute the major theme. The three main stages are: the forced
association of men to protect themselves from wild beasts, their
association to protect themselves from each other, and the invention of letters, essential to the establishment of laws.[3] Mandeville attributes most of the development to the slow, gradual
improvement of one generation after the other, the "joint labour
of several ages" (2:321–22, etc.), aided by the plasticity in body
and mind of the children and the double tendency of men,
rooted in the family, to revere (as children) and to dominate (as
fathers). This gradualness, which Kaye praises, is intended not
only to replace the innovations of great men by the product of an
anonymous social process, but also to bridge over the discontinuity between animal and human life and between men as
Individuals and men as social beings, which the existence of
language most uncomfortably underlines.

More important: Mandeville insists, against Shaftesbury, that
he conceives society, not "as a Herd of Cows or a Flock of
Sheep" drawn together by "natural Affection to their Species or
Love of Company," but as a "Body Politick" under a government (1924, 1:347). The passage links the point with Mandeville's
psychology, and it is reminiscent of Hobbes in every detail
but one: man under government "is become a Disciplined Creature, that can find his own Ends in Labouring for others." Mandeville thus introduces economic activity, division of labor, in a

social framework characterized by subordination. This he never forgets, but his posterity will. Thus "each Member is render'd Subservient to the Whole, and all of them by cunning Management are made to Act as one."

Man is not naturally sociable, but only teachable. He has to be taught sociability by society itself, through the ages. (In that sense Tufts's dictum is right.) Given man's pervasive and universal selfishness, this training entails hypocrisy (1:349). From the start, Mandeville proclaimed that "the imaginary Notions that Men may be Virtuous without Self-denial are a vast Inlet to Hypocrisy" (1:331), and he went on to suggest that Shaftesbury deceived himself: he believed he was spontaneously virtuous, while actually he was simply of a "Quiet Indolent Nature."

Mandeville was probably not an outstanding economic analyst, and Schumpeter mentions him only cursorily. It is clear from a detailed discussion of trade with Turkey that he was, like many of the mercantilists, in favor of *freer* trade, and not of free trade altogether (1: Rem. L.). Yet Kaye singles out what he calls a "definite anticipation" of laissez-faire. Provided "nobody meddles with it," an equilibrium would spontaneously establish itself in regard to one particular: "In the Compound of All Nations, the different Degrees of Men ought to bear a certain Proportion to each other, as to Numbers" (1924, p. cxxxix, from *Fable*, 2:353). What I find most remarkable here is the combination of the international level of consideration with the unusual and vague notion of a proportion in the numbers of the "different Degrees of Men": we have seen that some mercantilists had arrived at the notion of an automatic equilibrium in the flows of money in international trade. We have here something more abstract and general, and I am tempted to take the passage for a statement, not of a particular theory of laissez-faire, but of its underlying ideological principle, something like the ideologeme of free trade, if I may risk the term, say, "There must be a universal spontaneous order of a sort." This is all the more remarkable in that we have seen Mandeville fully recognizing, in general, the necessity of government and subordination in society. Of course, the statement is a mere corollary of the more general "harmony of interests," but to disregard national boundaries in a matter only indirectly connected with international trade would seem to require ideological abstraction.

In conjunction with his moral—or antimoral—preoccupations, Mandeville presents an overly simple view of the motive forces of the economy. For him, consumption commands all
the rest: we have been shown the diversity of wants at the
root of society, and his belief that luxury is a boon because it
encourages the production of goods. The demand creates the
supply, and so the demand for work creates the workers, as,
according to others, the amount of available subsistence creates
the population to consume it. This is the "make-work fallacy,"
as Kaye puts it: the Great Fire of London was not an unmixed
evil, since it created work for many craftsmen. No one is less
concerned with investment or saving. Only, by reason of the
universal interdependence of opposites, the miser accumulates
so that the spendthrift may better and more usefully dissipate.
The animus falls on frugality, a virtue for theologians, which
makes for a small and stagnant society, not for a large and pros-
perous one.

It is perhaps too much to speak of a theory of the division of
labor in Mandeville. Yet he is fascinated by the phenomenon;
and when, in the index of the second volume, he lists "Labour,
the usefulness of dividing and subdividing it," he refers to a
passage where one can read "dividing" as meaning the distinction of different industries, and "subdividing" as meaning the
division of labor within each industry. Kaye thinks that Adam
Smith here followed Mandeville (Mandeville 1924, p. cxxxiv);
Smith's picture of the making of pins is anticipated in the *Fable*
in the making of watches; but the latter is widespread, being
found in Petty, as Marx knew (*Capital*, I, IV, xiv, 3), and in the
Considerations of 1701 (Stephen 1962, 2:255), a fact that one
would like to associate with the deists' predilection for the Great
Clockmaker! (On the same point, see also Bonar 1927, p. 93 and
note.) Mandeville also mentions the plain coat of the peasant as
embodying a considerable degree of division of labor. In general, Mandeville delights in showing how vast a chain of workers exercising different skills contributes to a given product or
machine, such as a man-of-war, or is set to work by a single
intemperate consumer, such as a drunkard.

Kaye is correct in locating in his philosophy of individualism
Mandeville's first and foremost bequest to the economists (p.
cxl): the idea that passions are so arranged that "their apparent

discords harmonize to the public good" does represent a step
further in the emancipation of the Individual. We are now in a
position to return to Adam Smith, to see how he managed to
reconcile the two irreconcilable foes, Shaftesbury and Mandeville, as Bonar said (1927). It is enough to recall that Smith is
also the author of *The Theory of Moral Sentiments*, written a great
deal earlier than the *Wealth*. In the sphere of morality, the
human subject is made a social being through the operation of
sympathy. This notion is in line with Hutcheson and Shaftesbury, even if, for Smith, sympathy is to a large extent composed
in a Mandevillean manner of egoist elements, and if he replaces
Hutcheson's predominance of altruistic tendencies with the
predominance of egoistic ones. On the contrary, in the sphere of
economics, what we would call in our jargon the "socialization"
of man's deeds is effected by an automatic mechanism, a non-
conscious property that is equated with the operation of the
Invisible Hand. The economic sphere is the particular domain
where the predominant passion, egoism, can with good justification be given free rein under the form of self-interest. Globally, Adam Smith has differentiated economic action within
human action in general as the particular type that escapes morality without being contrary to morals in a wider sense. This
happens with the *Wealth* and was not yet accomplished in the
1763 *Lectures*, in which, as Halévy shows, both principles are in
play according to the question at hand (1901, 1:161). Yet the
place of the *Wealth* was marked in advance in the *Moral Sentiments* (for instance II, ii, 3), where it was said that society can
subsist without love and affection and be based only on utility,
or justice, a "mercenary exchange of good offices according to an
agreed valuation," etc.[4]

Up to now we have considered only some aspects of Mandeville's views. We must now come to their core, to the center of
Mandeville's argument: "Private Vices, Publick Benefits." There
is no doubt about what Mandeville is actually saying, but there
is ambiguity about what he wants his reader to conclude and
about what he himself thinks about it. According to Leslie
Stephen,

> [He] has overlaid a very sound and sober thesis with a
> number of shadowy paradoxes which, perhaps, he only half
> believed . . . . He is, in fact, radically opposed to the ascetic

doctrines of theologians. Accept in all sincerity the doctrine of
contempt for the world and its wealth, and the further
doctrine that all natural passions are bad, and we should
be a set of naked savages.... And it is perfectly true that
the industrial view of morality is, on this point, vitally
opposed to the old theological view. (1962, 2:30–31)

That some of Mandeville's contemporaries saw traditional
morality in danger is shown by the refutations of men like Den-
nis, Law, and Berkeley. Selby-Bigge (1897, 1:xi ff.) takes a different view, which is also convincing up to a point. For him,
Mandeville is a satirist, and a satirist should not be asked to
produce "speculative validity and completeness" (p. xv). His
"constant indulgence in paradox enables him to give a maximum
of offence, while keeping in the background a few unexception-
able principles to which he can appeal in case of need" (ibid.).
And Mandeville did so, abundantly, in his rejoinders to critics.
The satirist denounces the sham, and this implies adherence to
the code. Yes; but is this adherence sincere or feigned in Mandeville's case? Selby-Bigge asserts that it is indeed sincere, and
he is thus led to turn the argument upside down: "When he
[Mandeville] is maintaining the odious thesis of 'private vices
publick benefits,' he is really concerned to argue the converse,"
that is, to attack "the complacent cant which sees in the accumulation of private wealth the height of social virtue" (ibid.). There
is no reason to suspect "backhanded attack upon ascetic and
theological ethics" (p. xvi). This seems to be making Mandeville's
argument simpler, more one-dimensional, than it is. Now,
Selby-Bigge distinguishes the satirist and the skeptic, not to
speak of the cynic, and there is ample reason to find some skepticism in Mandeville, who was, in the first place, a disciple of
Pierre Bayle: the interpretation is too narrow. Indeed, it seems
impossible to maintain that Mandeville's treatment of luxury is
evidently ironical (p. xvi), for it is intimately linked with his
interest in the division of labor and in economic phenomena in
general.

We are much indebted to F. B. Kaye for his monumental critical edition of the *Fable* and especially for his painstaking collec-
tion of sources—documented or hypothetical—of Mandeville's
thought, and for parallel passages in previous writings, on the
one hand, and his catalog of references to Mandeville in the

subsequent literature, on the other. He has generously enabled us to form a conspectus of Mandeville's place in the history of ideas. Clearly, the interpretation by a scholar who has immersed himself so painstakingly in the Mandevillean climate is of great weight. On which side, he asks, do Mandeville's sympathies lie? No doubt he is with the empiricists against the rigorists. There is plenty of evidence for that. He is simply not to be believed when he states, "If I have shown the way to worldly Greatness, I have always without Hesitation preferred the Road that leads to Virtue" (1:231). We have only to look at "his insistence on the animal facts of life," which expresses "such complete faith in nature that he feels no need for any beliefs by which to lift himself above it" (p. lv). Rigorism is not congenial to Mandeville, yet Kaye does not believe that he was attempting a conscious reductio ad absurdum of it. It appears consistently in all his major works "and seems to have become part of his mind." Finally, such a "coupling of contradictory attitudes" is not unknown in other authors of the age.

We come, thus, to the conclusion that it is not easy—and perhaps not apposite—to try to condense from the *Fable* a theory that would both be Mandeville's own and be consistent. We shall be on surer ground in trying to focus on what is happening in and through Mandeville, in plotting his position in the history of ideas. Kaye's minute inspection of the literature confirms the reader's impression that there is little originality in Mandeville's points, taken separately. He is, in the first place, the disciple of Pierre Bayle, the skeptic author of the *Dictionnaire historique et critique*—that bible of the Enlightenment. Either through Bayle or directly (demonstrably so for La Rochefoucauld and Erasmus), Mandeville imbibed a whole trend of Continental, especially French, psychology. Skepticism, relativism, antirationalism found in him an eager disciple. He combines Gassendi's sensualism with that of Hobbes and Locke, and his Hobbesian emphasis on self-love is armed with the sharp scalpels of Jansenists like Pascal and Pierre Nicole. Several authors have noted this confluence of two national traditions, French psychology and British philosophy and political economy (North and others) (Mandeville 1924, 2:446 ff.), which probably contributes to the effectiveness and pungency of the "debunking" in the *Fable*. Mandeville's originality lies in his manner of amassing in force a number of contradictions which he found, scattered in the literature of at least two countries, and of which his contemporaries were not totally unaware. He concentrates them, as it were, into a single contradiction between moralistic pretenses and a behavior oriented to material advantage and worldly satisfactions. We must now look more closely at the achievement.

In the first place, we noted in the "Enquiry on Virtue" the separation between morality and religion. Morality in its essential mechanism (the passions, and pride and shame in relation to social esteem) is common to civilizations that differ deeply regarding religion. Morality is of this world, as linked with universal conditions of social life; religion is not, and for this reason it is put out of court. Here we may remark that the same is exactly the general effect, or direction, of Bayle's criticism, which consists, according to a French historian of philosophy, in "depriving the metaphysical and religious theses of every support in human nature and human reason," with the result that "The metaphysical truths are placed so high, that they have scarce any interest for men: religious life, reduced to itself, separated from rational and moral life, isolated in its majesty, is left hanging in a void" (Bréhier 1960, pp. 308–9). Religion is thus, for practical purposes, expelled, cast out, and it is noteworthy that a consequence of this position in Bayle is a concrete, historical conception of human nature and a sociological view of man. Thus Bayle attributes to Nihusius (s.v., Rem. H) this reflection: "What would be the use of abandoning the *denomination that has produced and raised us* if, by leaving it, we were only to exchange one disease for another?"[5] (My italics; quoted ibid.) We see here a close parallelism between Mandeville and his master.

Kaye designates as "rigorism" Mandeville's amalgamation of two contemporary currents, the ascetic and the rationalistic view of morality. But let us start from Mandeville's most complete and formal definition: those acts alone are virtuous "by which Man, contrary to the impulse of Nature, should endeavour the Benefit of others, or the Conquest of his own Passions out of a Rational Ambition of being good" (1:48–49). Moral action being defined through its *motive* (which is of course essential), three characteristics are here identified among themselves in contradistinction to self-love or the passions in general: self-denial, conformity to reason, and orientation to the good of others or to the public good. The third aspect is important, because it will allow the transition from a moral to an economic point of view, ' as implied in the subtitle, "Publick Benefits." In Mandeville's argument, moreover, the moral norm will be seen in relation to the actual action. There is more to his argument than the point of view of a satirist, as seen by Selby-Bigge, for the stress is definitely on the fact and not on the ideal. After religion has been eliminated, this earthly world of fact will be established as an absolute, and morality itself will—paradoxically—be judged according to whether it is more or less actualized, according to the degree of its correspondence with the actual deeds of men.

How can we make logically explicit the central argument? Mandeville considers the relation between men's actions and the public good in two perspectives. From a moral point of view, the relation to the public good is normative: a given action is oriented to the public good if it is in accordance with the moral rule. But observation tells us that, in fact, no action is ever so oriented; it is never altruistic, but always egoistic. The second point of view considers the consequences for the public good of the action as observed; here observation tells us that the action as it is, that is, the egoistic action, serves the public good. Several consequences follow, which Mandeville tends to restrict rather than to make quite explicit: (1) the claim of morals is false, insofar as it is not through it that the public good is attained in fact; (2) in general, moral precepts have no influence on conduct, insofar as they prescribe nonegoistic action; (3) the public good is realized only through an action that is not consciously oriented toward it. Therefore, man is not social by nature, for it is when he does not will it that he works for the public good; (4) on the contrary, on the level of fact, there is a natural harmony of interests. On the whole, morality is expelled from the real affairs of men as religion had been already. Mandeville may well protest that he has not tried to establish vice in the place of virtue: morality is entirely subjectivized; the mixture of subjectivity and objectivity that characterized it has been severed into two. As to the fact that *some* vices, namely, crimes, must be punished by the government, this matter is no longer a question of morality but of law.

Let us note that to compass, as he says, this result, Mandeville has, on the one hand, pushed moral rigorism to extremes by refusing to admit as virtuous any action that would in the slightest degree favor the agent; on the other hand, he has identified economic prosperity with the public good, without more ado. The thesis is in itself quite implausible: there must have been particular circumstances and a quite peculiar passion in Mandeville to lead him to such a position. One would be inclined to admit that Mandeville, as a disciple of Bayle, was deeply disturbed and shocked by the contrast between the current moralism and the ubiquitous immorality of his surroundings; he resented it as a hypocrisy he felt called upon to unmask. At the same time, turning with some cynical relief to the coarser aspects of life, he perceived a vigorous growth of material interests and was one of the first observers to feel the optimism of economic growth and to express it in the ideologeme of the natural harmony of interests. His genial trick was to connect the two things in a satirically very effective, superficially coherent manner.[6]

Be this as it may, one cannot help sensing that one is faced here with a crucial issue. What aroused a scandal among Mandeville's contemporaries appears to us retrospectively as a critical transition. I shall now endeavor to lay bare some of its aspects. The author himself implies in his argument some equivalence between two systems, the moral and the economic, representing two views of the social system. In the social system of morality, we see the subjects or agents internalizing social order under the form of moral rules, each subject defining his conduct indirectly, by reference to the society as a whole. In the economic system, on the contrary, each subject defines his conduct by reference only to his own interest, and society is no more than the mechanism—or the Invisible Hand—by which interests harmonize. It is a mechanism that is not conscious to begin with and that, once discovered, as by Mandeville, will justify the egoistic, asocial conduct of everyone. In other terms, the transition from traditional morality to utilitarian ethics (when fully accomplished) represents the expulsion of the only and last form under which, in the modern world, the social whole still constrained individual conduct: the individual is free, his last chains have fallen from him. A very similar transition, that between the law of nature and utilitarian philosophy, seems to have gone unnoticed. Thus, in Schumpeter's *History of Economic Analysis*, continuity is assumed and utilitarianism is seen simply as a development of natural law theory. This view hides what is to my mind a very serious change: natural law theory has no doubt greatly served the emancipation of the individual; in it, social and political institutions are considered and discussed by reference to an ideal state of nature in which men are given as Individuals, and the theory consists in trying to deduce the principles of society and polity from the characteristics of the Individual so given. There is thus in natural law theory, as in traditional morality, a basic *normative* transcendent reference that disappears in utilitarian philosophy, where an immanent, empirical criterion replaces it, namely, the greatest happiness of the greatest number.

It is this kind of transition that we perceive when Mandeville no longer refers to morals, to the ideal society of all human beings (as in Locke), but instead to each concrete society. At first sight, one has the impression of a sociological gain, but it is not true, for the concrete society resolves itself into its sole economic aspect (and social good is identified with economic prosperity or development). And society resolves itself into economics because only Individuals, that is, men stripped of all social characters, are considered. The reduction of society to individual agents, which was ideal and normative in natural law theory, is here taken for granted on the level of the *description* of social life. Who can say that nothing has happened and that there is an unbroken line from medieval Scholastics and their sound recognition of the social whole?

There remains something opaque in the transition we are discussing, a heterogeneity between the moral point of view and the economic that is not only a matter of the actual versus the ideal and that we can grasp by observing that the transition is from relations between men to relations between men and things as the focus: morals regulate the relationships between men, *whether or not* goods are involved, while Mandeville focuses on gain, wealth, material prosperity, as the core of social life. We can look at the *Fable*, and especially at the poem itself, as dealing throughout with this change in primacy: morality fits (perhaps) the small and stagnant society (of yesterday), not the large and powerful society (economy) of today. We shall see that Locke and Hume were concerned with the same shift at different levels. It should be clear that this is a major axis in the transition from traditional to modern ideology.

But we must also come back to the question of the relation between norm and fact. Hume complains of the confusion between the two points of view that he found, he says, "in every system of morality I have hitherto met with" (1875, *Treatise*, bk. III, pt. I, chap. 1, at end). Our contemporaries also often complain of the absence of this distinction in, say, Hobbes or Locke; and we have at hand an enlightening essay by Alasdair MacIntyre, who convincingly shows that Hume did not state that the transition was impossible, but only that it should not pass unnoticed or unjustified. He recalls that the absolute distinction under whose spell we labor was the work of Kant (MacIntyre 1971, chap. 13; see also the important conclusion, pp. 123–24). Where does Mandeville stand in that matter? We found that, outdoing Bayle, he severed the moral norm, together with religion, from the sphere of actual life, thus no doubt paving the way for Kant. At the same time, however, he appeals from the norm to the facts, and he finds on the level of fact that certain actions contrary to the norm have satisfactory social results. He thus indirectly justifies egoism. We cannot say that egoism becomes the norm, but we can say that the norm is found in public prosperity, that is, the norm is found in the relation between men and things, in contradistinction to the old norms bearing on the relationship between man and man. At this point, Mandeville surreptitiously reinstates an immediate passage from fact to norm: he does not ask whether prosperity, by itself and bought at the price of general corruption, is a good thing or is sufficient as the end of human action. To justify the passage, one might equate prosperity and the happiness of the greatest number and might posit that this happiness is the moral end. This was done very soon by Hutcheson, notwithstanding his general disagreement with Mandeville, and later on, explicitly and in terms of interest, by Hume.

We can now return to Tufts's statement and more precisely appreciate the truth it contains. We must first acknowledge two views of society in Mandeville: a contemporary view, in which society boils down in fact to the economy, and a view of

the origin or beginnings of society, through which, although all
the reasoning is based on man's contemporary psychology,
there emerges a general and vague recognition that man is what
society makes him. This recognition represents the acme of
Mandeville's abstract reasoning, and though it may be taken as a
possible germ of future sociological developments, it is found,
not in the *Fable* itself, but in its second volume. This later work
represents a quite distinct speculative adjunct to the *Fable* and as
such, as far as we know, does not share its predecessor's impact
on contemporary readers. The contemporary view is the core of
Mandeville's message, and the following remarks will concentrate on it.

Mandeville's achievement is more complex than Tufts has
seen, as can be shown by distinguishing a factual and a normative view. Factually, it is clear, as compared with Hobbes for
instance, that there is a recognition of something that lies
beyond and outside each particular man and that may be called
provisionally, for this reason, something social. This something
is the mechanism by which particular interests harmonize: a
mechanism (as in Hobbes, but on an interpersonal, not a personal, level), that is, not something willed or thought by men,
but something that exists independently of them. Society is thus
of the same nature as the world of natural objects, a nonhuman
thing or, at the most, a thing that is human only insofar as
human beings are part of the natural world. Normatively, on the
contrary, the particular human subject is emancipated from
moral constraints, or from the reference to the ideal state of
nature, which were the last remnants in his consciousness of his
dependence on something beyond him: he is made the Individual, the complete embodiment of humanity at large. To appreciate the importance of the transition, one need only recall
the central role played by moral obligation in Locke's political
theory. (It is true that moral obligation in Locke was a substitute
for subordination and that Mandeville, in line with Hobbes,
accepts subordination as ontologically given: his political theory
thus jars with his economic theory.) In other words, if we may
say with Tufts that, in Mandeville and throughout the whole
period, there is a growing recognition of society, we must immediately add that it is a recognition of society demoted from a
fact of consciousness to a fact of physical nature. Everything

points to the supremacy of the Individual having been bought at
the price of degrading relations between men to the status of
brute natural facts. This change is consonant with the primacy of
relations to things, to which I shall return. It is consonant also
with Mandeville's predilection for the coarse and the
scurrilous—what Kaye calls his reliance on "the animal facts of
life."

We are actually dealing with two transitions, one narrower
and one broader. The first consists in the emancipation of
economics from morality, and here there remains one observation to make. If the economic domain escapes the general
supremacy and jurisdiction of morals, it is through the recognition of its having a moral character of its own: the automatic
mechanism makes for the public good. Thus it is that the normative reference will cling to the domain as Gunnar Myrdal has
insisted: the moment it could be shown that the mechanism
does not work, or does not work that way, general morality
would reassert its claim on it and authorize political intervention. This situation creates a powerful incentive to assume the
consistency of the domain and to believe that the simplest correlations that come to mind must, in fact, hold. No wonder that
the crude or wild assumptions thus produced or favored bewil-
der the historian of analysis who restricts his purview to the
domain in itself as separated from the ideological universe.

The broader transition we are faced with is that between the
rationalist and the utilitarian philosophy, between, on the one
hand, a deductive and normative rationalism or what we might
perhaps call the "natural complex"—natural law, natural religion, natural morality (Shaftesbury)—and, on the other hand,
"philosophical radicalism." Admitting with MacIntyre that in
the tradition of Aristotle the normative doctrine is linked with
the observation of moral facts, we might begin by saying that the
eighteenth century and Mandeville himself readjusted the norm
to the changed facts, but the change goes deeper: on the one
hand, Kant will completely detach the norm from the fact; on
the other, Bentham will reduce morality to a calculus of a peculiar sort. To appreciate the different dimensions of the change,
we may try to locate Mandeville in relation to a few thinkers
who preceded and followed him.

In relation to Hobbes there is a great deal of continuity, but also a notable break. The continuity is obvious, whether in the conception of man and his psychology, in the recognition of government or subordination in society, even in the theory of the artificial origin of morals, which Selby-Bigge calls the worst sort of Hobbism; the *Leviathan* is mentioned more than once, although it acquires, as we noticed, a new, an economic, dimension. The main break is in the complete replacement of deduction (still present in Locke) by empiricism. Far from saying that man can know only what he makes or, with Locke, only what he has in his mind, Mandeville refers the norms to the observed facts. Where Hobbes deduces subordination, Mandeville induces economic harmony. Contrary to the artificialism of Hobbes (and Descartes), we are invited to admit the existence in human society of an involuntary automatism, a natural fact.

The controversy with Shaftesbury puts forward the aspect of Mandeville that caused a scandal: hedonism, pleasure, or happiness as real—if not avowedly ultimate—ends. Predominantly until then, happiness had been the natural sanction of the moral law, but the Protestants had tended to separate the two (MacIntyre). Mandeville deepens the divorce and emancipates the subordinate element. Very soon, Hutcheson himself will accept happiness as the moral end, "utility as a criterion of virtue" (Stephen 1962, 2:52), and in the British tradition the utilitarian principle will attain predominance, while Kant, with the categorical imperative, will reinstate morality by cutting it off definitively from the realm of facts. We must, with MacIntyre, be wary of it; if we think of morality, we think of Kantian subjective morality. Let us be just to Mandeville: after all, he has expressed in dramatic terms this sundering of goodness and happiness that is our lot and that would have been incomprehensible to Plato.

It is perhaps as against Locke that Mandeville's innovation stands out most clearly. Mandeville follows Locke in many things. Notwithstanding all his relativism, he would almost agree with Locke about the "eternal and unrevocable character of right and wrong" (cf. 1924, 2:221–22), but this, although remarkable, is not central. More important is the fact that Mandeville develops Locke's empirical method and that, like him, he takes the moral sense to be, not primary and sui generis, but derivative. But Mandeville cuts the Gordian knot that halted

Locke.[7] In Locke hedonism, the will of God as legislator, and the deductive, mathematical demonstrability of morals still coexisted. Mandeville disjoins hedonism from morality as he separates morals from religion. He gives hedonism a precise character by establishing the primacy of the relation of man to goods over the relations between men—if not in principle, then in the actual life of a large and powerful society.

Here we touch again on what I believe is a major continuity: Locke, Mandeville, and Hume move in the same direction, Locke in replacing subordination by property (plus obligation) as the principle of society, Mandeville in promoting material prosperity to the status of a moral end, Hume in seeing in the common interest the foundation of moral obligation and, still more distinctly, in making of property and justice the basis and prototype of social virtue (1875, *Treatise,* bk. II, pt. II). In Hume, justice owes its origin, on the one hand, to the egoism and limited generosity of men, on the other, to the fact that nature provides for their needs in only a limited manner. The primacy of the relations to things over the relations between men cannot be more forcibly and naively put forth. This is the decisive shift that distinguishes the modern civilization from all others and that corresponds to the primacy of the economic view in our ideological universe, and it is the shift that, whatever his intimate convictions may have been, Mandeville has expressed, for us as well as for his contemporaries, in the *Fable of the Bees, or Private Vices, Publick Benefits.*

6 The Wealth of Nations: Adam Smith's Labor Theory of Value

That *The Wealth of Nations* contains elements or aspects hailing from Quesnay, on the one hand, and from Mandeville and Locke, on the other, is widely recognized. But the manner in which these elements combine in Adam Smith is not simple, and it has received less attention. Quesnay's influence is clear, for it lies on the level of the economic consideration proper; the Mandevillean pedigree of some basic statements is unmistakable. This observation led me to locate Mandeville's influence in the very point of articulation between Adam Smith's general theory of social life, his *Theory of Moral Sentiments,* and his particular theory of economic phenomena, *The Wealth of Nations.* (To the end of his life Adam Smith had in preparation a political treatise.) Fundamental as the point is, I shall not return to it, while of necessity I shall look toward Locke when analyzing Smith's theory of value.

Locke's influence is, I think, minimized by Schumpeter on account of his strictly defined point of view, because it lies on a metaeconomic level. Fortunately, other authors have fully recognized it. Hasbach admitted that the natural law foundations of Smith are those of *The Second Treatise of Government* (1893, p. 761), and, independently of each other, Halévy and Myrdal reached the same conclusion. Halévy insisted on the difference between the theories of value of Pufendorf and Hutcheson (utility plus scarcity) and that of Locke (labor) (1901–4, 1:173–75). He added: "[Locke's] theory of value is at the same time and indivisibly a juridical theory of the right of property." Actually—*pace* Schumpeter—there is in Locke at least the germ of a theory of value in his statement that " . . . 'tis *Labour* indeed that *puts the difference of value on every thing*" and in his surmise that labor constitutes nine-tenths or perhaps ninety-nine-hundredths of the value of goods (*Two Treatises,* II, § 40). Halévy added: "If

Adam Smith follows . . . the tradition of Locke, is it not because
he obeys, consciously or not, the same preoccupation [re prop-
erty]?" and he insisted on the normative aspects in Adam
Smith. That Myrdal insisted on the same point will be seen in
our detailed study of Adam Smith's text, in which some close
parallels with Locke are apparent and on which Myrdal's observations bear (see below, Appendix, §§ a, c). To return to
Halévy's remark that Adam Smith departed in the matter of
value from his master Hutcheson and the traditional view in
order to follow Locke is an important point, as Ricardo was to
follow him: Adam Smith made here, so to speak, the first step in
what Schumpeter called "the Ricardian detour."

Regarding the link between Quesnay and Adam Smith, we
are on sure ground, thanks especially to three authors: in the
first place, the editor of Smith, Edwin Cannan, and then Marx
and Schumpeter. Cannan published, from the manuscript of a
student, Adam Smith's *Lectures on Justice, Police, Revenue and
Arms* of 1763 (thirteen years earlier than the publication of the
Wealth) (Smith 1896), in which, as the title indicates, economics
is not yet disembedded from statecraft. These *Lectures* are valuable for tracing the progress of Smith's ideas. A much later draft
of the *Wealth*, relatively short and incomplete, has been published more recently (Scott 1937). According to the editor, the
draft is anterior to the voyage of the author to the continent,
where he met Quesnay and some of his disciples. It is thus
possible to measure in some manner the impact of the encounter
on the *Wealth of Nations* as it is. Actually, Cannan had surmised
before the discovery of the manuscript for the *Lectures* some
aspects of this impact (notably, the scheme of distribution "in-
serted" by Smith in the middle of chapter 6 of the first book; see
Cannan 1898, pp. 186–88); the text of the *Lectures* confirmed and
enlarged the view. We have thus from Cannan, in his introduc-
tions to the *Lectures* (1896) and to the *Wealth* (1904, pp. xxix ff.),
with a precise concordance between the two texts, a clear acknowledgment of the extent to which Smith's acquaintance with
Quesnay's theory influencèd the *Wealth*. The influence looms very
large indeed.[1] Much was already known: the account of the physiocratic or "agricultural system" in book IV (chap. ix), following
the much longer discussion of the commercial or mercantile system, well characterized as "patronizingly benevolent"

by Schumpeter (1954, p. 186); stray passages and occasional contradictions resulting, as Marx remarked, from Smith's juxtaposing a physiocratic tenet and his own (for instance, II, ii, § 2: "the whole annual produce of the land and labour of every country . . . "); the preoccupation with the distinction between productive and unproductive labor (II, iii), inherited from Quesnay and destined to a long career (see Marx's book-long discussion in "Mehrwert").[2]

But the comparison of the *Wealth* with the *Lectures* affords more decisive facts. In the plan of the work, book I, which is essentially Smith's and which grounds everything in labor, is followed by book II, on stock, which looks very much like a new beginning with, Cannan observes, an introduction that offers an uneasy transition. Schumpeter explains (p. 565): Smith borrowed from Quesnay the conception of advance economics (as against synchronization economics); his broad model of the economic process is Quesnayan. This is due also to another aspect to which Marx drew attention: the neat distinction between production (Quesnay's annual produce) and the other aspects of the process (distribution) survives the shift from land or nature to labor as the essential factor in production.

Here is perhaps the crux of Adam Smith's originality—which Schumpeter for one did not recognize—the point at which he welds together a global model of the economic process that comes from Quesnay, including the production/distribution dichotomy, and a view of production, that is, a theory of value as based on labor, that comes from Locke[3] and represents an *unfettered individualism* unknown to Quesnay—as I shall try to show. Here the search for what Marx called the "essence of wealth" goes one step further. Marx contrasted the mercantilists, who, according to him, acknowledged only the "objective essence of wealth" (money or treasure), to Adam Smith, who discovered in labor its "subjective essence," while Quesnay, who had not reached labor in itself—abstract labor—was seen in an intermediate position. Borrowing from Engels, Marx called Adam Smith "the Luther of political economy" (1844 "Manuscripts"; see Eng. trans., 1961, pp. 119–20; later, in the *Grundrisse* from a slightly different angle, see McLellan 1971, pp. 37 ff.). This of course corresponds to a shift—I should say, an ontological shift—from value in use (Quesnay) to value in exchange

(Smith). Let us also note that, if the search was throughout for a unique factor, a self-sufficient entity, a substance (the "substance of value," says Marx more than once; see, for example, "Mehrwert," French trans., 1:173), the question was less about wealth than about the increase in wealth, the *creation* of wealth (Schumpeter uses the word in the passage on Quesnay). Thus it seemed to require a *living* agent, nature (in Quesnay), and then man (from Adam Smith unto Marx) (Myrdal 1953, pp. 72–74). Moreover, Smith's solution—the individual man as creator of value—is closely parallel to the deists' emphasis on God as Creator (the Great Architect, Clockmaker, etc.), which is not absent from his *Moral Sentiments*.

Tentatively, I shall venture to attribute to Quesnay still a supplementary influence on Smith's value theory: that of a catalyzing agent. There is little of the theory yet in the 1763 *Lectures*. I find only two statements: "In a savage nation every one enjoys the whole fruit of his own labour" (p. 162) and "Labour, not money is the true measure of value" (p. 190, one of the rare occurrences—the only one?—of the word *value* in that text). More: on the negative side, the idea of natural price is extended to labor in a passage (p. 176) that, as the last word on wages, contrasts strongly with the interest for the question in the *Wealth,* as seen in the long empirical inquiry in book I, chap. viii, etc. Even in the later draft, the labor theory of value does not appear. The fact is the more striking, since the development on the division of labor is there from the start, in keeping with the British tradition. It is tempting to suppose that it is the encounter with Quesnay that spurred Adam Smith, by reason of his opposition to Quesnay's land theory, to develop his incipient view based on labor. The role played in Quesnay by use value passes in Adam Smith to exchange value. For Quesnay, wealth consists essentially in the use values afforded by nature for the satisfaction of human needs. Nature must be aided by labor, but the point is secondary. Adam Smith does away with use value in a few lines (I, iv, at end) and grounds wealth in the exchange value created by labor. The notion is elaborated on a Lockean basis, as will be seen in the textual study (see Appendix).

Given the direction of our interest, we are drawn naturally—as it were by an invisible hand—to Adam Smith's theory of value. Also, the topic is central to the relation between Smith and his followers, and a continuity can thus be traced from Locke to Marx through Smith and Ricardo. This continuity has a pronounced metaeconomic, value-oriented character: here is an area where the themes that interest us crystallize, to to speak. Moreover, the topic is highly problematic: Adam Smith has been charged with inconsistency by his own followers, and he seems to have remained uncomprehended to this day, with the exception—perhaps the partial exception—of Marx. Here then is a choice ground for testing our approach: by taking Adam Smith seriously, as the anthropologist does a good informant, by accepting his concern for what it is, and by applying our small set of tools, we can make sense of a body of statements that have been very influential although they were seen as contradictory.

Another attraction is the fascination exerted on the modern mind by the quantity-of-labor theory of value. It is easily understood, taking, if not Marx's definitive theory, at least a vulgar Marxist form: that all commodities, since they are exchanged against one another in the market in certain proportions, must of necessity contain one and the same *thing*—a social thing, at that—in the same proportions, seems obvious to a mind accustomed to think in terms of substances and not in terms of relations. The fact that there is more value at the end of the labor process than at its beginning is easily understood as a surplus value if one admits that labor is a commodity—the only commodity—that can produce a greater value than it is worth. The argument is tight, and the idea of man as an individual acting creatively on some part of his environment is by no means uncongenial to individualist thinking. An anthropological parallel is brought forth by Lévi-Strauss in his criticism of one detail in Mauss's classical essay on gift (Mauss 1950, pp. xxxviii ff.). At one point Mauss discusses a Maori notion, the *hau*, a quality inherent in objects that would explain all the obligations (to give, to give back, etc.) he has noticed in connection with the complex exchange of gifts. The critic observes that this solution is fallacious, in particular because there is no advantage in tracing back a complex of relations to a supposed substance that will be nothing but the reification or hypostasis of the relations themselves.

*

Before coming to the topic of the labor theory of value, I shall locate it in the *Wealth* by outlining the place of labor in the first book of the work. *Labor* is the first substantive the reader encounters, for the introduction begins with this dogmatic assertion:

> The annual labour of every nation is the fund which originally supplies it with all the necessaries and conveniences of life.

These very words evoke Quesnay, who would have said, "The annual produce of the land and labor." Then the title of book I begins: "Of the Causes of Improvement in the Productive Powers of Labour...." Here, apart from the major theme of labor, we encounter a secondary theme of importance: the *Wealth*, in its first book, is permeated with the idea that there has been and there is taking place a process of improvement, development, increase, progress (cf. MacFie 1967). This dynamism or optimism supports and orients the whole inquiry. We already had something similar in Mandeville, and for once it is difficult not to see expressed here a perception of the growth of British economy preparatory to or on the threshold of the Industrial Revolution.[4] Be it as it may, this perception softens, for instance, that of the conflicting interests of the workers and their employers; for in a period of growth, as Adam Smith expounds in chapter viii, the increasing demand for labor keeps wages well above the minimum subsistence level.

From the start of book I, the reader is put under the spell of the division of labor and its development. Halévy remarked that Smith had inverted the order of factors found in his master Hutcheson (1901, 1:163–66). With Hutcheson the division of labor is the cause of exchange, while in Smith it is the exchange, "the propensity to truck, barter, and exchange" that calls forth the division of labor and its development. Halévy shrewdly concludes that Smith thus offers a demonstration, or an illustration, of the natural harmony or the "theorem of the identity of interests": exchange arises from self-interest, and self-interest— not, say, a desire for cooperation—is thus the cause of the blessings brought by the division of labor. Schumpeter stated that Smith had added nothing to Petty on the subject (1954, p. 214;

cf. Marx, *Capital*, I, XIV, iii, n. *c*). It must also be remarked that here is the first example of another ubiquitous feature characteristic of the *Wealth*, I mean an association between labor and exchange so close that it invites reflection. Thus, at the beginning of chapter iv (end of § 1), the importance of exchange in our society leads Adam Smith to write: "Every man becomes in some measure a merchant" (and see Appendix, § b). The first chapter is a sort of hymn to the division of labor and its progress: an English peasant lives far better than an African king. As I have commented, this had become a kind of commonplace—witness Locke for the passage just cited (Bonar 1927, p. 93). Smith goes further: the process has ethical results, for the real (as opposed to the nominal) price of labor increases with it, and the worker sees his lot bettered in proportion to the increasing productivity of his labor, which is in conformity with equity (I, vii; 1904, 1:80).

The first three chapters of the first book deal with the division of labor in itself and in relation to the extent of the market; the fourth chapter is devoted to money, a technical necessity; and the three following chapters deal with value (exchange value, of course) and price. The order is anything but linear: chapter v essentially asserts that value consists in labor and that only labor can really measure it, a largely metaphysical assertion. Chapter vii, on the contrary, is very empirical: it describes the oscillation of market price around what is defined from observation as "natural" price. In between, chapter vi attempts to present as logically as possible the transition between chapter v and chapter vii.

At this point, I must refer the reader to the Appendix, to which I have relegated the detail of the indispensable *explication de texte* in order to make the present development a little less heavy-going. A reader who so chooses may neglect the Appendix, to which I shall refer only sparingly; not so, if he wants to find out how far the statements in the text are substantiated in the detail.

To get at the principle of value, Adam Smith starts from what is actually the state of nature. He finds the principle of value in labor, where Locke had found that of property, and he proceeds to try to apply this finding to the civilized or contemporary state of things. In this development, he has been charged with inconsistency. There is a transition in his definition of value from the quantity of labor contained or embodied in a good, to the quantity of labor its owner can exchange it against, directly or indirectly—the quantity it can purchase or command. This is well known as an important juncture, where Ricardo and Malthus took opposite stands (Schumpeter 1954, p. 590). We may ask why Adam Smith introduced the second formula. In the initial conditions of barter the two formulas are equivalent, but the second is superior in two ways: first, in the abstract it encompasses production *and exchange,* and from what I said of the link between the two in Smith, we may surmise that the point is not negligible. Yet the main thing is that the second formula alone allows, *in Adam Smith's idea,* for generalizing from the original to the civilized state. In the latter, the price of a commodity is made up of three elements (see Appendix, § e; 1904, p. 52), and "wages, profit and rent are the three original sources of all revenue as well as of all exchangeable value" (1904, p. 54). This is actually Smith's operational formula, which has nothing to do with the quantity-of-labor theory. Yet in chapter vi, where he tries to effect the transition, he concludes by asserting that, in the last analysis, labor measures the value of all those elements (Appendix, § e), and this is possible only through the second formula, which alone allows Smith to proclaim that labor is the ultimate substance out of which all these things are made. In his actual comparisons he uses corn for long periods and money for short periods—not labor. It is more, for him, than a mere matter of measure; it is a matter of the essence of production or, as I prefer to say, of the single productive substance. It is obviously essential for him that the actual situation is seen in the light of the standard or norm derived from the original state. The norm is metaeconomic, as Schumpeter says; yet, to be sure, Smith's message is that it was all-important for him.

There is another and deeper difficulty in the detail: we do not understand—and neither did Ricardo—why it was that Adam Smith found his first definition (by the labor embodied) inapplicable to the observed process. Moreover, he expressed this difficulty in a form that is both complicated and, for us, contradictory (see Appendix, § e). It is a recurring paragraph, made up of two parts (for convenience, Part A and Part B). Part A states, roughly, that the laborer must share the produce of his labor with his employer. Well and good; it represents a modification of the original state, in which he kept the whole for himself. But Part B reads, *on the face of it,* that the quantity of labor contained in the goods does not entirely make up their value: "an additional quantity must be due for the profit of the stock." At first sight we might suppose that Part A is the real Smithian statement and Part B a statement of physiocratic influence (the stock), but this won't do. In Part B the expression "the quantity of labour ... employed in acquiring or producing any commodity" actually designates the salary paid to the worker producing the commodity, or more exactly the value of that salary. It thus looks as if Adam Smith was confusing the value of the salary and the value produced by the worker. Of course he does not do so, and this is how he can juxtapose Part B to Part A. As will be seen from the Appendix, § f, Part B can be taken as a statement relating to *price* but expressed in terms of *value.* It may be put under the form of an equation (Appendix, § g):

$$Q1 + \text{Profit} (+ \text{Rent}) = Q2,$$

where $Q1$ (quantity of labor no. 1) represents the wages and $Q2$ (quantity of labor no. 2) represents the price in labor, so to speak, of the good produced. The equation—that is, Part B—presents only the contemporary situation, but expressed in terms (quantities of labor) designed to bring it as close as possible, by the intermediary of the definition of value, to the original situation. The essential part of the statement corresponds to "= $Q2$," that is, the good exchanges against a certain quantity of labor (definition of value *through exchange*). But our question remains: why did Adam Smith think that this equation contradicted his first conception of value, value *in production,* or embodied?

It is time now to turn to Marx, who has much to tell us about our question. Marx was very preoccupied with it, and in his manuscript notes on the history of economics, published posthumously as "Theories of Surplus Value" ("Theorien über den Mehrwert"), which are considered as a draft for what was to be the fourth book of *Capital,* he discusses the point at least thrice.[5] The first discussion took place when he was dealing with Adam

Smith, the second when dealing with Ricardo about the cost of production (*Kostenpreis*), and the third, again with Ricardo, about the theory of rent. It is characteristic that, in the last instance, Marx not only comes back from rent to value but also reverts to the very plan of the first book of the *Wealth* in a renewed effort to capture the movement of Adam Smith's thought. (This he does not quite accomplish because, like Schumpeter, he is preoccupied at the same time with separating what is analytically sound from what is not.) Throughout, Marx is busy with Smith's contradictions; he isolates the principle of some of them—the juxtaposition, mentioned above, of a physiocratic tenet to his own—and he repeatedly characterizes the main one:

> Smith himself, with much naivety, lives in a permanent contradiction. On the one hand he tracks down the inner relations of economic categories or the hidden structure of the bourgeois economic system. On the other hand, and close by, he sets down the apparent relations given in the manifestations of competition, as they appear to the unscientific observer or to any one interested and confined in the process of bourgeois production. (*Werke*, 26.2:162)

> Smith on the one hand speaks out the soul of the agent of capitalist production and expounds the things purely and simply as they appear to him, as he thinks them and is determined by them in his practice, and as they in fact in all appearance happen, while on the other hand he reveals here and there the deeper relation, and this naivety makes the great charm of his book. (Ibid., p. 217)

Elsewhere, Marx contrasts the two views as esoteric and exoteric. This contrast applies strictly to chapter v as against chapter vii, and in our particular paragraph to Part A as opposed to Part B, except that Part B presents the exoteric view clad in esoteric language. But Marx saw more in the matter. An isolated fragment tells us:

> The contradictions of Adam Smith are significant in this, that they contain problems, problems that he certainly does not solve but that he expresses by contradicting himself. That he is instinctively right is best seen from the fact that his followers oppose each other by taking up one side or the other. (Ibid., p. 121)

As more or less final on the part of Marx, and issuing from an endless struggle with the detail of the *Wealth*, this is a very gratifying judgment regarding not only Adam Smith but Marx himself; and, I would add, it justifies my present effort and corresponds to the feeling one has when one tries to take Adam Smith whole, even on a limited scale. I must now sum up briefly what Marx says about our problem. According to him, there is a hidden truth, which Ricardo did not see, in Smith's muddled formulations. What he has in mind is not just the exchange of one commodity for another, but especially the exchange between the capitalist employer and the worker, an exchange of goods or money—that is, *realized* or solidified *labor*—against *living labor*. Only remember Adam Smith's favorite expression: to "purchase or command" labor. Now, says Marx in substance, in this particular exchange it is correct to say that the quantity of labor contained in the wages the capitalist pays is less than the quantity of labor the worker gives in return, and that the difference or, in Smith's language "an additional quantity," corresponding to Marx's surplus value, "must be added" to account for the profit of the capitalist. This statement follows closely that of Smith, and the equation above can certainly be read in that fashion, especially as $Q2$ must stand for labor and not for a commodity (whose price or value would again fall into the three elements). Yet, it will be asked, if this is really what Adam Smith is saying, why does he put it in such an obscure form? Why does he resort to value through exchange and abandon value in production? Why does he confuse—or, as I said above, appear to confuse— the value created by labor with the value of labor (wages)? Because, says Marx, he has not distinguished, from labor, the labor power (*Arbeitsvermögen*)—which is what the employer actually buys. On the whole, Marx is not vindicating Smith's statement as it is, but is only showing that, albeit bungled, it makes some sense from his (Marx's) point of view.

Can we reach any further, can we account more completely for Smith's statement? If, as I conclude in the Appendix (§ g), not only the stress on labor as a *measure* of value, but also the preference for the definition of value through exchange is rooted in the statement I have singled out, why then did Smith not rest content with the special statement he could have made, according to Marx, instead of merging it into a general statement

that, apart from being cumbrous, led to such dubious propositions? Was he more perspicacious than Ricardo and therefore
afraid of the consequences? Did he dimly perceive what were
later to become the socialistic implications of his ontological
thesis, the contradiction between it and the property-based lib-
eral view? Was he therefore content to bypass the difficulty and
assert the claim of labor on a superior level only—the level of
measure? The surmise is unwarranted. There was perhaps
another way out: one could have imagined that not only "living
labor" but also "realized labor" has in certain conditions—as
capital—the faculty of producing value. Perhaps John Locke
might not have shied away from such a view. Actually, one
author took such a path subsequently in order to better Ricardo's theory (see Schumpeter 1954, p. 595, n. 16).

It is safer to start from Marx's view of the ubiquitous contradiction in Adam Smith and ask why Adam Smith chose to
stick to the "appearances" in this particular case. I hope to have
shown in the Appendix (§ g) that the two parts, A and B, of the
paragraph in question operate the transition from the "original"
to the civilized state of things, each part doing so in relation to a
particular "role," as we would say. Part A identifies the modern
worker and the original hunter *as producers:* "the whole produce
of labour belongs (or: does not belong) to the labourer." As for
Part B, it identifies the capitalist employer with the original
hunter *as engaged in exchange.* In a first step the employer spends
a salary, as the hunter his toil, in order to acquire a good; in a
second step he exchanges the product as the hunter did his
game. Seen from this angle, not only are the two parts, A and B,
not contradictory, but both are necessary, together, to ensure
the complete passage from the original to the contemporary
scene. It is clear that *labor and exchange* taken together are central
to Adam Smith's thought. This pair runs like a red thread
throughout the beginning of the *Wealth* (see above, pp. 87–88;
App. §§ a–c). We must therefore, by rejecting from our mind
the more thoroughgoing distinction between production and
exchange that the followers will introduce, try faithfully to follow Adam Smith's own view. What do we see on the level
of the observation of economic facts? Transactions. In relation
to *production,* the transaction consists in the payment of wages
against the delivery of labor: labor is bought by the employer

presumably at its value. And that is all that we can say from "production." To learn more, we must go to the market where the produced good is *exchanged* for others; it is there that we can ascertain its price, hence its value, that is, a "quantity of labor" that we can compare with that ascertained from production, as in our equation. (Similarly for profit and rent: they are ascertainable from transactions.) All this makes sense, for the value of the good cannot be predicated before it is exchanged on the market: if by chance more labor than is "socially necessary" in Marx's terms has been expended in the production of the good, that labor will be not paid but lost.

If we rewrite the equation in Marxian terms, replacing profits, etc., by "surplus value," we shall have:

Value of labor + Surplus value = Value produced by labor as made real only through exchange.

Here we have the similarity that Marx perceived, but in a general statement about any commodity: Adam Smith preferred his second definition of value (through exchange) because, from his point of view, soundly based on the observation of transactions, it was necessary to consider the exchange to bring forth the equivalent of Marx's surplus value.

To all appearances, Adam Smith could not yet think of value, or surplus value, as already present in the good produced, in anticipation of its future destiny on the market. This further step, by the way, modified the distinction between production and exchange and attached to production a feature that appears empirically, as Smith saw, only in exchange. This step is of course in keeping with the general inspiration of classical economics as tending to see the economic process as rooted in a substance (production, labor) rather than in relations.

Yet, the same tendency was already present in Adam Smith on a more general level, that is, in his ontological doctrine of labor, and the difficulty that has detained us so far marks precisely the point at which the tendency, as present in Adam Smith, is held in check: the produce of labor does (or does not) belong entirely to the laborer; but in terms of value, and starting from the actual transactions, we must put it another way. Here labor is not enough, for value is inseparable from exchange. It is only with his disciples that exchange will be demoted to secondary status as against production, or labor. True, Adam Smith had already hierarchized his pair of concepts, finding in the "original" state the secret of the preeminence of labor. Yet he had a strong feeling that in fact labor alone was not enough. At the beginning of his chapter on wages (chapter viii) he speculates at length on what would have been the blessings of the division of labor if it had come about without accumulation of stock and appropriation of land. He then observes that accumulation and appropriation were present "long before the most considerable improvements were made in the productive powers of labour," which is a way of acknowledging that the division of labor is linked with the forms of appropriation and that labor or production is not self-explanatory. And yet he did push as far as he could the preeminence of labor. One observation remains to be made regarding Part B, which has claimed so much of our attention. We concluded that the seeming confusion of that passage had its roots in Adam Smith's wish to build as complete a parallel as possible between the original and the observed state of things. This is the preoccupation that has compelled the author to identify a quantity of labor with a salary, i.e., with the value of labor. Yet this particular identification was possible only through his having confused these two sorts of concepts throughout. Other passages (detailed in the Appendix, § d) present the same confusion between labor as a value and the value of labor. If our analysis is right, it is not this confusion itself that has commanded the form of Part B, as has probably been generally believed: it only made it possible.

We may go one step further and ask whether we cannot reverse the order of the two factors. Suppose that it is the difficulty encountered in the application of the labor theory of value to the modern case that has caused Adam Smith to become confused and, in general, in order to bypass the obstacle, or by way of overcompensation, to put forward excessive claims in the name of labor, to exaggerate or extrapolate the identification of value with labor. I feel that the point is obvious in this very chapter regarding the introduction of labor as "measure," and it might be extended step by step to the other passages (quoted in the Appendix, § d). It cannot be demonstrated, but it is likely, that the need to make labor the *deus ex machina* of the whole story, held in check by the facts, or, as Marx said, by the "appearances," has led Adam Smith to err as to "the value of labour" (as everywhere and always constant, etc.). Here may lie the explanation for part of the dogmatic exposition and stentorian tone which are so striking in the whole development.

The stumbling block Adam Smith encountered was his inability to dissociate value from the transaction in which it appears in fact, namely, the exchange. It is noteworty that his followers, heirs to his ontological conviction, will see nothing of the sort in their way and will wonder at Smith's inconsequence. We may then say that the initial, the Smithian, formulation of the labor theory of value was not so remote as the subsequent formulation from a view that would not separate production from exchange; for if Adam Smith distinguished and hierarchized the two aspects, he did not as yet, at this level, *construe production into a self-sufficient entity.*

At this point, I must go back to a surmise I made above. I noticed that the Lectures of 1763 already contained two statements: "In a savage nation everyone enjoys the whole fruit of his own labour" and "labour, not money, is the true measure of value" (see above, p. 85). According to the present hypothesis, the latter proposition would have resulted from the difficulty in generalizing to present-day conditions the identification of value with the quantity of labor contained in the commodity. What I have previously contended as to the physiocratic system's having catalyzed the Smithian theory of value should then be qualified: the encounter with Quesnay would have spurred Adam Smith to expound at any cost a theory which, in view of its difficulty, he had left implicit until then. If this was so, it would show how strongly Adam Smith needed to posit labor as *the* value.

This exaltation answers immediately an ethical need. This was clear to everyone, Schumpeter included (1954, p. 558, etc.). Marx twice mentions in "Mehrwert" Adam Smith's sympathy for the productive workers, and once Smith's illusions in that regard. I have insisted, after Myrdal, on the metaphysical, or metaeconomic aspect of the theory, and it should be stressed as a conclusion.

In Adam Smith the labor theory of value is essentially a natural law argument. He did not manage to make it operative for his empirical inquiry, or did so to only a limited extent; but he felt the need to erect it as an aegis under which to carry out his concrete descriptions and discussions of the economic process as factually observed.

It is not enough to say that Adam Smith juxtaposed esoteric and exoteric views. Regarding value, at any rate, the reason for this juxtaposition lies in the fact that Smith was so convinced of the profound truth of the esoteric view that, when it ran against obstacles in the factual analysis, he could neither renounce it altogether nor yet would he force the facts as he saw them into it.

He could not bring himself to obliterate the rights of exchange as against those of labor, and he was led to construe the two elements into that curious pair on which we had to insist. He exerted himself greatly, now bringing together as forcefully as he could the esoteric and exoteric views; now, on the contrary, heaving up above the obstacle the great principle which was to rule over the whole scene to the point of losing himself in a maze of identities; or, again, hedging this principle with a set of rhetorical defenses and proclaiming what he had been unable to demonstrate.

We have looked for the message. It can be read at several levels. Man is the creator of wealth, of value: man, and no longer nature, as with Quesnay. This active man who creates value is the individual man in his living relation to nature, or the material world. Moreover, this natural relation between the individual and things gets somehow reflected in the egoistic exchange of things between men. And this exchange, in turn, albeit a substitute for labor, imposes its law on labor and allows the progress of labor. As with property in Locke, we see here the elevation of the individual subject, of man as "self-loving," laboring-and-exchanging, who through his toil, his interest, and his gain works for the common good, for the wealth of nations.

At this point, I should like to return briefly to Schumpeter's treatment of our topic. At first sight, Schumpeter seems to deny any close continuity between Locke's theory, which bases property on labor, and Smith's theory, which bases value on labor.

Actually, if we bring together a number of stray passages, we find that what Schumpeter does is to distinguish sharply between a labor theory of value, in the strict sense of economic analysis, and other views related to labor or the laborers, such as Locke's juridical doctrine (1954, p. 120) or his vaguer declarations or declamations extolling the role of labor and the claims of the laborers (ibid., p. 310, on Locke and Adam Smith; p. 558, on Adam Smith and others; p. 479, on Locke, Adam Smith, and the Ricardian socialists). But then, does Adam Smith have any labor theory of value at all? Notwithstanding a passage to the contrary (ibid., p. 590) the final answer is no. The decisive passages are on page 310 and in the note on pages 188–89: Adam Smith "claimed no validity" for the labor theory of value beyond the "special case" of primitive barter. (The discrepancy is probably due to the fact that Schumpeter had not reached a definitive formulation of all this; cf. the editor's notes, p. 181, n. 12, and p. 308, n. 16.) That labor alone produces the whole product (p. 558) or is the only factor of production (p. 479) is not an economic proposition (p. 558), hence not a theory of value. Nor is the proposition that the value of a commodity is measured by the quantity of labor for which it can be exchanged, for it simply asserts the choice of a measure or *numéraire* (pp. 310, 590).

Whatever may be the case from the point of view of economic analysis, all this is highly unsatisfactory for the understanding of Adam Smith and for the history of ideas. For what Schumpeter has done is to cut up a chain or complex of assertions that clearly belonged together for Adam Smith, in order to sort them out into his own pigeonholes. As he wrote about Marx: "We lose something that is essential to understanding him when we cut up his system into component propositions and assign separate niches to each" (p. 384). In the deepest sense, it is not true that Smith intended to limit his labor theory to the natural state. Quite to the contrary, the propositions (1) that labor produces the whole product; (2) that, if not the labor embodied, at least the labor obtained through exchange accounts for the value of a commodity; (3) that all the components of price can in the last analysis be measured in terms of labor—these three propositions result from the obstacle encountered in the generalization of the labor theory of value to the civilized case; they are something like *residual statements of this theory*. As for the filiation of ideas, if it is admitted (p. 310) that a passage of Adam Smith that does not contain a (proper) labor-quantity theory of value is the source of such (proper) theories in Ricardo and Marx, then why could not the "juridical" assertion of Locke be recognized as closely linked with Smith's (attempt at a) labor theory of value?

Moreover, Schumpeter's treatment hides a similarity of great import between the theories of Smith and those of his two followers. I mean their failure. It can be argued that Ricardo no more than Smith had a real labor theory of value. His theory was no more operative than Smith's. He had to be content with giving it as an approximation, a 93 percent approximation. Partly for this reason, Marx in his turn took the field. Did he succeed? He was able to establish more firmly than ever the concept of value, to make value absolute in a sense even Ricardo had not (Schumpeter, p. 597), but this was accomplished only by completely severing value from price, which it was intended to explain. The very expression *exchange value* lost all meaning; *value* became a metaphysical entity unrelated in actual fact to the exchange of anything but agricultural goods and unrelated as well to the individual producer. To wit, in Schumpeter's terms—that is to say, in strictly economic terms—there has never been a labor theory of value worthy of the name. It has always been a very imperfect affair, rooted in metascientific needs.

This imperfection does not make the topic any less significant for the present inquiry. To the contrary. I shall therefore briefly outline the fate of the idea, up to Marx. I hinted above at a post-Smithian step, reserved for a generation already familiar with labor as the productive substance. It consists in thinking of the value of the product as already present—under certain conditions—in production; or, in other words, it consists in importing into production a feature—value—that Adam Smith had properly seen as arising only through exchange. Although I insert a proviso, "under certain conditions," it will probably be objected that my characterization of the post-Smithian step does not apply to Marx, who, for one, took fully into account the "social conditions" of production, the quantity of labor "socially necessary," etc. This is a typical situation; it will crop up repeatedly when we deal with Marx at length, and I do not hope to clear it up entirely at this point. I argue that, under the cover of the social context, production itself is separated, reified, or construed into a metaphysical object far removed from experience and that it can be assailed regarding the functions it performs and the distinctions on which it rests and can be seen in the light of alternative constructions. The crux of the matter is that the substantialist inspiration I have shown to be at work in Quesnay and Smith—in other words, the individualist tendency—survives all qualifications, formal or real, addressed to "social conditions."

Marx's criticism of Ricardo's theory of value, coming from a follower of the approach, is decisive and is particularly interesting for us because Marx shows that the rigorous Ricardo, if he sees some of the limitations of his theory, is blind to the most immediate and decisive ones. As to Marx, it is widely if not perhaps generally admitted that, in his definitive economic theory (the "Critique" and *Capital*, I and III), he completely severed his theory of value from his theory of prices (Baumol 1974). This is so even if Marx avoids, in the initial stages ("Critique" and *Capital* I) telling the reader outspokenly that the value of a thing has nothing to do with its price but in fact largely implies the contrary.[6] Less widely acknowledged is, first, that this is not true of agricultural products, and, second, how Marx came to that position and what it means for the general inspiration and impact of the theory. The position resulted obviously from a long work bearing precisely on the difficulties and imperfections of Ricardo's theory. We see it reflected a posteriori in the notebooks dating, we are told, from 1863—already mentioned here in connection with Adam Smith—the "Mehrwert" or "Theories of Surplus Value" (*Werke*, 26.2).

Fundamentally, Ricardo's theory of exchange value as based on the quantity of labor embodied in the commodity came up against the uniformity of the rate of profit, given the differences in capital investment in different industries (and this is what Ricardo actually did not see!). This can be understood immediately in the rough: the profit, supposed to be uniform in rate throughout the economy, bears on the total investment, while the surplus value produced is supposed to be proportional to the investment in labor alone and varies, therefore, for an equal total investment, according to the proportion of fixed investment and wages paid (fixed and variable capital, in Marx's terms). If the profit is made up of the surplus value produced by the workers, there must then be a redistribution between the different industries producing surplus value at different rates if profit is to be uniform.

Marx manages to articulate and perfect the theory on many other points, including the introduction of the concept of surplus value itself. But this interposition of a sort of general pool that receives the integral sum of all the surplus value produced within the economy (excepting agriculture) and redistributes it according to a common rate of profit so that the price of each good (*Kostenpreis,* or cost of production) is more or less that calculated by the capitalist according to his expenses and his profit and no longer depends on the value incorporated in it by the labor that made it—this is the basic change introduced by Marx, and with its help he thought he had salvaged the labor-quantity theory of value. It is of course to his honor as a scientist that honesty compelled him to introduce such a thoroughgoing complication, but it means an important shift in the function of the theory. It is the apotheosis of value, made absolutely absolute (Ricardo's "real value" representing an intermediary stage; cf. Myrdal 1953, pp. 61 ff.), but at the cost of having nothing more to do with exchange and of leaving almost completely this economic earth for an empyrean existence.

Except for agriculture and the explanation of rent, the economic function of the theory is replaced by a political one, and for this reason it may well be that Marx did not realize the dimension of the change he had effected. The theory was there to explain the rate of exchange between different things (their "normal" price) and to relate it to the quantity of socially necessary labor expended on these things each time by individual workers. This is brushed away—which is to say, purely and simply, that, in its original form, the theory failed. I take one aspect to be essential: *an individualist theory was compelled, in order to survive in name, to combine with a holistic scheme and thus find refuge in the heaven of the unfalsifiable.* What remains is, on the one hand, the metaphysical notion that the creation of wealth is still in our days the work of the individual man and not—contrary to all evidence—of teams of men judiciously assembled and helped by their own creations, and, on the other hand, the notion that

the workers, as the creators of wealth, are collectively dispos-
sessed of a part of their produce, are exploited by the owners of
the means of production in proportion to the relation between the
surplus value they create—an entity supposed to exist but
forever impossible to measure—and the wages they receive. In
perfecting the theory, Marx had been led to introduce the concept of "socially necessary" labor, which already meant resorting to the social whole. But what is the bearing of such a concept
when it is admitted that the value of a thing does not manifest
itself in its price, except for the fact that whatever surplus value
it contained has been pooled with all others to enable them to
reach the price they command?

I said that Marx's theory of value still had a strictly economic
function regarding agriculture. Its link with his theory of rent is
sometimes overlooked. Here, Ricardo has been drastically
amended. He granted only relative rent, while Marx admits that
there exists an absolute rent, and he accounts for it by imagining
that agricultural products escape the capitalist law of exchange
at production cost and are or can be exchanged at their value.
Since agriculture requires, as compared to industry, a smaller
proportion of fixed capital, the value of agricultural products is
superior to their production cost; and since the landowners
enjoy a monopoly of the land, they are able to push up the
prices and gather a rent from the difference between value and
production cost (*Capital*, III, section 6). The theory transcribes
very ingeniously the historical relation between the classes as
Marx saw it: the heirs of a defunct domination are able, through
their "monopoly" of a natural factor of production, to escape the
law of the market to which their victors are subject, and to
exploit an otherwise submerged property of the goods that come
to the market, thanks to the relatively great quantity of labor that
enters immediately into agricultural production.

*

We are coming to the end of the first part of this inquiry, which
has been focused on some landmarks in the genesis of economics.
The study is too incomplete to bear the weight of a full array of
conclusions, and I shall not here recapitulate all the major questions raised. Yet, I want to underline a few points that have not
been made explicit enough or that the limited focus on value in

the preceding section has removed from the center of our attention, while the subsequent study of Marx might obliterate or
obscure them.

I have insisted throughout on the substantialist approach that
pervades the whole movement by which economics emerges. I
mean by that expression the tendency to stress a single agent or
element as a self-sufficient entity, to the exclusion or covert
subordination of others—this self-sufficient entity affording the
rationale or the vital core of the domain as a whole. This feature
is of the essence of the "Ricardian detour," which begins with
Adam Smith; and Schumpeter's reader cannot help seeing it run
like a red thread all through this part of the *History of Economic
Analysis* (see, for instance, the fate of the triad of factors, pp. 557
ff.). It explains, it seems to me, a good deal of the discontinuity
that Schumpeter, as against Marshall, lays at Adam Smith's
door with regard to "many of the most promising suggestions"
of his predecessors (p. 308). We have seen the fate of the category of value at the hands of three of the classics. How could the
first outspoken representative of this substantifying tendency
possibly do justice—supposing he had had knowledge of it—to
Galiani's definition of value "to mean a relation of subjective
equivalence between a quantity of one commodity and a quantity of another" (ibid., p. 301)? The relational aspect was just the
thing to be eliminated, and, unbelievable as the feat may seem,
it was progressively expurgated in successive steps by Smith,
Ricardo, and Marx. Also, the "subjective" aspect ran contrary to
the basic inspiration of our classics, for it meant locating value in
the exchange relation *between men* while they were busy locating
it more and more *in things* as produced. The two aspects of
course go together, and, on a different level, there is the same
revolution in thought between Galiani (who actually himself
had both!—Schumpeter, p. 301) and Smith, as we found on
record in Locke's *Two Treatises.* The new mode of thought was
obviously in accord with the mood of the times. No wonder,
then, that Ricardo got the better of Malthus in their controversy,
not only as the better dialectician, but also as the more analytical
versus the more sociological thinker: the one who isolates one
variable, one factor, versus the one who tends to keep the others
in mind.

The second point has a tautological air: there is a strict

congruence between the general ideological constraints bearing on nascent economics and the orientation and major contents of economic doctrine. On the one hand, we see emancipation from politics and establishment of a special relation to general morality, on the other, the natural harmony of interests, laissez-faire, or free trade, and, finally, economic liberalism as a universalist doctrine. In other words, these doctrines could not possibly have been replaced by others; they were implicated in the very existence of economic thought as an ideological category: they are nothing else but the direct assertion in concrete terms of the economic dimension. Therefore, they will on occasion be found more widespread in the general public than among the specialists. Much of this will change subsequently, once the economic category has been firmly established, though Gunnar Myrdal has shown how the normative aspect, albeit suppressed and hidden, survived and clung to the discipline (1953).

There is need here for a footnote qualifying this general statement as regards Adam Smith. Halévy had recognized the limits of the "natural harmony of interests" in the *Wealth* (1901, 1:172 ff.). We should expect that, under the aegis of the ontological, Adam Smith would make room for the empirical. In a paper of 1927, "Adam Smith and Laissez Faire" (1958, pp. 213–45), Jacob Viner shows first that the harmonious order of nature rules without qualifications in the *Theory of Moral Sentiments* but not in the *Wealth*. There, not only is the harmony often incomplete or revealed solely on a statistical level, but there are outright flaws in the natural order—conflict between masters and workmen, etc. Thus, even though the government is by nature unable to remedy many—perhaps most—economic evils, yet Adam Smith concedes that its intervention is warranted in some cases, of which Viner has compiled an impressive list. (Viner is not alone on this point; cf., e.g., Rosenberg 1960.) On the whole, Adam Smith gives the impression that he is perfectly aware that economic life and progress rest on institutional preconditions, more so perhaps than his direct followers.

I come to my third and main point. It deals with largely unsuspected relative valuations or hierarchical judgments in the ideology. The birth of economics actually implies a shift in primacy, which we have witnessed in some examples, from the

relations between men to the relations between men and nature
or rather between *man* (in the singular) and things. A corollary is
a change in the category of wealth, or rather, I should say, the
accession of the category of wealth as such, to which I referred
in the introduction (p. 6). The latter change has left a deposit in
economic thought in the theory of rent. If only we could pause
and look at that theory, I think my point would be illuminated,
but in any case an informed reader or someone reading through
Schumpeter on the question will easily grasp it. In conjunction
with the substantialist stress on labor (and, subsidiarily, capital)
in classical economics, property in land and rent occupy a marginal and anomalous position indicative of a deep heterogeneity. As Marx perceived, they stand there as remnants
of a former epoch very uneasily accommodated in the capitalist
framework, that is, in the framework of wealth *emancipated from
political power.* This is readily understood, as property in land is
the new form of what was an *indissoluble union of right in land and
power over men* in a system in which movable wealth was subordinated and disparaged. As the transition from Quesnay to
Adam Smith must have suggested, land ownership and rent on
the one hand, industrial capital and profit on the other, are so
incompatible that it is a matter of either-or: either the one is
acknowledged and the other disparaged, or the reverse.[7] This
situation continues with Ricardo and others, in the sense that
rent remains an extraneous element that one must dispose of by
one device or another. Ricardo does so first by recognizing no
absolute rent and then by explaining relative rent through the
law of decreasing returns. *Nota bene:* a differential or more or less
"marginalist" consideration is thus reintroduced at the margin
of a substantialist system.

The case of rent is an illustration of a particular aspect of the
general shift in values from relations between men to relations
between man and things. Yet economics is not technology: it
deals with human relations considered as a corollary of the
stress on things and of the increasing mastery over them (cf.
J. S. Mill's definition). The point to be borne in mind is that the
stress on things, the mastery over things, is throughout a property of the individual, not of the society as a whole. It begins
with private property in Locke, but it goes on, down to Marx

himself, with the agent of production remaining—against all likelihood in manufacturing and in modern industry—the individual man of the state of nature or of traditional handicrafts.

I conclude that the rise of economics, i.e., the shift in value from one kind of relation to the other, and the full accession of the modern Individual (remember Mandeville)—the latter prepared and made ready for this last step from long before—are solidary aspects of one and the same phenomenon. On the level of the general ideology, this Individual is ourselves, for I do not see any deep modification that has intervened and separated us from him. For all practical purposes we are those who have, with Locke, enthroned private property in the place of subordination, or, for that matter, have chosen to be possessing and producing individuals and have turned our backs on the social whole, because of the subordination it entails, and on our neighbor, at least insofar as he would be superior or inferior to us. An important consequence follows for us, I think. It will be my fourth and last point.

There is one event that separates us from Locke and Adam Smith. It is the development of economics as a science. This development, however, is irrelevant to our discussion, just as our study of the relation between the general ideology and the beginnings of economic thought as a distinct kind of thought is irrelevant to the scientific attainments of economics. The way a scientific statement was arrived at is irrelevant to its status as such, if it is not irrelevant to the history of ideas in general. That the progress of the discipline has allowed it to free itself from the presuppositions, prejudices, and limitations of its beginnings and to develop an analytical apparatus free from value imputation may well be the case, but it is a question beyond our reach and purview.

Nevertheless, the present state of economics may be alleged as an objection to a consequence I want to draw from the above. Well-meaning thinkers, especially economists like John Maynard Keynes, sometimes suggest that we should cease to behave as slaves of the economic process, that we have for too long looked at economic questions as final questions, and that the time has come to downgrade the economy to the status of a means for the real human ends, which are social. This proposition has probably more than one meaning, but, taken at its face value, it perplexes one who has pondered on the beginnings of economic thought. For, if the link with the Individual as an idea and a value is as close as I have said, then either such a program will confront the best-rooted and most central and unanimous of modern values and be defeated, or if, contrary to expectation, it proves the more powerful, it will undermine, weaken, or destroy that value; and then, what of us? The only answer history suggests is that, in such a case, we should return to subordination, unless we are able to produce at short notice a consensus bearing on a still unseen third path. In other words, "the economic" is a major category of our thought, and the constraints inherent in our ideology are such that we are not at liberty to decree that, from now on, it will be downgraded to the rank of a servant.

Is this view far-fetched? On the contrary, we need not indulge in recondite speculations but only look around in order to see that what happened or is happening in our world is, at first sight, verifying and sharpening the surmise. Some socialist or totalitarian countries, certainly, have put an end to the autonomy of the economy and have applied it to the service of political or social ends. To think that it is possible to do the same without a similar oppression—that is, involuntary or imposed subordination and the disregard of the Individual as value—is a view devoid of foundation for the present. I am not trying to present in a new form a defense of private enterprise; I am merely bringing together in an admittedly fleeting manner our findings and some happenings of the present day. It will be objected that the attachment between economic things and views and the Individual is a thing of the past. The most important economic agents in real life are now large organizations of different sorts; and, science following in step with reality, the individual has ceased to be the darling child of the economist, so that my picture of the interrelation, even if it should be admitted to hold for the beginnings, would in any case be outrageously out of date.

I would rejoin in the first place that my point is essentially neither about the reality "out there" nor about the science. It is about the ideology of the common people, of you and me, which has not markedly changed since our beginnings, although it may be that the discrepancy between it and the two other factors is felt and presses perhaps toward the proposal in question. As to the science, that economics has ceased to be anchored in the individualist valuation does not necessarily result from its adaptation to recent developments; it would have to be demonstrated. On the face of it, it is unlikely; at any rate, the concepts it receives from outside, from economic common sense, could, I think, be shown not to be so emancipated. I hope I am not misreading some developments of Kenneth Galbraith if I say that what is true of a specialized development in a very particular branch is not true, at the same time, wholesale of general economics. Also, the study of Marx that follows should show how it is possible to descry an individualistic basis in constructions that are granted sociological, not to say holistic, status by practically everyone and from which, it is also sometimes claimed, the individual has evaporated.

Beyond this I must keep silent, for lack of expertise. But after all, the point about economic science is, as I said, irrelevant, and the facts before us are weighty enough to warrant reflection. Totalitarianism is lurking in that zone where an unsuspected or minimized individualist background is unwittingly mixed up with holistic pretense, and it emerges when the mixture reaches the critical mass or the critical proportion (cf. p. 12, above). Here, even the generous doctrinaires who claimed to deliver us from "possessive individualism" appear as apprentice sorcerers. Today we know that social representations beyond the dictator's control have more power than he does in the long run, but in the meantime many lives have been destroyed and many conditions of a human life endangered. There are other limits to modern aritificialism than those ecology has begun to teach us, limits that follow from the social nature of man as a thinking being. The time has come to begin understanding this kind of necessity, which escapes our notice because it apparently goes against our dearest dreams of the last centuries,

> For it is not what is that makes us irascible and resentful, but the fact that it is not as it ought to be. But if we recognize that it is as it must be, i.e., that it is not arbitrariness and chance that make it what it is, then we also recognize that it is as it ought to be. (Hegel 1964, p. 145)

II

The Accomplishment:
Karl Marx

7

From the Revolutionary
Vow of the Young Marx
to *The German Ideology:*
Individualism Predominant

Whatever the controversies surrounding Karl Marx, it will be readily agreed that no author looms as large as he does in the borderlands between the general ideology of our times and economic science, that is to say, precisely in the area on which the present inquiry is focused. I need therefore no justification for devoting to him the longest of the few soundings of which this study consists. Common sense even suggests at the very beginning what our conclusion is likely to be: that, whatever may be the case from the point of view of economic science, Marx has brought economic ideology to its point of maximum power and scope, to its apotheosis. With him, the economic consideration is not content with flourishing as a specialized pursuit; it conquers sociology, history, and politics. Moreover, without engaging in political controversy, it can be calmly stated that in his central and most general point Marx has stated what was to become in the century following him a matter of largely common and universal belief. It may be that the theory of infrastructure and superstructure is not universally admitted among scholars, but for the man in the street the predominance of economic phenomena in social life is one, perhaps the first, article of his creed. Even social scientists in America often give European students the impression of "being Marxists without knowing it," as a friend once told me. I know that such notions are most generally taken as matters of fact, as the simple and honest reflection in the mind of the tremendous development of the economy "out there." I think there is more to it than that; but even if this were the case, it would not diminish Marx's merit and importance.

Our question is: How did Marx accomplish this? It so happens that his intellectual itinerary is of the utmost interest for our inquiry. As the inquiry is limited in scope, the focus will be on the works of Marx's youth and on that one of his mature works which is more explicitly sociological, the *Grundrisse* of 1857. The choice is thus quite different from that of Raymond Aron (1967), who concentrated on the classical works of the mature period and particularly on the *Capital*, in order to give a general picture of Marx's historico-sociological thought as Marx himself saw it and willed it. The difference here is similar to that which I noted about Schumpeter's masterpiece. My modest inquiry is concerned with setting economic analysis back into its context—in this case, the thought of Karl Marx or, rather, the basic presuppositions and articulations of his thought. I am aware that such a limited inquiry is beset with risks. Our concern will sometimes bring us dangerously near recent controversies: whether there is basically a continuity or a discontinuity between the earlier and the later works of Marx; whether Marx ceased to be a philosopher and became something else; whether Marx remained fundamentally a Hegelian all his life; or whether he developed by straying further and further from Hegel and owed more to others, etc.

Up to a point I think it is easy to answer such questions: I shall insist that Marx remained faithful all his life to a moral commitment made in his youth and that his intellectual development was fundamentally determined by that fidelity. The commitment commanded him to abolish philosophy; but in a Hegelian perspective, what is abolished is present in another form, and no serious reader of Marx can maintain that Marx ever ceased to think in a Hegelian mold—whatever the modifications he introduced—and that this is part of his strength as well as of his weakness. This does not discount numerous other encounters by Marx or influences upon him. Here lies a shortcoming of the present study: the originality, the personality of Marx, and hence his very thought would be better understood by someone more familiar with all the authors Marx read in his formative period and with his environment.

Beyond a certain point, however, these questions are not the real questions; they are questions for the classroom, for coteries or factions, which at best express sociointellectual movements. Aron is right to contrast the masterpiece on which Marx relied with a formless draft written in his youth, when he was still

ignorant of economy and history. We need to distinguish between what Marx published, what he left unfinished, and what
he wrote at one time for his own use, which was then published
long after his death as the result of a kind of indiscreet adula-
tion. Of such texts I shall make use—and extensive use of the
"formless draft," the "Manuscripts" of 1844. I view them not as
finished products but as precious evidence relating to the question of how Marx became Marx, of how, in particular, he built
up his basic presuppositions regarding the place of economic
phenomena among social phenomena in general.

I in turn have a question to ask in conjunction with the major
one mentioned above. It springs immediately from the comparative approach I have taken. Is Marx, in our terms, individualist
or holist? At first sight, the collectivist or communist aspect of
his thought appears to put the stress on the social whole so
much that, if we ask our contemporaries, they will classify him
spontaneously as holist. I contend that this is only an appearance, reinforced perhaps through the fact that the person who
asks the question perceives Marx as more holist than himself.
For instance, this would seem to be the case for a student in the
United States. My thesis, which I propose to test here, is that
Marx is essentially individualist. This insight emerged a few
years ago in connection with studies in the social history of
India. As I wished to draw a sharp distinction between sociological thought (in my view, essentially holistic) and economic
thought (essentially individualistic), I was led to doubt the
acccepted view that Marx was one of the founders of sociology
and to conclude that he is not an economic *sociologist*, but a
sociological *economist*.[1] At the point we have now reached, I
hope the question will be seen as meaningful in relation to the
question of Marx's attitude to economic thought. The two
themes will interlock in what follows.

The outline of the plan results from the major question I am
asking and from the chronology of Marx's writings. The general
orientation of his thought was set before he began to study
political economy; it will be dealt with in this, the first of the
three chapters devoted to a study of Marx. The second, chapter
8, will be devoted to the encounter with political economy and
to what it becomes in the hands of Marx, in relation to the global

framework of his thought. The third chapter (chapter 9) will sum up the results of the inquiry regarding the ideology in general and will end with an excursus, into which some by-products of the study will be collected.

It is not too arbitrary to take Marx's theoretical sociopolitical writings as beginning in 1843. His thought crystallized around a criticism of Hegel's thought, especially in his *Philosophy of Right.* In his criticism Marx extended to the State the theory of alienation developed by Feuerbach for the criticism of religion. The initial period is marked by three texts, two of which were published by Marx in 1844: the "Introduction to the Critique ... " contains his revolutionary profession of faith, and "The Jewish Question" complements it brilliantly in relation to a particular problem. The third text is the "Critique" itself, a detailed study of the State in Hegel's *Philosophy of Right* that Marx hoped to complete but finally left unpublished.

Shortly afterward, in 1844, came his encounter with the economic literature, which is known to us through Marx's Paris "Manuscripts of 1844." *The German Ideology,* written by Marx and Engels in 1845–46 (and left unpublished only by chance), or, more precisely, its first part, expounding in Engels's own words "the materialist conception of history," combines in the first approximation the two lines of thought, if one leaves aside altogether less important influences. In actual fact *The German Ideology,* although later in time than the "Manuscripts," continues the line of the earlier writings in the sense that, while giving an important place to the economic aspects, it integrates them within a general view of history. The economic view is used to give a firm outline, a decisive character to what was already there. It is thus possible to proceed in two stages. In a first stage we shall pursue the development of the general theses from the first writings to *The German Ideology,* while remaining alert to the connection between it and the "Manuscripts." In a second stage we shall single out the "Manuscripts" as the record of Marx's discovery of economics.

In the first stage, a complication will arise as our second theme is allowed to intervene. On the one hand, the texts here considered predominantly express or imply an individualistic view; on the other hand, the contrary view, of man as an essentially

social being, is also present, very explicitly, in a few texts or
passages. It is necessary to study the latter texts in the first stage
of our consideration, wherever they may be found—and they
are found mainly in the "Manuscripts"—in order to throw into
relief the problem posed by the juxtaposition of the two opposite
conceptions and by their subsequent fate. (It must be said at
once that, if there is here a problem for us, there is none for
Marx himself—and we shall have to understand that fact.)
Therefore we shall, after considering the first three texts, insert
at their chronological place the relevant passages from the "Manuscripts" that present the sociological apperception before we
go over to *The German Ideology*, where it is submerged and disappears forever.

The brief text called "Introduction to the Criticism of Hegel's
Philosophy of Right" (exactly: *Zur Kritik der Hegelschen Rechtsphilosophie: Einleitung;* I shall distinguish it throughout as the
"Einleitung") was written by Marx at the end of 1843. He
was twenty-five and had married in June 1843 after seven years
of engagement. The text was published in the spring of 1844 in
Paris in the first and only issue of Marx's and Ruge's *Deutsch-
Französische Jahrbücher* (Marx, "Einleitung," *Werke,* 1:378–91).[2] It
can be called Marx's revolutionary profession of faith. Essentially, it proclaims the alliance of Philosophy with the Proletariat
for making philosophy real and abolishing the proletariat. Apart
from Marx's usual dialectical brilliance and a sort of clarion-call
eloquence—"the weapon of criticism cannot altogether replace
the criticism by weapons" (p. 385)—this well-known text is remarkable in one regard: it focuses on Germany and there is a
distinctly Fichtean ring about it.

It does not refer to Hegel's *Philosophy of Right* only in its broad
relation to German history—or rather, with Germany's lack of
recent history, apart from the realm of thought. Hegel's work is,
actually, as the crowning part of the German philosophy of right
and of the State, "the only German history standing on a par
with the official modern present" (p. 383). The theme is well
known, indeed it is a stereotype of German literature: while the
other peoples act on the stage of history, the German people
(*Volk*) is excluded from it and reduced to thinking what the
others live. As Fichte had, more than thirty years earlier, Marx
takes this very deprivation as the basis for an unprecedented

accomplishment. The parallelism with the situation of the proletariat elsewhere—if it is true that it was then nonexistent in Germany—justifies an identification. The parallel with Fichte is very close: as Germany is "fundamental" (*gründliche*), it cannot revolutionize except from the very "fundament" (*von Grund aus*). Thus, "The emancipation of the German is the emancipation of man" (p. 391). As for philosophy, it has accomplished its task (in Hegel's *Philosophy of Right*); it cannot go any further without abolishing itself, and it cannot be abolished without being realized, nor realized without being abolished (p. 384). Given a social class whose chains are "radical," the alliance is in the nature of things: "the head of this emancipation is the philosophy, its heart is the proletariat." There is a precedent, for Germany's revolutionary past is the Reformation: "As then the monk, so now it is the philosopher, in whose brain the revolution begins" (p. 385). If weapons, that is, physical power or violence (*materielle Gewalt*), are necessary, "the theory becomes physical power as soon as it catches the masses " (p. 385). The proof of the radicalism or practical energy of German theory is found in the conclusion of the criticism of religion, "that Man is the highest being for Man," whence follows "the categorical imperative to throw down all the conditions in which Man is a humiliated, enslaved, abandoned, and despicable being" (p. 385).

We know from earlier texts that the radical stand, the basic attitude expressed in 1843, was not new. It can be traced back to Marx's philosophical dissertation of 1841 ("to make the gap between the ideal and the real intolerable") and even to the extraordinary letter to his father of November 1837 with its rejection, among other things, of the duality between *is* and *ought* (see McLellan 1971, pp. 1–22).

This rejection inevitably calls to mind the Hegelian criticism of Kant's morality. The general attitude of the young Marx is highly significant. On the one hand, it offers an example of a typical phenomenon of our world, the revolt of the educated young man; on the other, it is in continuity with German romanticism in the widest sense, namely, with that "intensification of the dignity of man" (*Steigerung*) which is, according to Dilthey, one of the defining features of the German intellectual movement around 1800 (Dilthey 1968, p. 204, etc.). The parallel is

striking with the orientation of the young Hegel, which Marx
could not know, but which is echoed in some manner in the
later *Phenomenology of the Mind*, in which Marx found the core of
Hegel's philosophy ("Manuscripts," 3d Ms., fols. XI–XXXIII).
Hegel, when working on the "Spirit of Christianity" in 1798–99,
was keen on surmounting all forms of separation, which is pain,
and on recovering the spontaneous unison of the Greeks. He
searched for a new religion, as Marx for a new society, and we
shall hint more precisely at the parallel further on.

It is noteworthy that the revolutionary vow of the young Marx
is presented not on an international but on a German plane, as
growing specifically from German conditions. The point is in
keeping with German tradition in general, in which one is a man
through being a German, and it evokes, beyond Fichte, a widespread German attitude to the failure of the French revolutionaries as due to their lack of moral fiber, in contrast to the
serious and faithful character of the Germans, who alone could
have brought such a grandiose task to fulfillment.

I believe that this German allegiance of the young Marx
should be taken quite seriously. Beyond the pregnant reference
to Luther, there is an intimate link between Marx and German
philosophy. We shall see an essential aspect of it, thanks to
Robert C. Tucker, but even in very general terms one cannot
understand the development of Marx if one does not see him
carried along, as it were, on the wings of that philosophy. His
intellectual boldness and his revolutionary project itself are inseparable from the speculation of those Titans who thought they
had gone beyond all contradictions and transcended all distinction between finite and infinite, subject and object, nature and
spirit.

At the same time, as Hyppolite noted (1955, p. 153), Marx
substitutes class for the Hegelian nation (or *Volk*) as the actor on
the historical stage. Instead of an elected people being called to
dominate other peoples, as described by German thinkers in
general (even by such an equalitarian as Fichte), the proletariat
will put an end to all domination or subordination. On this
point, then, Marx transcends the German tradition.

In close connection with this "German" aspect is the intellectual character of Marx's formulation: it is not the proletariat
that seeks and finds an ally in the German philosopher, it is the

German philosopher searching for a solution to the national problem in terms of the relation between national thought and national life who finds a quasi-providential tool *cum* ally in the proletariat. The revolution begins in the brain of the (German) intellectual: from Luther through Fichte and Marx the filiation leads to a really international figure: the professional revolutionary of the twentieth century. Lenin was to demonstrate that the intellectual was not bound to wait for the development of a proletarian class.

All this is perhaps not essential for us here. What is essential is that Marx will remain faithful all through his life (in spite of all the hardships it brought upon him) to the revolutionary vow thus rooted and justified, but for all practical purposes universal in its content. Even those who prefer to read Marx's message from the works of his maturity—whether predominantly or exclusively—cannot deny that here is the great motive force of his later achievements. I am going to exploit to the utmost this continuity for the understanding of Marx, to stress as much as possible the entailments for Marx's thought of this initial and capital step, which I shall continue to call his revolutionary vow. Here is a young romantic scholar, publicist, and rebel who wants to reconcile and indissolubly unite thought and action, and who to this end commits himself to the emancipation of man under the motto, "Man is the highest being for Man."[3]

It should be noted that what is in question is not essentially the reform of society or the deliverance of one class from oppression. The class with "radical chains" is only the precondition of absolute emancipation for all men or, rather, of the emancipation of Man as an abstract being, of Man, that is, as a self-sufficient being and the incarnation of the highest value—as an Individual in the perfect, modern sense of the term. Moreover, the person who takes the vow obviously does so as an Individual in the same sense, as an independent being whose paramount value is precisely the Individual—man rid of his chains, purged of any dependence. It is thus clear that the revolutionary vow of the young Marx affords a first answer to our question: whether Marx conceived of man essentially as an individual or as a social being. At this stage our answer to that question must be as radical, as absolute, as Marx's commitment. And insofar as Marx kept faithfully all his life to this commit-

ment, there is a strong presumption that his view of man remained fundamentally the same, unless we can convict him of
inconsistency or unless we can detect a change in that regard. We
may surmise that any other views Marx may have been led to
take in the course of his long studies of economic and social life
will, on analysis, be found to have been relatively secondary,
limited, and superficial as compared to this one, which was
rooted in the very orientation he chose to give his life.

To test this hypothesis, we shall turn, first, to the other works
of Marx's youth, for the most part unpublished in his lifetime,
all written within the short span of three years (1843–45). First in
time as well as in importance for the subsequent development of
Marx's thought is his manuscript "Critique of Hegel's
Philosophy of Right" (Aus der Kritik der Hegelschen Staatsrecht).
We know that Marx held Hegel to be the greatest thinker of the
times, and it is by reference to the Philosophy of Right that he
defined and planned his own work for several years. We have
here a long, painstaking criticism, paragraph by paragraph, of
the central part of Hegel's consideration of the State (§§ 261–313
[Werke, 1:203–333]; for a summary and a fair judgment, see Hyppolite, 1955, pp. 120–41). Marx's close reading is by no means
useless, to begin with, for the understanding of this difficult
text. As to his criticism, its most incontrovertible aspect consists
in showing that Hegel does not really, in many places, grasp the
object philosophically but juxtaposes abstract logic and empirical admissions: "Hegel gives to his logic a political body, he does
not give the logic of the political body" (p. 250). Marx derides
Hegel's "deductions," especially regarding the monarch, the
bureaucracy, and the two chambers, and he denounces the
mediations and transitions, many of which deserve such treatment.

The basic and general criticism consists of two observations,
which bear on different levels. First, Marx reproaches Hegel for
inverting the subject and the predicate: "What should have been
the starting point becomes the mystical result, and what should
have been the rational result becomes the mystical starting
point" (p. 242). Hegel takes as subject the State as Spirit and
predicates unto it, as its phenomenalizations, every social institution or aspect, from civil society to the constitutional
monarch. According to Marx, the real concrete subject is the real

man of civil society, and the State is only its predicate (Hyppo-lite, p. 127). This is the well-known Marxian criticism of Hegel-ian idealism, dialectics, and consciousness in general as in-verted, as walking on its head and having to be put back on its feet.[4]

The second point bears on the relation between civil society and the State. Hegel describes them as separate institutions. "Hegel starts from the separation between 'State' and 'civil soci-ety,' the 'particular interests' [of the latter], and 'the general in itself and for itself' [of the former]" (p. 247). For Marx, this is true as a description of the modern state of things, and we have seen that, in the published "Einleitung," he vindicated Hegel's achievement in this regard. But Hegel is not content with de-scribing; he approves of this situation, and, accepting civil soci-ety as given, he delineates—indeed, he prescribes—his State accordingly. Marx, on the contrary, denies that this separation is in conformity to reason. And this denial of course corresponds to his revolutionary attitude. In Hyppolite's words, Marx "proposes to solve this contradictory dualism by . . . the absorp-tion of the State in the society, the society transforming itself at the same time in order not to be lost in individualist atomism . . . . The real man, the one who lives and toils, must express himself as such in the State, which will then lose its transcendent character" (Hyppolite, p. 126).

This is a momentous proposition, which Marx does not di-rectly justify in this place; he simply admits that the absorption is possible. One might suppose that this lack of justification results here from the critical aim of the text: Hegel's adverse view is criticized, and Marx's own view is barely indicated; other texts will perhaps be more explicit. There is more to it than that; the rejection of any and all transcendence is a basic characteristic of Marx's thought. Hegel's followers (Feuerbach) here continue and intensify a feature already found in Hegel. It hardly need be recalled that Hegel's logic culminates in the Idea, where the concept (*Begriff*) is incarnate, where rational and real coincide. In this very same *Philosophy of Right*, the State is extolled as con-trasted to religion by reason of its immanence as opposed to the latter's transcendence. (See the long explanation added to § 270, on the relation between State and Church; Marx announces [p. 214] that he will take it up later on; apparently he did not in this work, but see below, p. 215, n. 6.)

To Marx, the State is not at present immanent, or not absolutely or sufficiently so. In relation to civil society, it is transcendent, and therefore Marx condemns it. (About the merciless war
of Marx against transcendence, see Cottier 1959.) This is all of a
piece with the revolutionary vow; indeed, it is identical with it
and reveals its real philosophical dimension: the "emancipation
of man" is conterminous with the destruction of transcendence.
On this very point, the theological writings of the young Hegel
offer a precise parallel. Hegel is concerned there with ridding
Christianity of all transcendence, with reconstructing a purely
immanent message of Jesus, who would have preached, for
example, "virtues without domination or subjection, [mere]
modifications of love" (Dilthey 1968, p. 94; cf. Hegel 1971, p.
244). Cottier has admirably pointed out that this attitude is a
sequel of the Reformation, which banished God from this
netherworld and thus made transcendence intolerable.

The sociologist has every reason to ponder this trend in Marx;
for if society is admitted to be a whole, it transcends as such its
elements in the same way as an organism does its components.
Marx shows at length that Hegel's philosophical determination
or deduction of the State does not go beyond that of an organism in general and that this is the point where the empirical
fleshing out of the philosophical outline begins. As far as I can
see, however, he does not protest against the assimilation itself
(see ibid., pp. 209 ff., on Hegel's § 269). Precisely this notion is
an important aspect of Hegel's construction, arbitrary and imperfect as it may be in other regards.

It can hardly be denied that Hegel's State as Spirit (*Geist*) is
the social whole as conscious of itself or, if one prefers, as present in the consciousness of the members of the society. (Indeed, only the expression "social whole" that I just used is not
literally present in Hegel's text.) The relation Hegel posits between civil society and the State is not only one of separation, it
is also one of contradiction insofar as civil society is dominated
by egoism and individualism, the State by altruism and holism;
and it is, if I may use my own terms, one of hierarchy or
encompassing/encompassed. For Hegel's State is the totality encompassing its elements, including the one element that is formally contradictory to it, as freedom is formally contradictory to
law. (On contradiction in hierarchy, see my paper, 1971*b*, pp.
80–81.) It is hard to think that Marx was blind to this aspect.[5] We

are confronted with an event so dramatic and of such historical import that it is worthwhile looking into the detail of this rejection by Marx of Hegel's holistic aspect. I take one paragraph of Hegel and Marx's commentary on it: Hegel, § 274 (T. M. Knox, trans., 1942, pp. 178–79):

> Mind is actual only as that which it knows itself to be, and the state, as the mind of a nation [*Volk*], is both the law permeating all relationships within the state and also at the same time the manners and consciousness of its citizens [*der Individuen:* of the individuals]. It follows, therefore, that the constitution of any given nation [*Volk*] depends in general on the character and development of its self-consciousness. In its self-consciousness its subjective freedom is rooted and so, therefore, is the actuality of its constitution.

Marx's commentary (Marx, "Hegel's Critique," J. O'Malley, trans., 1970, p. 20):

> The only thing that follows from Hegel's reasoning, is that a State in which the character and development of self-consciousness and the constitution contradict each other is no real State. That the constitution which was the product of a bygone self-consciousness can become an oppressive fetter for an advanced self-consciousness etc., etc., are certainly trivialities. However, what should follow is only the demand for a constitution having within itself the characteristic and principle of advancing in step with consciousness, with actual man, which is possible only when man has become the principle of the constitution. Here Hegel is a *Sophist*.

Hegel's first sentence is clear: the State is the Spirit of a people. As such, it is at the same time a political institution and the general principle or law of social relations in general, hence the mores or values (*Sitte*) and the consciousness of the individuals that compose it. Hegel calls "State," at the same time: (1) what we call by that name; (2) the global society or community as a symbolic system, the same thing as Durkheim's "collective consciousness." Rousseau had said similarly that mores (*les moeurs*) are what makes up "the veritable constitution of States" (*Contrat Social*, 2:xii); and in his commentary on Rousseau, Durkheim insisted on this "fixed, permanent orientation of the minds and activities in a determinate direction" as underlying the *volonté générale* and explaining the possibility of its apparently sudden emergence (quotation and reference in Dumont 1965, p. 47).

This is a point of central import, and yet one that is not always seen, or stressed, by Hegel's commentators. One misses a crucial aspect of Hegel's theory if one sees in his State only the political aspect. If this were so, then Marx would be right in refusing to see in Hegel's State anything but an institution juxtaposed to the other social institutions (the family, civil society). If, on the contrary, we substitute the global society for the State, then it becomes evident that there is an intimate connection between it and all the particular institutions found within it, and that it not only subsumes but animates and sustains them. At least this is the basic postulate of holistic sociology.

But, we may ask, why is it that Hegel resorts to that indirect presentation of the global society under the guise of the State? This certainly obscures his thesis, and it may be partly responsible for the apparent "sclerosis" shown by Hegel in the *Philosophy of Right*, according to such an expert as Hyppolite. The reason, by and large, is the same as that which prevented Rousseau from distinguishing between global society and State. Due to their emphasis on consciousness and freedom, these authors moved essentially within an individualistic universe, and their opposite perception of man as a social being, or of society as a whole from which the human person is born and fed, took, paradoxically, the form of political consideration. In Rousseau's *Social Contract*, holism is reinstated as against individualism through the seeming miracle of the *volonté générale*; in the *Philosophy of Right*, the *societas* or juxtaposition of individuals of civil society is transcended in the *universitas*, or whole, of the State in its unity and corporateness as the incarnation of Spirit (ibid., pp. 49, 59).

Marx's relatively brief comment on this paragraph of Hegel is remarkable. He focuses, not as Hegel does on the principle of interdependence of the different spheres within a society, but on the case in which a discrepancy has to be recognized between the state of social consciousness and the political constitution. He implies that such is the fact in modern society, and he advocates as a remedy a constitution based on man, which is just what the program of the French Revolution had been. He does not consider Hegel's holistic plea; he abruptly opposes it with the individualistic creed, and in so doing he clearly misses the point I insisted upon for the understanding of Hegel's thesis. This is remarkable, for in his long commentary Marx is anxious to analyze Hegel's text with the utmost care and displays no little ingenuity in his efforts to lay bare its intricacies. In this case, Marx seems to have been irked by the assertion of a correspondence between consciousness and constitution and to have missed the essence.

History displays here, if not its Hegelian cunning, yet one of its minor tricks; for when he stresses the discrepancy between the established institutions and the present state of consciousness, Marx unwittingly reproduces a central motive of the young Hegel. The closest parallels are found in the latter's political writings. The short tract on the affairs of Württemberg deals precisely with the institutions "from which the spirit has flown" (Hegel 1964, p. 244; cf. 1958, p. 12). The fine fragment meant as an introduction to "The German Constitution" is wholly devoted to the "ceaselessly increasing contradiction between the life which men unconsciously search for and the life that is offered and permitted them" (1958, p. 16). The same notion plays a central role in the religious studies. The positivity of religion is defined as an obsolescence which calls for authority (1971, pp. 167 ff.). Jesus appears among the Jews at the moment when "the spirit has disappeared from a constitution, from the laws, when it has changed and does no more agree with them" (1907, p. 385); and again, when Hegel explains the victory of Christianity over paganism, his schema is identical with that of Marx.

To return to Marx, I find a similar blindness on his part in a passage near the end of the first part of "The Jewish Question" (*Werke*, 1:370) where he quotes (at length, with two short but perhaps significant omissions) the famous and illuminating passage of the *Contrat Social* to which I alluded above: "Whoso would undertake to institute a People . . . ." Marx is stressing the separation between *real* man as the member of civil society—the egoist individual—and *political* man as the abstract citizen—an artificial, allegoric person. He quotes Rousseau as showing the abstraction of political man and concludes, briefly but memorably: "Any emancipation *refers back* the human world, the conjuncture, to *man* himself" ("Alle Emancipation ist *Zurückführung* der

menschliche Welt, der Verhältnisse, auf den *Menschen* selbst"[p.
370]). (Note, in passing, that this sentence confirms my thesis
of a fundamental individualism of Marx being rooted in his
emancipation vow.) The passage shows a complete incom-
prehension of Rousseau that, in contrast to Marx's usual penetration, requires an explanation. For Rousseau does not show
anything like "the abstraction of political man"; quite to the
contrary, he says that man must be completely transformed, as
it were, in the crucible of political constitution and must "receive
from the whole his life and his being." Clearly, Marx passes over
this remarkable holistic statement and goes straight to the result
as he sees it, namely, that by the side of this new creature the old
individual lives on. Rousseau is thus made responsible for the
divorce between the real man and the abstract citizen, a separation that Rousseau certainly never contemplated any more than
he sponsored anything like the Rights of Man. The absurdity is
complete when Marx concludes from Rousseau's fusion of the
individual with the social and political whole that "emancipation" leads back from social relations to the individual.

To understand the strange way in which Marx reads Rousseau, we must recognize that, for Marx, the Individual and the
social whole are not incompatible. The point will occupy us at
some length, and I must here anticipate. Marx cannot understand the pains that Rousseau takes to surmount this incompatibility and to offer a transition in the passage from the "particular will" to the "general will"—which is not the "will of all."
For Marx, the divorce between the two aspects is merely a
pathological social fact. After acknowledging it, one should not
construe it in thought, as he thinks Rousseau is doing, but just
destroy it. There is, in Marx's reading of Rousseau here, an
element of self-deception and a close parallelism to Marx's reaction to Hegel's § 274. Provisionally, I conclude that in both cases
Marx was inhibited from taking holistic statements at their face
value. He could not see in them anything beyond their political
import, which he immediately referred to his own conception of
the political sphere as being, in modern times, separated from
and contradictory to that of civil society.

"The Jewish Question" is contemporary with the "Einleitung," was published with it at the beginning of 1844, and is
only slightly later than "Hegel's Critique," according to the

biographers (*Werke*, 1:347–77). This text is quite explicit about Marx's conception of the relation, factual as well as ideal, between the State and religion. It is, in its first part, a brilliant reply to a Young Hegelian, Bruno Bauer, on the question of the emancipation of the Jews in Germany. What appeared only indirectly in the criticism of Hegel is here explicitly and clearly set out. We perceive how Marx extends to the modern State the method developed by Feuerbach in his criticism of religion and thus generalizes the latter's attack on transcendence.

Just as man separates himself from himself in religion by attributing his own qualities to an imaginary, otherworldly being whom he worships, so also he is separated from himself in the modern democratic State. For this State is characterized by the disjunction of his real and his ideal being: there is, on the one hand, the individual of civil society, independent and egoist—real, but not true to the essence of man, an untrue phenomenon (*unwahre Erscheinung*); on the other is the citizen of the political community, true to the generic essence or social essence (*Gattungswesen, Gemeinwesen*) of man—a moral but abstract, artificial person, deprived of his real individual life and filled with an unreal universality. The political State is to civil society as heaven is to earth: "Man is acknowledged as *real* only in the form of the egoist individual [*Individuum*], and as *true* only in the form of the abstract citizen" (pp. 355, 370).

There is thus a deep affinity between the modern democratic State and the Christian religion. Indeed, the modern State—as exemplified in the contemporary United States—is the only form of State that is true to the Christian spirit. It does not acknowledge religion on the level of the State,[6] but it presupposes it on the part of the subjects, that is, on the level of civil society (Tocqueville is named, his friend Beaumont quoted). This is so because the democratic State, on the one hand, and the Christian religion, on the other, are expressions on different levels of the same thing, namely, a certain stage of development of the human mind. Religion remains the ideal, nonworldly consciousness of the members of the State because it is the ideal form of the stage of development that is actualized in the State. Just as the Christian religion is the acknowledgment of man in a roundabout way, through a detour (*auf einem Umweg*), through a mediator (*Mittler*), "so the modern man proclaims himself an

atheist only through the mediation of the State, only in a roundabout way, and remains for the rest confined in religion." Or
again: "As Christ is the mediator whom man burdens with his
whole divinity, his whole religious confinement, the State is the
mediator in whom man transfers his whole un-divinity, his
whole human un-confinement" (p. 353).

Marx thus arrives at a clear contrast between political emancipation, as realized in the modern State, and human emancipation, which will consist in doing away with all detours
and all mediators. We see here more concretely to what Marx
committed himself in his juvenile enthusiasm—or should I say
en-anthrop-usiasm? It comes out as nothing less than the realization of the Hegelian *Idee* as the fusion of the ideal and the
actual, the utopian program of a complete, material, absolute
identification of value and fact. For the detour to be abolished is
in essence the recourse to idea and value for designating, judg-
ing, and shaping the raw datum of life.

Even while leaving aside the issue of Jewish emancipation,
there is more in "The Jewish Question" for our purpose. From a
long and on the whole magisterial discussion of the Declarations
of Rights of the French Revolution, it is useful to extract the view
Marx takes of the historical development since the *ancien régime*
with respect to the sphere of politics. Marx begins by stating
what he calls the enigma of the French Revolution: "that a
people, which just sets about ... to found a political community [*Gemeinwesen*] solemnly proclaims (Declaration of 1791) the
legitimacy of the egoist man, divorced from his fellow men and
from the community" and even degrades the community to a
mere means for the maintenance of the so-called Rights of Man
(p. 366). Marx finds the solution of this enigma in the general
historical development. In feudalism, civil society[7] had an immediate political character (pp. 367–68); political emancipation
has consisted in separating the two aspects: here the actual man,
there the citizen as an artificial, if "true," man. The French Revolution has differentiated the political community from the civil
society (p. 369). Real human emancipation will consist in reunit-
ing men's empirical life with their universal or social essence,
the latter ceasing to appear in political guise.

Thus, the movement as a whole is for Marx the suppression of
politics through a first stage, isolating it, and a second stage,

dropping it altogether. But what is the meaning of *politics* here? It is, implicitly, subordination: under feudalism, subordination permeated all aspects of social life; the Revolution isolated, confined it, to a distinct sphere; what remains is only to suppress it in a free association of men, an association without subordination or mediation, where the whole will not transcend its parts but only be immanent in them. This is the outline; this is the design.

To recapitulate: all that we have seen until now shows Marx adopting a predominantly individualistic view of man—I mean a view according to which humanity is embodied in each particular human being. In his profession of faith, Marx vows to emancipate that being; in his critique of Hegel he makes light of Hegel's perception of global society as prior to the particular institutions and to the human agents as found, for instance, in civil society; in "The Jewish Question" he rejects as insufficient the political emancipation that, while excluding religion from the State, presupposes it on the part of its members: the real, human emancipation will do away at one and the same time with religion and with the State.

Yet in all this, it can be argued, society itself is not negated. Man is called predominantly a generic being or essence (*Gattungswesen*, from *Gattung:* genus, species; a current expression, found in Feuerbach, that evokes from earlier generations the species as the universal society of mankind in Kant).[8] But man is also called occasionally a social being (*Gemeinwesen*, which means both a community, particularly a political community, and "a common essence," that is, a being living in community). Thus we find in these texts (as also in Lorenz von Stein) a prefiguration of Tönnies's distinction between *Gemeinschaft* (here the State) and *Gesellschaft* (in civil "society"). The contemplated emancipation will not put an end to man's life in society (how could it?) but will actually amount to a reform of society, especially regarding its present-day political aspects.

All this is true, but it is clear that the basis of this reconstruction is the individual person. For instance, civil society is real in a sense that the State is not, and, as we have seen, all emancipation is the reduction of relations to man himself (the Individual!). There is a deep-seated paradox in the fact that what Marx calls "common," or "community," must be eliminated,

while what he calls "society," that is, the mere juxtaposition of
individuals, will only be modified. Yet, in one detail, the holism
predominant in German thought in general (and so extraordinarily brought back into its opposite in Hegel himself) has not
been expurgated: the emancipation of man will be attained, as it
were, on German soil, through the solution of a purely German
problem; it will be German emancipation and, *by virtue of it*, that
of all men. I think we may conclude that, although the antithesis
between individualism and holism has not been seen, as is clear
from the "enigma" of the French Revolution, yet here Marx is
clearly—and unavoidably for an emancipator—thinking of man
in terms of the Individual.[9]

We shall see in the sequence that the same view holds of the
first elaborate statement of "historical materialism" in *The German Ideology*. But before proceeding to that book, I must make
some mention of certain texts, chronologically intermediary between those already considered and *The German Ideology*, where
a different view is found regarding the nature of man. The main
text is found in the 1844 "Manuscripts," which will be considered as a whole at a later stage. For the moment I shall only
extract and briefly highlight one single theme from the "Manuscripts."

In the third Manuscript (fols. V–VI), after a discussion of the
various sorts of communism comes a development that abounds
in categorical affirmations of the social nature of man. "Therefore the whole movement (of production by man of himself and
of the other man) is essentially social; just *as* society itself produces *man* as *man*, it is produced by him." "Activity and enjoyment ... are social activity and social enjoyment ... ; society is the achievement of the essential unity of man with nature." Even if my activity is scientific, etc., and if I engage in it
mostly in isolation, "I am *social* because I am active as *man* ... ;
my *own* existence *is* social activity" (*MEGA*, I.3:116, corrected as
in *Werke*, supplementary vol. I, p. 538).[10]

The last passage in particular leaves no room for doubt: here is
an articulate statement of the perception of oneself as a social
being—what I call "the sociological apperception." It is interesting to note that the French translator of 1969, obviously a Marxist, understood it otherwise. As an orthodox individualist, he
appended a note of his own to "society itself produces *man* as

man" to explain that Marx had in view here the "true" society, that is to say, not the society in which we live, but the communist society of the future ("Manuscripts," French trans., p. 89). Unfortunately for the simplicity of our inquiry, this view is not tenable. It is true that the paragraph opens with the "assumption of private property having been positively abolished," but, as my quotations already show—and as the context abundantly confirms—Marx soon shifts to a more general viewpoint. In the long development that follows, and that would deserve a detailed commentary, Marx deals with our relationship to nature, and he insists on the fact that our senses are educated and developed socially—for instance, that is how our ear becomes musical—and he writes: "The *formation* of the five senses is the work of all past history." Clearly, the "true society" of the French translator does not account for this.

In fact, what the text as a whole says is that the social nature of man will receive only in communism its perfect expression, its complete development. Private property prevents the full development of man as a social-and-sentient being: "*All* senses, physical and intellectual, have been replaced by the simple alienation of *all* these senses, the sense of *having*" (*MEGA,* I.3:118). (This is again a clear example of the social determination of man here and now.) We are thus faced with a double problem. We had already encountered the question of the relationship between man's generic or universal essence (*Gattungswesen*) and his social nature (*Gemeinwesen*). Now appears the relationship between this social nature and the communist society. On this point one passage is essential. Marx, who has just written, "My *own* existence *is* social activity," adds, "and therefore what I do of myself I do for the society and with the consciousness of myself as a social being" (*MEGA,* I.3:116). Even though this passage can bear a wide interpretation, it is impossible not to see in it an allusion to the revolutionary commitment. There follows an explication that is worth pondering:

> My *universal* consciousness is only the *theoretical* form of that whose living form is the *actual* common being, social being,[11] even if at the present day this *universal* consciousness is an abstraction from real life and, as such, confronts it as an enemy. It follows that the activity of my *universal* consciousness as such is also my *theoretical* existence as a social being. (Ibid., pp. 116–17)

At first sight, we find here the answer to our first question: the social or common being (*Gemeinwesen*) is actual, while the generic or universal essence (*Gattungswesen*) is pure theory. In this sense, we should have here the transition, apparently definitive, from the abstract humanity of the philosophers to the concrete society of the sociologist. But this is not all. At present, "my universal consciousness," that is, the generic essence of man, confronts as an enemy my actual life as a social being. It is the communist society that reveals that both essences coincide at bottom and collide only as long as society has not been reformed. Thus, "the activity of my universal consciousness," that is, my revolutionary activity, is the expression of my social nature, for it is only through emancipation that the social nature will be fully realized in conformity with the universal or generic essence. The distance, the discord, between the "species" and the "actual society" is here transformed into a revolutionary motive. As we know, it is not a matter of understanding the world but of changing it. I conclude: if, on the one hand, Marx progresses here in principle from the theoretical view of the species to the sociological view of the concrete social being, on the other hand he keeps enough of the theoretical view to enable him to indict the contemporary society. All in all, both views are used—and destroyed. This subtle dialectic, which unites and identifies in some manner *Gattungswesen*, *Gemeinwesen*, and the revolutionary project, would be worth a long epilogue. Marx continues:

> It is first of all necessary to avoid positing once more the "society" as an abstraction facing the individual. The individual *is the social being*.

The first statement by itself might seem very happy, but actually it prepares the abrupt identification that follows: "The individual is the social being" (or essence: *Wesen*). Let us try to understand this identification. First, the sequence shows that it does not mean, simply, "Each particular man is a social being," but "In each particular man is found the human totality," or, in Marx's language, "the ideal totality, the subjective existence for itself of the society as thought and felt" (*MEGA*, I.3:117). In short, it is a matter of the Individual, in our sense of the term. Marx does not admit our distinction between individualism and holism; he claims to identify them.

Now, on what level does this identification apply? It is not a statement of fact, for Marx has just been telling us that in fact the two aspects are inimical. The statement is ontological, metaphysical; it is true in the depth of things, or in principle. In the final analysis it is a normative statement: one must act in such a way that the Individual and the social being should coincide; or, to use an expression of Marx that we have encountered, the thing is *true* and should be made *actual*. We see that Marx was not naive in the manner of his present-day followers; he knew what he was doing. With him, the distinction between individualism and holism is replaced by the distinction between the present society and the ideal society. In the ideal society, by hypothesis, free individuals will constitute a community and thus become complete or perfect social beings.

We thus obtain confirmation of something we had somehow perceived already: the vow to transform the actual society into the ideal society preempts under a purposive form and forestalls the intellectual recognition of the two opposed valuations, individualistic and holistic. Man is fully recognized as a social being only in the ideal society, because there only will have disappeared the contrariety between it and the free individual—who alone can bring about the revolution.

Incomplete as it is, our analysis of the theme of man as a social being in the "Manuscripts" prepares us to understand what is to follow: the theme will be completely absorbed in revolutionary activity; at the deepest level, it will disappear from the subsequent work of Marx. There is perhaps a symbol of that fate in the fact that here Marx has struck out the greatest part of the development on the social nature of the "physical and intellectual senses" of man.

A contemporary note of Marx falls into place here. It is found in his notebook on James Mill. It begins with the words, "If we suppose that we should produce as human beings ...," and Marx speaks in the first person as producer and addresses a second person as consumer: "In your enjoyment and use of my product ... , I should be conscious of serving as mediator between you and the human genus, of being known and felt by you as a complement of your own being and as a necessary part of yourself, of being acknowledged in your thought and in your love" (*MEGA*, I.3:546–47). I quote this more or less confidential fragment because it will contrast clearly with a corresponding

view we shall find in *The German Ideology*. It echoes an idea of
Feuerbach which Marx praises in a letter to him of August 1844,
"the unity of man with man based on the real differences between men" (cf. McLellan 1969, pp. 109–10; 1971, p. 184).

Actually, the two views of man that I have contrasted above
are found within the covers of *The German Ideology* as it has
become customary to print it, for the book includes, at the beginning, Marx's pithy "Theses on Feuerbach," which Engels first
published in his book on Feuerbach. The 6th Thesis obviously
links up with the passage of the "Manuscripts" quoted above
about "generic essence" and "social essence," and it presents a
quite categoric sociological statement:

> Feuerbach refers the religious essence back to the *human*
> essence. But the essence of man is not an abstraction [*ein
> Abstraktum*] inherent in the individual [*in dem einzelnen Indi-
> viduum*]. Actually, it is the whole of social relations.

Let me first remark that in this passage Marx, having to do
with the individual as a moral being, adds to the primarily
biological expression *das Individuum* the adjective *einzelne* (cf. p.
134).

In contrast to this statement, which is impeccable as we understand it, *The German Ideology* throughout considers individuals as primary subjects, adding their mainly economic relations
among themselves. The transition between the two views,
which shows that in Marx's idea there was no contradiction and
probably no real contrast between them, is afforded by the 8th to
10th Theses on Feuerbach. For Marx, stressing practical activity
was enough to transcend the "individualism" of the old
materialism. All social life is essentially practical, and therefore
the consideration of practical activity is sufficient for passing
from civil or bourgeois society to the "new" conception of "human society or social humanity." Thus, "the whole of social
relations" of the 6th Thesis will boil down, in *The German Ideology*, to production and the human relations immediately related
to it.

✳

I now pass to a consideration of *The German Ideology*, or rather,
of its first part, entitled "Feuerbach: the Opposition between
Materialist and Idealist Conceptions," which contains, according

to Engels, "the exposition of the materialist conception of history." The book, written jointly by Marx and Engels and one or two others in Brussels in 1845–46, remained unpublished, owing to adverse circumstances, but according to Marx the authors had achieved their main goal: to get a clear view of themselves and liquidate their old philosophical theories. The first part is taken as the work of Marx and Engels. The manuscript is in Marx's hand—entirely, as it seems. It looks as if the sociological apperception I have just stressed had gone overboard with the old philosophical theories and had been sacrificed to historical materialism for the sake of a clear, occasionally polemical contrast with the unhistorical materialism of Feuerbach as well as with the idealism of the "Critical Critics." I shall give in some detail the starting point.

The prime condition of human history is the existence of human beings. To begin without arbitrary presuppositions, one must start from the real individuals, their action and the material conditions of their existence (*Werke*, 3:20).

I must here explain an important point of vocabulary: the German word used is *das Individuum* (pl. *Individuen*), a current term in the literature, used, for example, by Hegel, which designates primarily the biological individual, whether human or not. In the German text, the moral individual appears—at any rate sometimes—as *"das einzelne Individuum,"* too uniformly translated as "the isolated individual" or "the singular individual." The individual could be simply *"der Einzelne (Mensch)."* It is well to bear in mind the Hegelian distinction: *Besonderheit* is "particularity"; *Einzelnheit*, "individuality"—that is, the particular as embodying the universal. The linguistic distinction between *das Individuum* and *der Einzelne* corresponds to my distinction between the empirical and the moral individual. In fact, however, German authors often confuse the two meanings under *das Individuum*, just as is currently done in English under "the individual." (So does Hegel in the quotation on p. 122, above: "the consciousness of the individual".) Only in certain cases or contexts is the need felt for introducing *der Einzelne*. This is true of Marx and Engels in this text and of Marx in general. This complex of occasional distinctions and lack of distinction in principle is highly relevant to the present inquiry, as we shall have occasions to notice.

To return to the starting point of *The German Ideology* and to
sum it up as far as possible in the authors' own terms: the first
point, the first historical fact, is the production of material life
itself. The second point is that, once the first need is satisfied,
the action of satisfying it and the instrument of that satisfaction
lead to new needs. The third point or relation consists in the fact
that men not only renew their own lives every day but also
create other men: they reproduce themselves, hence the family,
the first social relation. These three aspects are given together,
as three "moments," from the beginning. The fourth point is the
social relation, already present in the production of life: any
mode of production or any industrial stage is always accompanied by a certain social stage (ibid., pp. 28–30; trans., pp. 16–
18). "It is only now, after we have already examined four moments, four sides of the original historical relations or conditions
(*Verhältnisse*), that we find that man also has 'consciousness'"
and, in the first place, a language, which "*is* the practical, . . . actual consciousness." "Just like consciousness, language owes its origin to the need, the necessity of relationships
with other men . . . . Consciousness is thus from the start a social
product, and so it remains as long as there are men in existence"
(ibid., pp. 30–31). But, "This beginning is as animal as is social
life itself at that stage, a mere gregarious consciousness": instinct has become conscious instinct (ibid.). Consciousness
progresses with the increase of productivity, that is, of needs,
population, and division of labor.

Here then is what Engels called the "materialist conception of
history." In a sense the "four moments" are given together. Yet
among them the fourth, the social moment, is distinctly singled
out as relatively secondary, and this disposition will be maintained throughout Marx's work (see the corresponding passages
quoted below from the *Grundrisse*, pp. 164 ff.). Thus the relation
to nature, i.e., production, is given priority over the relations
between men, society, and consciousness. In other words, the
economic creed is already present, and crudely so: social life is
"animal"; consciousness is only conscious instinct. *The German
Ideology* thus presupposes the economic studies of Marx (and
Engels), which I shall consider further on.

We also note that, with the obvious aim of cutting the ground
from under the feet of any sort of idealism, the assertion that

language and consciousness are social phenomena is overdone
through what must be called an "arbitrary assumption" of
materialism: human society is first posited apart from any language and any consciousness, and it is only subsequently that
one finds "that man has also" a language and some degree of
consciousness, very little of it actually at the beginning—even
though the notion that instinct somehow became conscious represents a problem by itself. The effect is to throw off, with
idealism, the holism of the German romantics, the Herderian
notion of a cultural community of the people (*Volk*), of "a
people's spirit" (*Volksgeist*), or, in Marx's words, the "supposi-
tion" of a "special" (*aparten*) spirit of the society as a whole
(passage struck out by Marx, p. 26, note). This must be judged a
setback in the history of sociological ideas.

The choice of the biological individual as the starting point has
several functions: it agrees both with the adoption of an
economic perspective—the subject in economic thought being
the individual—and with the expressed intention to be strictly
empirical, which means in fact to resort to a materialism which is
neither empirical nor in the least historical at that stage, but bars
the door to anything that could lead back to the Hegelian "mystification." This is not all, for in the first part of *The German
Ideology* the stress on the individual goes far beyond the needs of
anti-idealist polemic and beyond the realm of political economy,
and is linked with the emancipation vow. Most remarkable is
perhaps a famous passage that gives a glimpse of the communist
society, as is rarely found in Marx.

And finally the division of labour offers us immediately the
first example of the fact that, as long as men find themselves
in the spontaneous society, as long, that is, as exists the split
between the particular and the common interest, as long as
activity is not voluntarily but spontaneously[12] divided, man's
own action becomes for him an alien power that stands in
front of him, that subjugates him instead of his governing
it. For as soon as labour begins to be divided, every one has a
determined circle of activity, which is imposed upon him and
from which he cannot get out: he is and he must remain
hunter, fisherman or critical critic if he does not want to lose
his means of livelihood—while in communist society, where
every one has not an exclusive circle of activity, but can train
himself in any branch he likes, the society regulates the gen-

eral production and thus makes it possible for me to do this today, that tomorrow, to hunt in the morning, fish in the afternoon, raise cattle in the evening and criticize after dinner, just as it pleases me, without ever becoming a hunter, fisherman or critic. That coagulation of social activity, that solidification of our own product into a material power over us that escapes our control, thwarts our expectations, annihilates our calculations, is one of the momentous aspects of historical development to this day. (Ibid., p. 35; trans., pp. 22–23)

A vast development of productivity, it should be recalled, is the presupposition of communist society. It is said repeatedly in this text that all social evils are conterminous with the division of labor and that the latter must be abolished for the former to disappear (for instance, p. 74). In this passage the theory is more subtle: a voluntary, as opposed to the spontaneous or "natural," division of labor is not excluded, and yet, in the concrete sketch that follows, it appears that the individual freely divides his labor—and thus takes the place of society in the precommunist stage—while the division of labor between individuals within the society, the *specialization*, has disappeared. It is not clear what remains for the society to "regulate"; indeed, the society would seem to have vanished at that level, for the sake of ridding the individual of everything that "escapes his control, contradicts his expectations, reduces to nought his calculations."

The Individual has here his apotheosis; he has become a society in himself. Society, insofar as it transcended the individual, has simply gone; there is no social whole left, *no collective ends apart from the ends of the individuals.* Marx certainly thought of a "community" as existing at that stage; but we see here that this community is nothing more than the negation of the historically given community. Marx falls back on the very configuration he condemned in the French revolutionaries: the society is reduced to a means for individual ends. There is no need to insist that it is a picture of emancipation: all subordination as well as domination, material and mental, has gone.[13]

At this point, the reader who has still in mind the quite different inspiration of the passage I referred to above, from the Notes on James Mill (*my* product being *your* enjoyment, etc.), may well ask what has happened. What has happened, more generally, to the fine and emphatic sociological apperception of the "Manuscripts"? How can we account for what appears to us as a contradiction and must, from the point of view of Marx, have been at the least a marked change? The question is the more important, as *The German Ideology* was ready for publication and only by chance remained unpublished, while the previously written Notes were not, as such, intended for publication. This particular discrepancy is actually only one element of a more general change that can be detected at this juncture. Without in the least wanting to split Marx up into chronological slices, one cannot help noticing a cleavage at this point. As contrasted with the "original" (Tucker) or philosophical Marxism of the first writings, we enter here into "mature" (Tucker) or militant, activist Marxism. The mold is set, and the *Communist Manifesto* will take up from *The German Ideology*; but this general aspect is beyond my purview and I shall touch on it only from the angle of our particular problem.

The German Ideology was a joint endeavor, and one might ask whether Engels's views have not here inflected those of Marx. This would be idle speculation, except perhaps in the sense that the associates wanted to get rid of their philosophical past, as Marx himself said, and to establish a position that would be effective in terms of the political struggle. And just as the people to be emancipated are individuals, it is only as individuals that people can be mobilized. Marx's finer insights become irrelevant at this point. Fundamentally, it does not matter for him, for he postulates, as we saw, that the individual and the social being are one and the same and will necessarily come to coincide, once the emancipation has been attained. Perhaps we put our finger here on the very spot at which the dimension of action, the revolutionary resolve, determines the fate of ideas. The individual is a lever, the sociological apperception a dream.

Precisely, the total abolition of the social division of labor is so implausible that it is easily seen as a basic demand of the unregenerate individual.[14] Now, the division of labor looms very large in the "materialist conception of history"; it is something like the main historical factor in *The German Ideology*, and as I said, its suppression is a leitmotiv of that work. But when Marx penned his nice fantasy in his notes on James Mill, he simply did not think of it. He thought then, as we shall see, in somewhat different terms; and at any rate he could "suppose that we should produce as human beings" without the division of labor having disappeared. That such a speculation disappears in the later work shows the predominance of individualism.

To this view of *The German Ideology* it can be objected that the work is in line with the "Manuscripts" on one point. The universal essence of man (*Gattungswesen*) has now been replaced once for all by his "common essence" (*Gemeinwesen*), that is, his essence as a social being. But if this is literally true, it is actually only a matter of the letter, for *Gemeinwesen* remains the kind of ideal representation that *Gattungswesen* was: the social nature of man is everywhere imperfect and will blossom only in the communist society. To show this, I shall consider two sorts of passages in *The German Ideology*, some dealing with the individual and some referring to what is supposedly common in a society: common interest, community, etc.

At a few pages' distance, two distinctions, different but convergent, that bear on the individual are presented. First (p. 76; trans., pp. 76–77), there is a difference in the life of each individual between a personal aspect and an aspect that is subordinated to a certain branch of work, etc.—between, literally, the individual as personal (*persönlich*) and the class individual (*Klassen-individuum*). This distinction was "still hidden" in feudalism and in the estate of the realm (*Stand*); it becomes manifest in the class, "itself a product of the bourgeoisie."

Clearly, then, this distinction relates to the partial emancipation of the individual of bourgeois society from subordination to social conditions. What is the justification for speaking of a sort of latency of the bourgeois individual in previous forms of society, if not the presupposition of a universal essence of man, which our authors criticize in the philosophers? We touch here on a general point: while Marx has an acute feeling of the discontinuity between feudalism and bourgeois society, he stresses and conceptualizes mainly the continuity, whether factual or supposed, between them. This attitude is determined, not only by the belief in a unilinear historical development, but also and in the first place by the compelling belief in the universal value of the proletarian revolution to come. It will be the emancipation of man in general also in the sense that the bourgeois period has merely developed and made explicit what was already there in some way, so that putting an end to it will end, by the same stroke, human "prehistory" in general.

The second distinction is more general (p. 71; trans. pp. 70–71). It is maintained that in each epoch the people themselves distinguish in some manner between the personal individual and the contingent individual (*zufälliges Individuum*). Each epoch is characterized, first, by its productive forces. Those human relations (later, *Produktionsverhältnisse*; in this text, simply "intercourse" [*Verkehr*] or, again, "civil society") that correspond to contemporary productive forces appear to the living persons—whose lives are essentially production—as part of their own activity, as personal. On the contrary, those social relations that exist only as a legacy or survival from former epochs appear to the living person as external to himself, as "contingent" impediments. This is a more ambitious distinction than the former one, little less than a social change theory of subordination. For whatever the individual perceives as limiting or potentially dominating him is due to obsolescence: oppression is the rule of the dead. It is a powerful prop for revolutionary action, when everything burdensome is presented as meaningless survival. We should not make too much of what is only a passing hint, but it is psychologically revealing. With the revolution, the voluntary union (*Vereinigung*) of individuals will replace their "natural" or unfree solidarity as members of a class.

Both of the distinctions I have just recalled are based on the belief that it is possible to do away with all factual domination or ideological subordination in society. Up to this point, the program is the same as that of the French Revolution. But at the same time it is believed that, in so altering society, one will not destroy the possibility of any community; on the contrary, one will bring about the real or perfect community, a community of equal and free human beings. Let us turn to this aspect: what do we read in *The German Ideology* about the global society in the past and in the present?

Near the beginning, immediately following the appearance of consciousness, comes a text of fundamental import in which the main features and implications of the division of labor are indicated: "The division of labour first becomes a real division at the moment a division of material and intellectual labour sets in," thus allowing for the separation of consciousness from "the

existing praxis." This is Marx's first general statement about the
topic, and he enlarges on it (pp. 31–32; trans., p. 20).

Then the division of labor implies private property—two expressions of the same thing, the one in relation to the activity,
the other to the product—and it implies a contradiction between
the interest of the individual person or family (*des einzelnen Individuums oder der einzelnen Familie*) and the community interest
(or: common interest, but the word is *gemeinschaftlich*, not simply *gemeinsam*) of all the individuals. This interest of the community exists "in fact in the first place as the dependence on one
another of the individuals between whom labour is divided"
(pp. 32–33; trans., p. 22).

> It is precisely this contradiction between the particular in-
> terest and the community interest which brings the latter to
> assume an independent form [*Gestaltung*] as State—distinct
> both from the real interests of the individual [*Einzelinteressen*]
> and of their sum [*Gesamtinteressen*]—and at the same time as
> an illusory communality [*Gemeinschaftlichkeit*].... [P. 33.
> There follows within the State the well-known clash of in-
> terests of the different classes determined by the division of
> labor.]

I should like to comment on these remarkable, if not altogether clear passages. It is recognized that, logically, in a stateless group in which the division of labor prevails, the conscious
interdependence of the members sets limits to the assertion of
their particular interests by particular persons. In other words,
each member must be the locus of a contradiction between his
private interest and the common interest. This situation, we are
told, leads to the common interest assuming the form of a State;
yet this State is at the same time an illusory community. I inter-
pret this to mean that, as a separate entity, the State cannot
remain identical with the common interest as such.

But a logical aspect seems to be left out; a differentiation has
occurred. The citizen no longer has to care immediately for the
common interest, since the State is now in charge of it; the
citizen, therefore, will be able to pursue his private interest
without qualms, in a manner that is impossible for the member
of a stateless group. In other words, there is a close interdependence between the existence of the State and the unrestrained

assertion of private interest by the citizens. Think, for instance, of Athenian democracy. If there is perhaps something illusory in the State as community, there is certainly also an illusion in considering the unabashed assertion of private interests unleashed by the existence of an arena for their ordered fight as if it were independent of that very arena, the State. It shows in the authors' mind a deep-seated tendency to take the individual as existing by itself. This logical mistake is surprising on the part of Marx, who excels in general in bringing forth all the facets of a given relation.[15] (And it explains perhaps in part a contorted and syntactically obscure paragraph that follows).

The passage quoted above is nevertheless valuable because it contains a recognition of something common to the members of a given society. At this stage, and all along, we are not told any more about language and consciousness as something common to all; but at least on the level of interest, which is the only one actually recognized, we are told of a common interest that consists roughly in preserving the framework within which the life and interaction of the members and the assertion of their private interests take place.

What becomes of this recognition in more advanced stages of society? We know, of course, a rough general answer by Marx and/or the Marxists to this question. It is obtained by an exclusive focus on economy and on class. What we are concerned with here is how the global society, and the State, are conceived in *The German Ideology*. In a section called "Relation of State and Law to Property," the State is defined as "the form under which the individuals of a dominant class pursue their common interests and in which the civil society of an epoch as a whole is summed up (p. 62). A few remarks: (1) "Civil society" (*bürgerliche Gesellschaft*) is taken here in its general sense as defined elsewhere: "the whole of the material relations of the individuals within a given stage of development of the productive forces" (p. 36). This usage is not isolated in this work. In the same passage the double meaning of the term is admitted: one more example of assumed continuity between the prebourgeois and bourgeois stages. (2) The definition does not absolutely rule out the existence of something, some minor degree of interest, common to all, even if the main interests are common only within a class.

Actually, the definition seems contradicted by what immediately precedes it in the text. To minimize the contradiction, we must construe it as saying, *"Where there exists a dominant class, the State is . . . ,"* for the preceding passage says, precisely, that in Germany, in the situation of transition between the Middle Ages and modernity, where estates and classes coexist, "no part of the population is able to dominate the others," and the State is thus "independent" (there, and nowhere else, nowadays) (p. 62).

The above definition thus appears as an unwarranted generalization from the modern situation, the more so as it is "through the emancipation of private property from the community" that "the State has acquired a separate existence outside civil society" (ibid.). Be it noted *en passant* that the remark about the same term being applied in a restricted sense to modern conditions and in an extended sense to other conditions applies here to "class" (opposed to "estate," on the one hand; encompassing it, on the other) and, elsewhere more distinctly than here, to "private property."[16]

Otherwise, common interests are discussed preeminently in passages relating to the replacement of one class by another as dominant. Thus:

> Each new class that takes the place of the class that dominated before it is constrained, be it only [N.B.: *schon*] in order to reach its ends, to represent its interest as the common [*gemeinschaftlich*] interest of all members of the society [*Gesellschaft*] . . . . Already [*schon*] from the very fact that it confronts a *class*, the revolutionary class presents itself from the start not as a class but as the representative of the society as a whole, it appears as the entire mass of the society confronting the single dominant class. It can do this because at the beginning its interest is still truly linked more [N.B.] with the common interest of all the other non-dominant classes and because, under the pressure of the antecedent state of things, its interest has not yet been able to develop as the particular interest of a particular class. (Ibid., pp. 47–48)

In brief, there is no common interest beyond the opposition between dominant and dominated except perhaps at the revolutionary instant when a new class comes to power.

In the margin facing this passage Marx noted among other

things "the illusion of common interests," adding, "In the beginning this illusion is right." There is something illogical or uneasy here, as in the quotation above (my brackets).[17]

Of course, the proletarian revolution must put an end to that state of things and reinstate a true community. How does this happen? In a remarkable passage on this question (pp. 74–75), the class is called a "community," but it is a community of the wrong sort:

> ... a community to which [those] individuals belonged only as average individuals, only insofar as they lived in the existential conditions of their class ... not as individuals, but as members of a class.... The apparent community, which the individuals had previously constituted, always took an existence independent from them, and at the same time, as it was the union of one class against another, it represented for the dominated class not only a quite illusory community, but also a new chain.... On the contrary in the community of the revolutionary proletarians who put under their control the conditions of existence of themselves and of all the members of the society, it is just the reverse: the individuals participate in it as individuals.

They do so by association or "union" (*Vereinigung*), a free and voluntary union. And again, "in the real community, the individuals acquire their freedom at the very time they associate, through their association and in it" in contradiction to the "surrogates of community one had had theretofore, the State, etc." where personal freedom existed only for the individuals of the dominant class.

All in all, we must conclude that the division of labor has initiated a drama of increasing intensity: it has created a divorce between particular and common interest which deepens with the increase in the division of labor. The result has been to isolate the common interest in illusory or insufficient institutions (the State, the class) which dominate the individual from outside. Only with the suppression of the division of labor and the conscious regulation of the economy by the voluntary association of individuals will they recover the sense of a true, immanent community.

It is clearly difficult for us to realize how a mind of the caliber of Marx's can have entangled itself in such an unreal construction under the bona fide claim of a soundly empirical, no-nonsense historical inquiry. Much more is involved than the relative ignorance of the young authors, as alleged by Engels. For one thing, we are wiser after the event, for we have the benefit of Tönnies's distinction between community and society and are thus enabled to see how Marx and Engels, who occasionally distinguished the two notions (see above, p. 143), have made a mess through their confusion. In this light, the work of Tönnies, himself an admirer of Marx, represents the advance of sociological thought emancipated from political bias and appears to us to be definitive on its own level, whatever developments or modification it demands at present. But if this is the form, or a main formal aspect, under which the failure of *The German Ideology* appears to us, the motive force leading to that failure should by now be clear: it is the imperative of emancipation that actually oriented and governed the whole inquiry. This is the reason why the sociological apperception found in the 1844 "Manuscripts" was not put to use in this endeavor and why the replacement of man's universal essence (*Gattungswesen*) by man's social essence (*Gemeinwesen*) did not develop the implications and sociological insights one could have hoped for.

In the realization of the design, there is no doubt that the economic perspective of society and of history has served powerfully in sustaining a purely individualistic orientation, notwithstanding the lip service paid to society, language, and consciousness as rooted in society. This is clear already from the small excerpts I made of the text; it would appear more forcefully if we could consider the work more completely. It is thus high time for us to turn to the "Manuscripts" of 1844, which record the first acquaintance of Marx with political economy.

8

The Encounter
with Political Economy,
and Its Reform

The "Economic and Philosophic Manuscripts of 1844," sometimes called the "Paris Manuscripts," is a richer and more complex work than those we have hitherto considered, a work difficult in places and tantalizingly incomplete. I shall not attempt to sum it up. For the present endeavor, the "Manuscripts" are important as the record of Marx's first encounter with political economy, and I shall consider them as such. Marx himself noted twice (in the foreword to the "Manuscripts" themselves, and in that to the *Critique of Political Economy* of 1859) how the criticism of Hegel's *Philosophy of Right* had led him to give explanatory value to the "material conditions of life" ("Critique": *Oeuvres*, 1:272) and to search in political economy for the anatomy of civil society. We know from his notebooks the scope and intensity of the study Marx did in Paris in 1844. (The "Manuscripts" proper are supplemented by the extracts Marx painstakingly made of his sources and by his own comments and reflections scattered through them, all in *MEGA*, I, vol. 3). We know also from the foreword to the "Manuscripts" that Marx thought he had made "a serious critical study" and was presenting "the results [he] had reached." He then contemplated similar critical works on law, morals, and politics, as well as one about "the unity of the whole"—all this as the development of his criticism of Hegel's book.

Marx was thus unaware at that time of the place the preoccupation with economics was going to claim in his life as a thinker and a writer or that it would become an obsession—in Rubel's words, "the haunter of his intellectual life" (*Oeuvres*, 2:xvii–xviii, lv). To explain this change in orientation, and perhaps also to express the moral tone of the "Manuscripts," Rubel speaks of a "traumatism" that Marx would have suffered in 1844. Our double study of the genesis of political economy and of Marx's beginnings should allow us to throw some light on the point. (It should be recalled at this juncture that *The German Ideology* was yet to come.) Between the Marx of the emancipation vow, of the criticism of Hegel, and of "The Jewish Question," on the one hand, and political economy as he found it in the writings of Adam Smith, Ricardo, and others, on the other, there was both an elective affinity and a difference so deep that it made for scandal.

An elective affinity: I scarcely need to insist on the point after having stressed, against the background of the preceding chapters, the individualism of the vow, the immanentist criticism of the State, etc. Civil society is the real thing, and the way is paved for the primacy of relations with nature as against relations between men, even if it is not yet quite explicitly present. At the same time, there is cause for scandal: I insisted above, in full agreement with Rubel and, I would believe, with all unbiased students, on the moral character of Marx's initial commitment. Marx turns to the economy as to something pertinent to his categorical imperative, to his revolutionary faith. What does he find? He finds a discipline that, in order to constitute itself as an independent science, has had not only to neglect moral issues but to proclaim that they are irrelevant within its precincts, where the facts will deliver the norms. The clash is pedestined, and at the same time its outcome appears predictable. The economic point of view is so germane to that of the revolutionary philosopher that he will need to remold economics to suit his purpose. This is what Marx, although he immediately begins the task, does not yet fully perceive in 1844, and what will make economics "haunt" his entire intellectual life. It is not to be wondered at that Marx found economic theory indispensable as affording a scientific demonstration of what had hitherto been an ethical norm (Rubel, in *Oeuvres*, 2:xliv).

What appears in retrospect a matter of wonder is, rather, how little Marx had to change in the operational premises of the founders. He could build upon the basic framework of Ricardo: he had not to reject it in toto. This fact, again, we can understand, as we insisted—after Myrdal—on the role played in the founders' theory by value judgments, which happen to be the same as those of Marx. More than a matter of scientific truth, it is a matter of general consensus on values in the modern world, a matter of Marx's remaining within the basic assumptions of our modern ideology. (See Hyppolite on the labor theory of value, 1955, pp. 153, 158.)

But first came the clash. Moral indignation is in full display in a short pamphlet by Engels, anterior to Marx's "Manuscripts" and published by him in his *Jahrbücher* in the spring of 1844, the "Sketch of a Critique . . . ." The pamphlet is replete with expressions of moral contempt and abuse addressed both to the practitioners of trade and finance and to political economy, presented, we would say, as a rationalization of the practice. The whole makeup of modern economy, with private property and competition at its basis, is immoral. Notwithstanding its occasional insights and its praise by Marx, who will take up some of its points, this pamphlet is a brilliant piece of journalism, interesting for the psychological background it reveals.

The impression we receive from Marx's texts is very different. Not that the moral feeling and judgment are less intense, but the reaction sparks off at several levels simultaneously. Marx uses, applies, furthers, interprets, corrects, and condemns, all at once. He condemns altogether sparingly if magisterially. His metaeconomic stand and radical distancing, his philosophical training, his moral commitment, give him an attitude of superiority, and he dashes into the enemy's camp for weapons and ammunition. He has no time to enter into a writer's mind. For instance, when Adam Smith concludes—against his subjective tendency, let it be noted—that the landowner's interest is always consonant with that of society at large, his statement is dismissed curtly as "a stupidity" (1st Ms., Rent; *MEGA*, I.3:72), for the young Marx knows better. He wants grist for his mill and plunges *in medias res* to get it. Thus, the first of the three manuscripts opens with a section on salary. Marx wants to paint the darkest picture of the industrial worker's lot and destiny, to establish that wealth and misery increase hand in hand—that the more wealth the worker produces, the more miserable he is. He has a few authors at hand who could give him ample satisfaction, and he could have invoked Ricardo, as Hegel had done very early. But his first author is Adam Smith—who said nothing of the sort—perhaps because Marx wants to take advantage of Smith's careful reckoning of the influence upon wages and profit of the dynamic tendency of the economy, whether it

is growing, decaying, or stationary. Marx's development is far
from being, as Marx says, a mere summary of Smith's views, for
they are not only developed but are also on occasion twisted,
misrepresented, and even replaced by their opposite. It is on
Smith's case of a growing economy that Marx's rendering is the
most inadequate.[1] We must admit that the revolutionary was
then blinded by passion and must add that it is perhaps
symptomatic of his initial reaction, for the case is exceptional; his
temper progressively cooled down. Here is the conclusion of the
disquisition: "That labour ... insofar as its aim is the mere increase of wealth ... is itself obnoxious and baneful, this follows, without the economist knowing it, from his developments" (*MEGA*, I.3:45).

This approach to political economy by Marx—hurried,
superior, and initially partial (in both senses of the term)[2]—
explains perhaps why Marx nowhere in the "Manuscripts"
comes directly to grips with the central issue that separates him
from the economists: the moral issue. One would have expected
an elaborate criticism of the notion of the "harmony of interests."
I do not find it, probably because Marx is convinced that the
facts are otherwise, and he does not bother to inquire *why* it is
that the notion is there—to inquire, that is, into the mode of
thinking of Adam Smith and others. We read, for instance, "[By
praising the social character of his science regarding division of
labor and exchange] the economist pronounces unconsciously
the contradiction of his science, the foundation of society
through the unsocial private interest" (3d Ms., fol. XXXVIII, § 3;
MEGA, I.3:144; cf. trans., p. 162). Later, in the *Grundrisse*, the
question will be confronted: "Rather it could be inferred ...
that everyone hinders the satisfaction of everyone else's interest; that, instead of a general affirmation, the result of the
war of all against all is rather a general negation" (*Grundrisse*,
trans. McLellan, p. 65).

A passage in a comment made while reading James Mill
shows Marx spontaneously projecting into political economy
what *he* searches for and what *it* had actually rejected from its
purview: "It is under the form of exchange and trade that Political Economy conceives the community of men or their humanity
in actu, their reciprocal complementation for a generic life, for a
truly human life" (*MEGA*, I.3:537; cf. McLellan 1971, p. 194, and

Oeuvres, 2:23–24). As we pondered on Mandeville regarding the relation to morality, it is interesting to find out how Marx perceived him. In the *Holy Family* he takes Mandeville as "characteristic for the socialist tendency of materialism" and also says that *The Fable* "was not an apology of the society" (*Oeuvres,* 2:401 n.; *MEGA,* I.3:308). The second statement explains the first: nonconformist materialism is equated with socialist materialism, and this is revealing of Marx's limited concern.[3]

In one place in the "Manuscripts" Marx expresses clearly both his attraction to economics and his disappointment with it. In two most remarkable pages at the beginning of the third Manuscript, subtitled by the editors "Private Property and Labor," Marx characterizes the progress of political economy and, in particular, the decisive advance made by Adam Smith. At the same time, he passes a moral condemnation on political economy as a whole. This development shows that Marx had already subdued his moral indignation enough to be able, while retaining his moral judgment, to enter not only into the development of economics but also, in some degree, into the mind of the economists. The passage is, as usual, so rich that, short of reproducing it and commenting on it at length, I must sum it up unilaterally.

To understand it, we must first recall that "private property" is, with Marx in general and in the "Manuscripts" in particular, a very complex concept. Where the economists say "wealth," Marx often says "private property." We saw in the first part of this study that the economists were searching for the essence of wealth and found it first in production and then in labor. Marx says that Adam Smith discovered in labor the "subjective essence of private property," while the mercantilists saw only the objective essence of it as an external object. But just as Luther had internalized religion, Adam Smith internalized private property, that is, political economy henceforth moved within the world of private property. This for Marx is anathema. He does not say why, at this time, but we can understand it in at least two senses. First, it is clear from other texts that the compartmentalization of science cannot avail where human values are at stake: the stand is metaeconomic; second, more immediately and in relation to action, the bourgeois world is rotten and private property is doomed. "Under the appearance of an

acknowledgment of man, political economy ... is rather the
consequent accomplishment of the denial of man" (*MEGA*,
I.3:107–8; cf. trans., p. 120). To comment: one expects to find
here an acknowledgment of man as a consciously acting, producing individual, but no: this individual is such only as private
owner:

> If then, that political economy begins with the appearance of
> a recognition of man, his independence, his activity by him-
> self, and if, transferring private property into the very es-
> sence of man ... it develops a *cosmopolitan* energy—
> universal, throwing down every barrier and every bond and
> setting itself instead as the *only* politics, the only universality,
> barrier and bond—then it must in its further development
> reject this *hypocrisy* and appear in all its *cynicism*, and it does it
> by ... developing much more *unilaterally*, and therefore
> more sharply and more *coherently labour* as the unique *essence
> of wealth* [N.B.: in this place Marx did not substitute "private
> property"], and by demonstrating, in contrast to the original
> version, that the consequences of the doctrine are *hostile to
> man.* (Ibid.)

It is not only that, from Smith through Say to Ricardo, Mill, et
al., the consequences of industrial development appear more
clearly; it is also that the later writers "go always consciously
further in the alienation with regard to man *only* because their
science develops more coherently and truly" (ibid.). Ricardo's
"cynicism" would then better be called honesty and
perspicuity,[4] were it not that Marx invests him with his own
ethical concern in reverse. This homage contained in a condemnation makes us sense why Marx could not recognize the similarity between his own values and those of Ricardo. In Marx's
perception of political economy, we can read at the same time a
recognition of what we called, above, the "emancipation from
politics," and Marx's disappointment at this (in his view) only
partial emancipation, which sets new barriers and new bonds
and is therefore taxed as "hypocritical."

It is characteristic of Marx's intensity of thought that, within a
few months of his first acquaintance with economics, he proceeds to transcend it. He does so, inevitably, as a philosopher,
and those who do not want to recognize him as such may shy

away from the "Manuscripts" and especially from the remarkable, though truncated, section on "Alienated Labour" that closes the first Manuscript. I turn to a brief consideration of this text in order to highlight an aspect of the troubled beginning of Marx's marriage with economics. Marx is immediately struck by the fact that political economy remains confined within the world of private property. It does not account for private property, nor is it able to show how the regularities in economic phenomena result from the essence of private property (First Ms., "Alienated Labour"; *MEGA*, I.3:81). In other terms, as usual for a science, it cannot by itself define its field or establish its legitimacy. (According to Cottier, Marx wants a Hegelian, and yet more-than-Hegelian, science; Cottier 1969, p. 268). Marx says this directly here, and indirectly at the beginning of the *Holy Family* (1845) in his eulogy of Proudhon: Proudhon had gone as far as was possible within the world of political economy.

What does Marx do in order to relativize this world and secure his own stand outside it, as he must do for his revolutionary purpose? He deduces private property from the concept of "alienated labor." The starting point is the "result" of the previous criticism: "The worker becomes the poorer as he produces more wealth.... [He] becomes a viler commodity [himself] as he creates more commodities," and so on (ibid., p. 82). The worker, thus separated, alienated, from his product, is as a consequence alienated from his activity as producer and, again, from the manifestation in him of the characteristic of the human genus—namely, the free, conscious action on nature. It is from this triple alienation that Marx deduces, among other consequences, private property. This sounds strange: one would have expected an author who is following Marx's path to start from the everyday facts of the matter—private property, the relation between the employer and the worker, etc.—and to build inductively anything like a concept of alienated labor. The reverse is true. Why? We have seen already that the recognition of labor as the subjective essence of wealth, or of private property, is taken as a great step forward for economics. But Marx himself explains his choice. Near the end of the development he expresses his satisfaction for having transformed the question of the origin of private property into that of the relation between alienated labor and the development of mankind,

for when one speaks of private property, one thinks one has
to do with something external to man. While when one
speaks of labour, one has immediately to do with man himself. This new way of asking the question implies already its
solution. (Ibid., p. 93)

A little earlier (p. 92), Marx admits that in actual fact there is a
reciprocal action between private property and alienated labor
and (p. 91) that he has extracted the concept of alienated labor
from observation, "from the movement of private property"
(another name for the economy). Yet, he adds, the analysis of
the concept shows private property to be a consequence of it,
just as the gods are originally not the cause but the effect of an
aberration in human understanding. We perceive here that private property, as something that appears external to man, is less
real than labor—that is, man himself, insofar as he is defined as
conscious activity or production. Why is property relatively unreal, like the gods? It is a human institution, a social phenomenon, while the activity of the individual as such is universal, as
constituting the essence of man.

I propose tentatively two almost identical formulations of
Marx's hierarchical judgment: (1) the individual is primary as
against society; (2) the relation between man and nature (work,
labor) is primary as against relations between men (private
property is a relation with nature, but mediated by human consensus). If I am right, there is something ironical about the result
of Marx's elaborate attempt. He succeeds in removing what
blocked the way to revolution: "Political economy begins with
labour as the very soul of production, and then goes on to attribute to labour nothing and everything to private property" (p.
92; cf. trans., p. 106), but he remains within the limits of
economic thought (primacy of the individual as the agent in the
relation between man and nature). Marx is already "haunted"
by economics.

It is also clear that alienated labor is a very general category
that, although derived from the capitalist regime of production,
can be and is taken more vaguely or implicitly as applying to
other stages of economic development—nay, to economic development in general. This is the advantage of a philosophical
category, a kind of ideal type after all, referring to the individual
human subject in largely psychological terms, much in the manner of eighteenth-century constructions, but derived from

historical social relations instead of from nature. The Hegelian parentage is obvious, and yet it is a great credit to Tucker to have traced back the ancestry and described the genesis of the concept with such precision and completeness that he has given the real answer to the question, "Why alienated labor?" His book must be read (Tucker 1972). Most immediately, it shows Marx's concentration on alienated labor to be the direct outcome of his Hegelian-cum-Feuerbachian philosophy. Hegel has the key to political economy, and conversely, Hegelianism has truth-value on that level (Tucker, pp. 120, 126). As to our particular inquiry, the first lesson is that the concentration on the human individual subject emphasized above is basic, issuing from philosophy— philosophy reconstructed insofar as it had strayed from that subject, while of course remaining rooted in it all along—and flowing into economics with perfect continuity.

Yet it is in this very same work that we find the deep perception of the social nature of man, which we studied above (pp. 129 ff.) and which is unique in the whole of Marx's works. It would seem that the narrow conception of human life entertained by the economists caused in him a revulsion and led him, in contrast, to dwell at length in the third Manuscript—as nowhere else—on the delights of a perfect social life, at the opposite pole from James Mill's "possessive individualism," and thus to stress psychological and aesthetic aspects that are absent from the works of his maturity. Let us recall, as a foil to *The German Ideology*, that in this text nature itself is reached by man only through the intermediary of society: "The *human* essence of nature exists only for man as social" (*MEGA*, I.3:116).

We must assign its place to this fine sociological apperception, and its place is secondary. The revolutionary militant closes again, with a firm hand, the door through which he had caught a glimpse of Paradise; a thick pencil strikes off big chunks of this text; the brief exploration must have no sequence. We have tried to understand why. By definition, individualism and holism, the individual and the social being, will coincide in communist society, where man will realize for this very reason his excellence as a social being. The present society is condemned on behalf of the Individual; it is so defective that one can acknowledge oneself fully as a social being, not by reference to it, but only by reference to the ideal society of the future, that is to say, by working for the emancipation of the Individual. Every other aim must vanish before this imperative. In this dialectic, it is clear that the Individual has primacy over the social being and that the revolutionary project replaces and forbids the full recognition of man as a social being here and now.

When I said previously that man is essentially "conscious activity," I pronounced what is perhaps the master word of the 1844 "Manuscripts": "Its mode of vital activity contains all the character of a species, its generic character, and the generic character of man is free, conscious activity" (1st Ms., fol. XXIV; *MEGA*, I.3:88). The novelty, compared to Feuerbach in particular, is in the transition from conscience, pure and simple, to conscious activity:

> The practical production of an *objective world*, the *elaboration* of non-human nature [exactly, 'nonorganic,' meaning what is beyond man's own body] is where man proves himself a conscious generic being, i.e., a being which behaves toward its genus as toward its own being or toward itself as toward a generic being. (Ibid.)

Another word for *conscious activity* is *production*. It is used profusely, far beyond the confines of the meaning of the word in economics. Here Marx follows closely in the footsteps of Saint-Simon, as Georges Gurvitch has shown (1963, vol. 2, chap. 12): man does not produce only material objects, but himself as well in the process: "Just as society produces *man* as *man*, it is produced by him" (*MEGA*, I.3:116).[5] On the one hand, "Production does not only produce man as a commodity ... but also as a *de-humanized* being." (2d Ms., fol. XL; *MEGA*, I.3:98); on the other, "In the hypothesis that private property be positively abolished, man produces man, himself and the other man" (3d Ms., fol. V; *MEGA*, I.3:115). "The history of industry ... [is] the open book of the essential human forces" (p. 121). Production is not only material, but also moral, spiritual, institutional:

> Religion, family, state, law, morality, science, art, etc. are only *particular* modes of the production and fall under its general law. The positive abolition of *private property* ...

signifies therefore the *positive* abolition of all alienation, that is
to say the return of man from religion, family, state, etc. back
to his *human,* i.e., *social* existence. (P. 115; cf. trans., p. 128)

Be it remembered: that production is *the* human activity explains why the alienation of the industrial worker is so radical. In
sum, *production* in the economic sense is used here as the prototype of a much wider category that tends to encompass the
whole of human life. Relations between men are subsumed
under a term that properly designates relations to things. It is a
choice example of a hierarchical judgment commanding the inordinate spread of the semantic area of a word. This usage is not
special to the "Manuscripts," and there is no doubt that Marx,
on this point, got hold of an aspect of modern mentality—
witness the very wide use of the word in current language at the
present day. The hierarchical judgment was already present in
economics: witness the strategic distinction, production/
distribution, and the classical distinction between productive
and unproductive labor; but this unprecedented extension in the
usage of *production* represents the apotheosis of the relation of
men to things.

The division of labor does not loom as large in the "Manuscripts" as it does shortly afterward in *The German Ideology.* The
role is played to a certain extent by alienated labor. Instead of
the question, "Why was the development of the division of
labor historically necessary, before it can be abolished as a bad
thing?," we have here the question, "How is the alienation of
labor grounded in the essence of human development?" It is
asked shortly before the first Manuscript as we have it ends
abruptly, and most unfortunately for us (*MEGA,* I.3:93). The
answer Marx later gave to this question is, roughly, that
economic development demands the production of a surplus,
and that men will not by themselves produce a surplus in excess
of their needs: they must be constrained by others—idlers, or at
any rate unproductive persons (*Grundrisse,* pp. 304–5). Again,
near the end of the third Manuscript there is a careful stocktak-
ing of the economists' views, in which Say is praised for admitting that the division of labor impoverishes and degrades the
activity of the individual. Again, the text breaks off after Marx
has listed the questions he wanted to treat and has announced

that he would prove what the economist cannot prove, namely, that labor is the essence of private property. Division of labor and exchange are formations of private property, and this proves that human life needed private property to realize itself and that it now needs its abolition.

For a non-Hegelian, there is something here that is highly arbitrary or paradoxical. The facts of the matter show that economic production is a social process. Marx has insisted, against the economist, on the social nature of man; yet he does not take society as the real subject of the production process but follows the economists in concentrating on the individual subject. Production in its reality, that is, in its development, supposes that one man works for another; how then can it be maintained that production, that is, the fundamental relation between men and things, is independent of the relations between men and exclusively a matter of man as an individual? Or again: if human truth resides in the individual, then it should not be searched for in production, which has progressed only thanks to the individual's alienation and is thus practically identical with alienation. From whence comes the hope, or the certainty, that this state of things can be upset, if not from the state of nature? I am afraid the real answer to such questions is that the deeper the contradiction under which mankind has labored until now, the grander the revolution—the redemption—promised to us. A rather involved paragraph shows that Marx sensed the paradox implied in a sociologist's rejection of the division of labor:

> The division of labor is the economic expression of the *social character* of labor within [the framework of] alienation. Or, since *labor* is only an expression of man's activity within [the framework of] alienation, expressing the externalisation of life as the alienation [extraneousness] of life, the *division of labor itself* is nothing but the *foreign, alienated* positing of human activity as *real generic activity*, or as the activity of man as *generic* being" (3d Ms., fol. XXXV; *MEGA,* I.3:139).

This passage is important as providing the transition from alienation to the division of labor, which alone will be retained in *The German Ideology*. To make it clearer, if we call work the free activity of man, and labor his alienated activity, then division of work would be all right as the expression of man's social nature, but unfortunately only division of labor is actually found. Yet, the "division of work" implies a will or control at the social level; how could it be, in fact, voluntary on the part of all? Between man as a social being and man as an individual for whom any form of social life will mean some sort of alienation (Gurvitch 1963), Marx has actually chosen already. The picture of man's free work in the communist society which we encountered in *The German Ideology* now appears as entailed by Marx's earlier choice.

*

There is a marked change of climate when one moves from the early to the late works of Marx. In the early works, Marx's self-definition or self-assertion has a pronounced polemical aspect, whether directed against the Young Hegelians, the economists, or Proudhon. In the *Grundrisse* and subsequent works, all discussion is certainly not absent, but the tone is much more serene. Moreover, if economic disquisitions and revolutionary design certainly remain close to each other, they no longer intrude upon each other. The foreword to the "Critique of Political Economy" (1859) closes with two verses of Dante, which Marx transfers from the infernal gate to the threshold of science. It is clear that the intention to work constructively on the level of science has absorbed the initial impatience with political economy as it was. Marx now conceives his scientific contribution as being of revolutionary import by itself.

Considering only the introduction of the *Grundrisse*, the general impression, in contrast to the dry schematism of, say, *The German Ideology*, is unmistakable: here is balance, maturity, mastery. Many examples could be adduced to show the author freely allowing qualifications and nuances that introduce a high degree of complexity but that, one imagines, he would have trenchantly repudiated ten years earlier.

Thus he says, "The bourgeois economy [as the most highly developed form] furnishes a key to ancient economy" etc.—and this is in keeping with his notion of a unilinear development—but he adds, "If it is true that the categories of bourgeois economy contain a truth valid for all other forms of society, this is to be taken only *cum grano salis*." This "grain of salt" accommodates at the same time, in my reading, Marx's perception of the specificity of each type (of which more below) and his view that bourgeois society is not the last stage of the evolutionary process but "only a contradictory form in the evolution" (*Grundrisse*, p. 26; cf. trans., McLellan, pp. 39–40). Yet, this passage might appear to differ only in style from previous writings. Let us take another example. Elsewhere in the *Grundrisse* Marx discusses the natural harmony of interests as the form given by the economists to the mutual dependence of the economic agents. He first reduces the so-called general interest to what it is, namely, "the totality of private interests"; then he not only suggests that, in fact, "everyone hinders the satisfaction of everyone else's interest," but he also adds,

> The point is rather that private interest is itself already a socially determined interest, which can only be achieved within the conditions established by society and through the means that society affords, and that it is thus linked to the reproduction of these conditions and means. (*Grundrisse*, McLellan trans., pp. 65–66; German ed., p. 74)

The first part of this statement would seem to point the way to Karl Polanyi's recognition of the exceptional character of bourgeois society and of the political conditions under which alone economic interest can fully blossom, but the statement is not in Marx a starting point but a point of arrival. In any case, statements such as this explain why the *Grundrisse* have been hailed as Marx's sociological masterpiece.

Self-directed humor or irony is perhaps not entirely absent from the introduction. Discussing at length the relation between production and consumption, Marx seems to conclude by expounding three modes under which the two are identical (p. 14), but he goes on:

> Hence, nothing is easier for a Hegelian than to treat production and consumption as identical. And this has been done not only by socialist writers of fiction, but even by economists . . . . [Yet] the important point is that . . . production forms the actual starting point and is, therefore, the predominant factor . . . . Consumption thus appears as a factor [*Moment*] of production. (McLellan trans., p. 27; German ed., p. 15)

Thus, a long-drawn-out Hegelian exercise is suddenly canceled by a brief statement of immediate positivity. This is part of a long and brilliant discussion of production in relation to consumption, distribution, and exchange (§ 2 of the introduction), the conclusion of which is worth pondering. There are two senses of *production:* one designates production as different from distribution, exchange, and consumption, while the other sense is much wider: "Production, distribution, exchange and consumption are ... all members of one entity, different aspects of one unit." This entity is called in its turn production because production predominates in it:

> Production predominates not only over production in the opposite sense of that term, but over the other elements as well.... A definite form of production thus determines the forms of consumption, distribution, exchange and *also the mutual relations between these various elements.* Of course, production *in its one-sided form* is in turn influenced by the other factors. (McLellan trans., p. 33; German ed., p. 20)

I find this conclusion very remarkable. In the first place it is a typical hierarchical judgment. Here is a whole made up of four elements, that is, the economic whole or, as we might call it, using an earlier expression of Marx, the whole of the "movements of private property." This whole receives the name of the one of the four elements which is thought to be predominant: production; and "production," in the *encompassing* sense, becomes so much the essential thing that the other, proper sense of the term is called "production in its one-sided form." Or, to take the structure in reverse: here is PRODUCTION writ large. It contains within itself four elements, namely, production (writ small) and three others, just as in the Book of Genesis Adam as first created is succeeded by two beings: the male Adam and his counterpart Eve, fashioned in the meantime from one of his ribs, that is, symbolically encompassed in him (cf. Dumont 1971, p. 72).

Such a hierarchical structure embodies a value judgment. Here there are two judgments implied: (1) that the economy as a whole has to be called by the name of one of its components; (2) that its predominant component is the one that embodies more immediately man's relation to nature as against relations between men. This Marx does not say here, but we may say that it underlies his thought (cf. below, p. 165).

It is to be noticed that Marx is led to this hierarchical conclusion by his honesty in trying to express the relation, as he conceives it, between production and the other aspects. The preceding development is replete with observations that, like the one
above, regarding consumption, could have led in other direc-
tions; but the conclusion to be reached is predetermined. Marx
must join Ricardo and the classics precisely in isolating production from the other aspects, for otherwise there would be no
necessity to consider value as issuing from production, to search
for its essence in the production process, and we might end—
who knows—with a marginalist theory of value.

One more remark: Is this conclusion of Marx not open to the
sort of criticism made by Marx, at least by the young Marx? If
we take a materialist, nominalist, empiricist stand, what can we
make of this hierarchical arrangement, of that production which
encompasses production and its contraries of one or the other
sort? Someone like the young Marx, if confronted with such a
statement, might well have called it hypocrisy or cynicism, if not
mystification.

We had already noticed in the "Manuscripts" how Marx, following Saint-Simon, tended to make production the prototype
of all human activity and life altogether. Here is a more clear-
cut, if more limited, case of encompassing, and this privileged
status is in strange contrast with the young Marx's impatience
with any subordination or transcendence, for transcendence is
indeed reintroduced with Marx's hierarchical judgment: "Here
is your god, ye moderns!"

The third and most significant section of the introduction to
the *Grundrisse* contains a statement which also has a hierarchical
aspect, but which I shall stress as the assertion of an important
sociological principle. It is the idea that in each type of society
one form of production predominates and gives its imprint to
the other forms that may coexist with it and to the whole
economy and, in Marx's view, society. This principle is accompanied by a truly structural consideration of the relative complexity of an element—here, a category—in relation to its place
in the whole. Marx argues that a relatively simple category can
express *either* dominant relations in a relatively undeveloped
whole *or* subordinate relations in a relatively developed whole
(p. 23). Abstract categories like labor (or private property) appear as the consequence of a complex historical development (at

the end of the line, in bourgeois society). While, thanks to their generality, they can be in a sense widely applied, yet they are fully valid only for the conditions in which they have appeared. Marx is especially concerned with the order of his general exposition: one should not begin with land ownership and land rent because in the modern period they are dominated and modified by the overall predominance of capital and profit. What I want to praise here is the recognition that the unity of a social system corresponds to the predominance in it of certain institutions which it is the duty of the sociologist to determine, not only as present by the side of others, but as giving its character to the social whole. In Marx's own words:

> Under all forms of society there is a certain production which by itself and by its conditions determines the rank and influence of all the rest. It is the general light in which all the other colours are dipped and which modifies them in their particularity. It is a special ether which determines the specific weight of everything that appears in it. (P. 27; cf. trans., pp. 40–41)

The aesthetic feeling is not so frequent in Marx. It marks here an intense perception of the specificity of each type of society and of its unity. We may call it a holistic and hierarchical perception.

Yet, the reader might say, these declarations, remarkable as they are, relate in the last analysis to the economy, or to the society perceived as or reduced to an economy. This is true; and when all is said and done, what I shall have to show is that all these blossoming developments, in which the bare bones of Marx's materialism almost disappear from view, do not in actual fact transcend the limitations set by the writings of his youth. They may well modify or even contradict the initial views on particular points, but the fundamental presuppositions are not replaced or doubted: they stand.

Regarding the social nature of production, the introduction to the *Grundrisse*—and especially its first part, which we shall now consider—is more articulate than the "Manuscripts" or *The German Ideology*. Actually, Marx opens the introduction by insisting on the need not to abstract the individual, as the agent or subject of production, from its social setting. This initial statement is directed in the first place against the adoption by

contemporaries—like Bastiat, Carey, and Proudhon—of the
eighteenth-century notion of the man of nature as an isolated
individual. Marx points out that this notion is part of the ideology of bourgeois society. There is only a short paragraph; yet
one is surprised that Marx, who had studied law, does not hint
at the link with natural law theories and assigns to the individual man of nature only a very short pedigree:

> The 18th century individual, constituting the joint product
> of the dissolution of the feudal forms of society and of
> the new forces of production that had developed since the
> 16th century. . . . (*Grundrisse*, McLellan trans., p. 17; German
> ed., p. 5)

What is more strange is that the word employed to designate
this mental construction, "the 18th century individual," is still
the biological word *das Individuum*, while it is clear that we are
dealing with *der Mensch als Einzelner*, with each particular man as
universal. Actually, the word appears a few lines further on,
when Marx says that in that period for the first time "the different forms of social interdependence confront the individual
[*dem Einzelnen*] as a mere means to his private ends, as an external necessity" (ibid., p. 6; trans., p. 17). Here the reference is to
the thinking subject, and therefore the biological expression was
untenable. The next sentence has still more: the view is called
that of the "isolated individual" or, better, "individualized individual" (*des vereinzelten Einzelnen*). It is clear that Marx has failed
to distinguish systematically between the individual as empirical
fact in relation to species or genus (*das Individuum*) and the individual as value or as self-sufficient, thinking subject (*der Einzelne*).

The point is not unconnected with Marx's general argument,
for we may ask: Which of the two sorts of individuals is the
subject of production? and Why is production referred to such
an individual as its subject, given the fact that production is
essentially a social process? A first answer is that the subject of
production is the empirical individual: we must think concretely, production is essentially labor or work, the working
agent is man as a separate agent, as a biological individual. As
Marx put it: "It is false to consider society as a single subject; it is
speculative" (ibid., p. 15; trans., p. 27). In that sense, then, Marx

is content at the start with cutting the individual to size as the empirical agent of production and insisting for the rest on the social determinants of production. But this is not quite the end of the matter.

Marx goes on: "The further back we go into history, the more the individual and, therefore, also the producing individual appears as dependent, and as belonging to a larger whole" (p. 6; trans., p. 17).[6] In this sentence as a whole, the individual (*Individuum*) is again clearly a mental construct and not a mere biological being. It is obvious that in such a state of dependence, not the particular agent, but the larger whole of which he is a part—the family, the clan, etc.—should be taken as the subject of production. The same is the case in a passage of *Capital* on primitive cooperation in which "the individual [*das einzelne Individuum*] is yet as little detached from the umbilical cord of the tribe or community as the individual bee from a swarm of bees" (I, chap. xi, quoted in Dumont 1970, p. 134). Here again the human individual is the mental construct.

Marx goes very far toward relativizing the notion—his own notion—of the individual, for he immediately notes that the ideology of the individual accompanies the highest development of social relations,[7] and he adds,

> Man is in the most literal sense a *zoon politikon*, not only a social animal, but an animal which can develop into an individual [*sich vereinzeln*] only in society. (*Grundrisse*, trans. McLellan, p. 17)

The evidence shows that Marx has actually generalized a modern category—the individual—without applying his own precept concerning the grain of salt. The grain of salt here would have consisted in distinguishing between the biological-empirical and the moral-normative individual. Marx did not do it, and he could not do it within his system.

On the crucial question of who is the subject of production, Marx in this introduction comes very near to transcending his initial view, and finally he does not. This can be seen from two passages found within four pages. In the first, it would seem that society is on the verge of winning the contest; in the second, the individual triumphs again. The comparison is instructive:

Therefore, whenever we speak of production, we always
have in mind production at a certain stage of social development [that is, in the last analysis a certain stage of production?], or production by social individuals [*gesellschaftlicher
Individuen*] [that is, simply, human beings living in a certain
society?]. (Ibid.)

All production is appropriation of nature by the individual
within and through a definite form of society. (Ibid., McLellan
trans., p. 21; German ed., p. 9)

The individual is the subject and society a mere determinant. In
the second passage, the main concern is property, or appropriation, and we thus get a significant indication that production is a
relation to nature, an "appropriation of nature." Now the ap-
propriator as such is clearly more than an animal: a moral person. We have seen that at the beginnings of society it would be
more proper to speak of the appropriation of nature by the family, etc., than by the individual. What about the other pole of the
development? Let us take one of Adam Smith's well-known
pinmakers, who is specialized in one operation among the many
into which pinmaking is divided. Can we speak meaningfully of
that man as appropriating nature, or is it not rather at the very
least the whole team of workers, or the manufacture, that can be
said to appropriate a part of nature or, better, to effect a first
stage in the appropriation that will be complete only when other
people will "consume" the pins? We know that such cases are
considered by Marx as alienated labor or the like.
    In any case, it is difficult to find a justification for maintaining,
from a universal point of view, that the individual is the subject
of production. As to the single human being, we may say only
that he is the elementary *agent* of production—or, should I say,
of a particular technical process?—and, as such, its main agent
as long as the techniques remain relatively simple and the division of labor little developed. As to the individual in the modern
sense of the term, who would be able to stand as the real *subject*
of production, we know on Marx's own admission that, on the
one hand, he is nonexistent—or at best only latently present—in
most societies and, on the other hand, that in modern society he
is not really the subject of production because alienation, or the

division of labor, estranges him from his product and from his productive activity.

The conclusion seems obvious: on the level of description, the individual has no place here, and production is essentially a social process. Properly speaking, society is the subject of production. Sometimes Marx comes very near to admitting this, as when he says in the same development, "It is always a certain social body or social subject that is active in a ... totality of branches of production (p. 8; trans., p. 19). Yet on the whole, he maintains his individualistic formula. Why? We must recall that he had posited from the start—remember *The German Ideology*— that the individual is the alpha and the omega. Society, language, consciousness, came far behind production in the determination of human life. Now Marx has found his way to stressing the social aspect more strongly, but even his most advanced statement, that man can individualize himself only in society, does not lead him to discard his nonsociological initial presupposition. All he can do is qualify it by speaking of "individuals producing in society" or of "the socially determined production of individuals," of "social individuals." There is a good reason for this: Marx's aim remains the emancipation of man through the proletarian revolution, and this aim is predicated on the assumption of man as an individual—as he thinks of himself, on Marx's own admission, only in the bourgeois era. Another formulation of production admitting another subject than the individual human being would appear to him, on the face of it, to sever the link between economic theory and revolutionary activity.

This may be one of the reasons why Marx, who perceived something of the question—the swarm of bees!—could not disentangle in the individual the empirical and the normative aspects: he could not look critically into his own valuation.[8] I hope to have made my point: extremely fine as many insights of the *Grundrisse* are, and whatever the progress from the early works in a sociological direction, yet all these insights and that progress remained confined within the old assumptions and could only enrich, qualify, partially correct—but could never transcend the framework which Marx had given himself, once for all.

At the risk of wearying the reader, I must conclude this chapter by highlighting once more, from the vantage point we have

now reached, Marx's identification with economics and its
deepest root, its ideological principle. I have just recalled that
Marx was wedded to the concept of the individual as the subject
of production by his revolutionary will. I had previously noticed
that Marx was forced by the ethical constraint embodied in the
labor theory of value to distinguish production as the
paramount aspect of the economy. These two are still partial
statements regarding Marx's relation to economics in general.
They must be completed and integrated. The theorist of revolution, on the one hand, and economics as he found it, on the
other, have first of all as their common ground the *individual
subject*. Only remember Marx's initial wrath against economics
remaining halfway in the "acknowledgement of man." This valuation of man as an individual is at the root of the labor theory of
value in Marx as in Smith and Ricardo; actually, it explains that
Marx accepts Ricardo's presuppositions or framework. The labor
theory of value presupposes that production is severed from
exchange, distribution, etc., as the essence of economics, or of
wealth, or of "the movement of private property." This corresponds to the search for the essence of economic phenomena in
one substance (wealth, production, labor), ideologically in keeping with the individualist valuation and which we are at liberty
to consider as the expression of a primacy of the relations with
nature as against the relations between men. Actually, Marx
himself not infrequently opposes these two sorts of relations. To
remain within the *Grundrisse*, while he states *en passant* that
"political economy is not technology" (p. 7), he also touches on
this aspect of production. Thus we had, above, the "appropriation of nature." Further on, discussing whether all the different
social forms of production have something in common, Marx
says that "it results already from the fact that the subject, mankind, and the object, nature, are the same" everywhere (p. 7;
trans., p. 18). But the main point is that production, that is, the
human relation to nature as paramount, is *of the individual*.
Please note: this is true universally, so much so that, without
knowing it, Marx is working within a kind of natural law concept of man as transcending all particular social constitutions
and stages of production. Contrary to all appearances we have
not left behind the "18th century individual."

On the whole, economics seems to be one of two alternatives:

it stands in opposition to the valorization of relations between men, which entails in one way or another the paramountcy of the social whole as against the individual, that is, holism, and hence—again in some manner—hierarchy, that is, the recognition of subordination, transcendence, etc., as rooted in man's nature. In brief, from Locke to Smith and from Smith to Marx, it is a matter of property, or value, or labor—against subordination, a willed order, the State. It is economics, not by the side of politics, but superseding it. Yet, if this hierarchical aspect is clear in Locke and in Marx, it is not so clear in Adam Smith, and we shall now consider Marx's achievement from that point of view.

9

Marx's Ideological
Achievement; Digression
on His Sociohistory

We can regard Marx's general theory of society and history as the affirmation of the paramountcy of economic phenomena. If such a paramountcy was, as I tried to show, implied from the start, and if it is so widely admitted in the modern world as to constitute an important or central aspect of its ideology, then Marx can be said to have brought economic ideology to its accomplishment, whatever may be thought of the scientific value of his economic theory or analysis. Although Marx's contribution in this regard seems peerless, whether the achievement is exclusively his own is irrelevant from the present point of view. I am contending essentially that the feature is present in Marx, and I am asking why.

Considering the whole development in retrospect and examining it in the abstract, it seems clear that a new view of the kind of the economic ideology cannot impose itself from one day to the next. Clearly, before the new point of view can rival, cancel, or dominate other points of view already established and firmly entrenched, it must first establish itself, that is, fight for and obtain its recognition—if not from the general public, at least within a circle of specialists who have some audience among educated people. Only then can the new *Anschauung* hope to rise above the horizon and become a sort of sun in the intellectual firmament. And this second stage might well require procedures and attitudes quite different from the first one. At least, such is the view that the sequence of events selected by me from the seventeenth to the nineteenth century suggests. The interest of this view lies in the light it throws on the difference of attitude between Marx and his predecessors. Given enough agreement on basic presuppositions, without which neither the former nor the latter could have worked at what appear historically to have been two stages in the same task, the second phase had to be imbued with a spirit quite different from the first; and we are now in a position to contrast them.

We saw by what process or movement political economy has constituted itself as a separate kind of consideration: the effort has been to emancipate one part of social activity from the encompassing subjection in which it had hitherto been accommodated and confined in relation to politics on the one hand, to morals on the other; and to constitute that part of social activity into a separate, independent, more or less autonomous domain. In relation to morals, autonomy was never complete, or rather, it was bought at a price, namely, the assumption that the new domain had a kind of built-in ethics of its own that rendered superfluous and even harmful the application to it of the trite rules of morality.

We noticed another feature of the phase, which now appears as another price that had to be paid: the emancipation of the economic domain demanded that it be considered as the arena where natural laws were at work, so that human intervention in it could only be obnoxious (at least, we may suppose, until the natural laws were sufficiently elicited). This position was indispensable in order to guard the domain against the intervention of the politician and the moralist, but at the same time it was at variance with the artificialist tendency, ubiquitous in the modern world and characteristic of it. With hindsight, these two sacrifices, which had to be consented to in favor of the emergence of the new kind of consideration—detachment from the common run of morality and from the basic modern artificialist pull—appear not only as exceptional but also as transitory in their nature. Dictated by necessity, they would be redeemed if destiny favored the newly born natural science of the individual in society, for it is what economics was to be—its focus on wealth, production, etc., being entailed by this point of view.

That Marx was unaware of all this is a minor reason for his clash with political economy when he first encountered it. The major reason is that he turned to the field with a deep motivation that was fundamentally opposed to the attitudes of the classics as egregiously incarnated in Adam Smith. Where they had been concerned with cautiously establishing their claim, reconnoitering the estate, and cordoning it off against marauding raids, here comes the young rebel who lays a claim to it in the name of the wholeness of man, as a base in his war against all established institutions and especially against everything that separates, mediates, partitions, mutilates, dominates, or humiliates man. Foremost in this man are perhaps his ethical commitment and his hatred of transcendence, bonds, and laws. With him, economics will become the scientific warrant of the most grandiose enterprise ever proposed to man's will. Economics is reintegrated with full rights in the society of doctrines. Indeed, it claims a right of suzerainty—or rather, of greater power—over the whole of human action and human history. Thus, by a movement precisely opposite to that of the founding fathers, economics comes to its maturity and its apotheosis as an ideology, and displays in full light what it had contained in the seed.

The evolution in the relation with politics is quite clear: economics developed from a humble maid (seventeenth century), to a kind of umbrageous rival (laissez-faire, etc., or, as Marx put it in the "Manuscripts," "the only norms and the only bond"), to nothing less than an abusive mother (Marx: men "produce" themselves and society, etc.). As we noted above, in this reversal of supremacy the content of primacy changes. It was a matter of hierarchy and teleology, economic means being subordinated to political ends; it has become a matter of factual primacy: the supposed cause is potent and hence superior in relation to the supposed effect.

In relation to morality, there has also been a reintegration, but the matter is more complex: the modern artificialist claim, which had been temporarily banished, is reinstated, and human intervention is now allowed in the name of morality—nay, it is advocated on an unprecedented scale on the very basis of economic findings. But this again is obtained at a price, namely, that economic science issues in a condemnation of the very society that gave birth to it. In other words, economic reality is contradictory, and it can be made humanly meaningful, or moral, only through its partial destruction, sifting as it were the good aspects, which will be kept, from the bad ones—that is, those that have survived their usefulness—which will be discarded.

We see here, as we found in the "Manuscripts," that the divorce between economics and morality is not really canceled.

It is only dialecticized, if I may risk the term: it becomes a call for action, since action alone will reconcile the fact with the norm. Not only is the articulation between socialism and economics dialectical, but also contradiction is enshrined at the heart of economic reality. If it were not, thought would not immediately issue into action. Do not ask why it is that throughout their long history men had to pay so heavily for their progeny to attain at last to a truly human life, for such a view is the necessary counterpart for mobilizing the maximum of energies in the present; contradiction is the nerve center, the power pile of a doctrine built as a weapon.

All in all, a built-in moral constraint has determined the development of economic inquiry in our authors. In this trend of thought, economics has not really succeeded in emancipating itself from morality. As to Marx himself, not only his economics but also his doctrine as a whole develops the initial moral commitment, the vow.

In closing this essay, I should insist on its limits, lest it be taken for what it is not. It does not pretend to completeness in any sense. It is selective regarding not only the authors but also the aspects that have been retained. Regarding its proper object—the relation between general ideology and economic thought—two misunderstandings should be avoided. The first would consist of assuming that the choice of authors corresponds to some kind of value judgment on my part, as if they were taken to be "more ideological" and "less scientific" than others. It should be clear that, as stated in the Introduction, nothing can be more remote from my mind than such a judgment and the dichotomy on which it rests. To take the example of Malthus, I hinted at the fact that in his controversies with Ricardo he seems much less characteristic than the latter of the ideological aspect I have been pursuing. But if we shift the ground to the theory of population, to the Godwin-Malthus controversy and to Malthus's *Essay*, especially in its first form, we have a clear example of an ideological controversy in which the naturalist view, as opposed to the artificialist, is strongly stressed. Indeed, there is so little ground for assuming a geometrical progression on the one hand, an arithmetical on the other, that one may well ask whether this genial trick is not at bottom a mathematical expression of nature's superior creative power as against man's. The second misunderstanding would be to assume that, within its limits, the present inquiry has exhausted its object. Here the reader is reminded of what I stressed in the Introduction as the partial, provisional character of the attempt, starting from the comparison of the modern with one particular other civilization and the few conclusions or hypotheses issuing from it as the modest tools of the present endeavor. The only claim that this study makes is that modern ideology, thus set—if imperfectly—in a comparative perspective, throws *some* light on the thought of our authors, and that, reciprocally, their thought so considered throws *some* light on our modern ideology in one of its major aspects.

*

Returning now to Marx, this section will gather some remarks which fall outside the mainstream of the preceding inquiry. They imposed themselves, so to speak, as the work went on and are in that sense by-products of the study. These notes are somehow intermediary between the foregoing limited study and a general study of Marx that will not be attempted. The standpoint is different: we are now concerned with Marx's final stand on general questions of sociology and history and its adequacy or inadequacy. The mature works should be in the foreground and the early works used only to supplement them.

One begins by noticing that, in the exuberant growth of Marx's brilliant, powerful, passionate, and painstaking, often recurrent analyses, the results or the insights are very unequally integrated into the general theory. Then one perceives the beginning of a pattern: there are recurrent sociohistorical perceptions that stand in an uneasy relationship to the theory. Marx's perception is wider than his doctrinal framework and bursts out of its limits here and there, but it also suffers in its development from the imposition of those uniform presuppositions that *The German Ideology* set out with perfect clarity. For scientific as against revolutionary purposes it is useful to recover those views in order to see where they would have led Marx, and where they would lead anyone who takes them seriously, if unhampered by the operation of a reductionist factor.

My remarks will bear on two general conflicts: first, the

conflict between a sociological or holistic view and an economic or individualistic view and, second, the conflict between the perception of the specific, original character of the different types of society and the assumption of a unilinear continuity and fundamental unity between them.

I concluded from the introduction to the *Grundrisse* that Marx had become sociological as much as his early personal starting point could permit without itself being canceled. We can adduce a few texts to show that the sociological recognition actually comes into conflict with the overall individualistic framework. Thus, in the *Grundrisse* themselves, in an excursus rightly singled out by McLellan under the title "Individuals and Society" and which should be read in its entirety, Marx introduces against Proudhon and the economists a sociological view of society: first, he notes—in different words—that society is present in the minds of its members; and second, he defines it precisely:

> Society does not consist of individuals; it expresses the sum of connections and relationships in which individuals find themselves.... To be a slave or to be a citizen are social determinations. (*Grundrisse*, trans., p. 77; orig., pp. 175–76)

And, we may add from the context, the reference is in each case to a given "historical form of society." Rubel, in a note in his edition (*Oeuvres*, 2:281, n. 1), marks the importance of this text and refers us to another one in "Salaried Work and Capital" (1849), an early but authoritative text connected with the *Communist Manifesto:*

> While producing, men are not only in relation to nature. They produce only if they co-operate in some fashion and exchange their activities. In order to produce, they establish between themselves precisely determined contacts and relations: their contact with nature, that is production, takes place only within the framework of those social contacts and relations. (*Werke*, 6:403)

This is perhaps the most explicit text we have—more complete in particular than the foreword to the *Critique* of 1859 or even the *Grundrisse*. I shall not insist on the general difficulty that arises from the fact that Marx most often equates social relationships and production relationships (*Produktionsverhältnisse*). But I shall ask whether the two fragments before us are compatible with the view that the subject of production is the individual. There would seem to be two distinct spheres or, rather, two incompatible points of view: *either* the social nature of man is fully recognized, as in these two texts, and in such a view production can only appear as a social phenomenon, *or* production, as the relation of man with nature, requires that the individual agent be privileged, and society falls into the background, as we saw in the *Grundrisse:* "Production is appropriation of nature by the individual within and through a definite form of society."

A fragment from the third book of *Capital* (*Oeuvres,* 2:1487; cf. Engels's edition, pp. 826–28, chap. 48, § III) shows, to my mind, the same uneasy combination:

> Just as primitive man, civilized man is compelled to struggle with nature in order to satisfy his needs. . . . With the development [of production] this domination by natural necessity widens because the needs multiply.

We see how fundamentally production depends upon the state of society. The multiplication of their needs obliges civilized men to work more or less on the same scale as did men in primitive societies. It is noteworthy that the fulfillment of such artificial needs is still called "the empire of necessity" and that the cliché of labor as the "struggle of man against nature" is not weakened in this context. (The image is central in modern ideology and as such would require careful study.) This is so because in this passage Marx is not actually concerned with society; needs, work, production—all belong to economics, that is, essentially to the individual man in his relation to nature. Thus we see how in actual fact the sociological consideration recedes in Marx's mind most of the time, while the economic consideration is in the foreground. This is to say that *at this level* there is a primacy of the relation between man and nature as against the relation between man and man. And of course it is in conformity with the general thesis, of which the initial postulate was that the former kind of relation is causally prior to the latter, whatever interaction between them is observable in a given historical situation. The passage shows that this primacy, built in from the start, is actually fact-proof.

This is not all. Marx denounces, in the society of *Capital,* the fact that human relations are disguised under the form of objects. Here the normative primacy would seem to be reversed:

relations between men are the real relations, and it is bad that they are not directly grasped as such, but only indirectly, through a detour, and are expressed in things, namely, in commodities as having exchange value. Here the "natural" aspect of things, of objects—their value in use—serves as a support of the human relations expressed as their exchange value. Our text here is the famous development on "the fetishist character of commodities and its secret" at the beginning of *Capital* (I, I, i, 4). What is of interest for us is the ethical superiority that is implied in favor of prebourgeois or precapitalist societies insofar as they expressed human relations directly—not indirectly. Take the society of the Middle Ages. Here, instead of everyone's being independent, everyone is dependent,

> and precisely because society is based on personal dependence, all social relations appear as relationships between persons. The diverse kinds of work and their products have in consequence no need to take a fantastic figure distinct from their reality. They appear as services, prestations and deliveries in kind. The natural, particular form of labour ... is also its social form ... the social relations of persons in their respective works are clearly asserted as their own personal relationships, instead of disguising themselves in the social relations of things, as products of labour. (*Oeuvres*, 1:611–12)

Marx is fully aware that the difference is accompanied by a difference in the perception of man. As he wrote, early, the lord always remains a lord, and the serf a serf, while the rentier is, although a rentier, at the same time a man (*The German Ideology*, p. 76; cf. above, p. 139). In the "Critique" of 1859 the contrast is clearly expressed: in the capitalist society "the labour represented in the exchange value is posited as labour of the isolated individual," while, in the early forms of society,

> It is *bel et bien* the community, posited before the production, which prevents the work of individuals to be private work and its product a private product; it is the community that makes individual work to appear as a direct function of a member of the social organism. (*Oeuvres*, 1:285)

And to return to *Capital:*

> These old social organisms [ancient Asia, antiquity in general] are, as regards production, infinitely more simple and trans-

parent than bourgeois society; but they are based on the
immaturity of man as an individual—whose umbilical cord,
uniting it to the natural community of a primitive tribe,
history had not yet cut—or conditions of despotism or
slavery. (*Oeuvres,* 1:614)

As with the swarm of bees, the moral individual is postulated
as being latent in the biological individual in nonbourgeois, even
in primitive, social formations. Apart from that point, one thing
is clear: social relations or relations of production become
opaque, hidden in objects—and the "social organism" is
occulted—when man becomes an Individual, independent, private, etc. It is strange that this concomitance has not led Marx to
doubt the appositeness of taking the individual universally as
the subject of production. Does not this recognition, moreover,
entail that the primacy of economics as against sociology fits
only the modern case and should be reversed for all others? The
first answer that comes to mind is that it is apodictic with Marx
that the bourgeois form of society represents the culmination,
development, revelation of everything that went before and
contains in the last analysis the *truth* of the development. Therefore, if the Individual appears with this society, then it means he
was not absent but latent or immature until then. Therefore, if
the modern form reveals the primacy of economic phenomena,
then this primacy *must* be uncovered in previous forms of society. To this argument again there is an objection, for, as Marx
told us, bourgeois society is "only a contradictory form of the
development," and not all bourgeois features are there to stay.
For instance, the form of commodity, or exchange value, that
social work takes in that period must go: the communist society
will return to a direct expression of work as a social function.
How is this judgment grounded in fact? How do we know that
the future society will not do otherwise and perhaps, on the
contrary, cancel the valorization of the individual and keep exchange value? It is tempting at this juncture to say that the
normative judgment of Marx—revolution as the primary
purpose—is the only answer. But this was probably not so for
Marx himself in his mature days.

We must at this point try to capture, albeit summarily and
imperfectly, the evolutionary and dialectic scheme that underlies Marx's doctrine: the global framework of history consists of

three fundamental stages. *Thesis:* The primitive community: social relations are satisfactory in themselves, but the undeveloped state of the relations with nature imposes, in society itself and in culture generally (religion), forms of bondage. *Antithesis* (of which bourgeois society is the culmination): Development of the natural power of man at the price of social subjection, division of labor, alienation, etc. *Synthesis:* On the basis of increased productivity, the social relations are remodeled on a human, transparent basis; the community aspect of the first stage is reinstated at the same time as the modern individual is maintained, only purged of its bad aspects.

The weakness of the schema lies in the place of the individual in it, for it appears in the historical evolution as contradictory to the community; therefore, how they can be reconciled should be problematic (or, for a Hegelian, should at least be described). But it was not so for Marx, as we have seen: he was so confident about the compatibility that he did not hesitate, from *The German Ideology* onwards, to stress forcibly the individualistic aspect at the cost of the insights gained in the "Manuscripts."

There is one aspect that is certainly fundamental and that my thumbnail sketch of the three stages does not capture. The first motto is: Man must be emancipated. The essential drive is probably toward the end of all subordination and transcendence—in brief, of all bondage. In the first stage, man's bondage was to nature; in the second, the society became powerful against nature, but the bondage was between man and man; and in the third, the second form of bondage should be abolished while the first is unable to reassert itself, owing to the development of productivity. Furthermore, the second stage is clearly distinguished into two phases. Thus, the *Grundrisse:*

> Relationships of personal dependence (which were at first quite spontaneous) are the first forms of society under which human productivity develops, though only to a slight extent and at isolated points. Personal independence founded on *material* dependence is the second great form: in it there developed for the first time a system of general social interchange.... Free individuality, founded on the universal development of individuals and the subordination of their communal, social productivity as being their social resources, is the third stage. (*Grundrisse*, p. 75; trans., p. 67)

The word "subordination" (*Unterordnung*) is surely important. On a collective or communal level, the formula is similar to that of Locke on an individual level: subordination is relegated to man-to-things relations. To comment: Men will be equal only if subordination is confined to things, and they will be free only if their wealth is common to all. History was able to rid men of dependence only toward men, that is, seemingly or incompletely, and a conscious submission of things to the community is necessary to purge them of their hidden content of human bondage. On the whole, the real axis of history is from dependence to independence through the contradictory bourgeois stage. Independence is the article of faith, located in the future, which allows us to see a continuity in all societies of the past. If we do not subscribe to this creed, then bourgeois society will stand in clear opposition to all others with their stress on human relations—which Marx approves as against bourgeois hypocrisy or fetishism—and hence on subordination and dependence—which Marx rejects because he has gone to the bourgeois school, or, I should say, to the Christian school, for the matter has old roots. Thus it is that Marx's value judgment is introduced among the objective facts of history, and it prevents him from recognizing the obvious fact that the Individual in his full development is historically a bourgeois phenomenon linked with commodities, etc., that is, linked with the *indirect* expression of the social nature of man.

Of course, Marx did not underestimate the stringency of factual dependence. He said in *The German Ideology:* "In the representation, the individuals are freer under the sway of the bourgeoisie than before, because their conditions of existence are to them contingent; actually they are of course less free because they are subordinated to the power [or violence: *Gewalt*] of things" (*Werke,* 3:76). The transformation begins with the division of labor, which transforms the powers or relations from personal to factual; therefore, the division of labor must be abolished and the factual powers must be again subordinated to the individuals (ibid., p. 74).

We have thus seen how it is that Marx did not exploit to the full his clear perception of the opposition between nature, or things, and men as the objects of human relations. But, the reader may ask, what would be the practical result of this perception as regards the postrevolutionary society? It is all very simple: according to what we know, *there must be* dependence of a sort in society. To suppress the indirect or factual dependence present in bourgeois society is most probably to invite the reappearance of the age-old direct dependence between men in its most arbitrary form. As Locke had already taught us in a manner, to do away with property must lead to the reintroduction of subordination. There is no merit in stressing this point in our time, but it is piquant to find that in one place Marx made the point, or very nearly so. In a passage immediately preceding the one last quoted from the *Grundrisse,* Marx wrote forcefully:

> [In modern society] each individual "carries his social power, as his relation with society, in his pocket" . . .

and, a little further on,

> Each individual possesses the social power under the form of a thing. Deprive the thing of that social power, and you must give it to persons over persons.

It should be clear that I am not ransacking the bulk of Marx's works for the sake of finding discrepant or contrary statements. We should never forget that Marx left his published work incomplete and that we are fortunate in having, from what he chose not to publish and from more or less confidential notes, so much more to enable us to reconstruct his mode of thought, so many reiterations, but also soundings, probes, trials, abandoned quarries, that testify to the unceasing effort of a tireless mind of rare power. It would be unfair, however, to treat these on a par with his finished products. What I am trying to do is to lay bare a few general features relating to the subordination, in Marx, of one line of thought to another and of many valuable or promising insights to a single aim. I want now to establish a single proposition: the concrete diversity of the types of society is finely perceived, but it is subordinated to the doctrinal elaboration of uniformity or continuity. I shall first recall the doctrinal generalization of bourgeois or modern features to nonmodern societies and then show how the scales are weighted in favor of continuity as against discontinuity, on the example of feudalism.

The first question was touched on above at its most general and fundamental level: the primacy of the economy and of the individual are generalized from the modern or bourgeois society to the others. More minutely, I drew attention, when dealing with *The German Ideology,* to a similar generalization of several expressions, and in the *Grundrisse* we found the problem posed squarely and, insofar as the assumption of a unilinear scale of evolution permits, deftly solved with the "grain of salt." The case of *The German Ideology* is interesting because it shows how the young authors, given their presuppositions, were naturally driven to extend the meaning of several basic terms and to conceive all societies on the modern model. Thus "civil society" occasionally designates the relations of production—so called later—before the accession of the bourgeoisie (also above, p. 127, n. 7); "class" is first opposed to "estate" before encompassing it and being generalized, as in the *Communist Manifesto;* private property is similarly generalized, as we noticed above (cf. pp. 139, 140, 142, 143 ff.), but the "grain of salt" is applied to it in the "Manuscripts": there are two forms of it. In the former (ancient Rome, Turkey), there is an opposition between property and nonproperty, which is not grasped as contradictory. Only in the latter, modern form does the opposition develop into a contradiction, "an energetic form which presses towards the solution of the contradiction." It is the contradiction between labor and capital: "labor, the subjective essence of property, and yet excluded from it; capital, as objectified labor and yet excluding labor" (*MEGA,* I.3:111).

Enough of these usages have gone into the mature works (the division of labor in general retaining some features characteristic of modern alienated labor) for me to recall once more that the basic rationale of this tendency is that the proletarian revolution should not only overturn the bourgeois society, but also at one stroke put an end to human prehistory in general. We on the contrary see the categories that are the offspring of the modern type of society as *therefore* problematic in their application to societies presenting other—not to say contrary—basic valuations, and we see Marx's stand as a justification of sociocentrism. But here comes the paradox: nothing is less sociocentric than Marx's genuine perception of feudalism or of Roman society. Were there two Marxes? At any rate, it is preposterous to attribute immediately to Marx's critical stand the quality of his pictures of nonbourgeois society: if he is a sociologist there, it is very much *in spite of* his revolutionary stand. Nevertheless, it is not psychologically unconnected with it, insofar as his empathy with, say, the Middle Ages is not unrelated to his negative attitude toward the bourgeois world.

My thesis is that Marx had a very acute perception of the feudal world and of the *discontinuity* between it and what follows, and that his insights remained limited and did not develop theoretically because the theory focused, on the contrary, on the *continuity* between the two eras. We saw it a moment ago with regard to personal versus material relations, an opposition close to that between a primacy of the dependence between men and a primacy of the relation between man and nature, between politics and economics. But the same is the case also in other respects, from "The Jewish Question" and the 1844 "Manuscripts" to the third book of *Capital*, with its very long section (§ 6) on land rent, not to speak of the long discussion of the same in "Mehrwert." The problem is intimately connected with the question of land ownership, and we know that Marx spent the last years of his life working on prebourgeois agricultural societies. There is thus plenty of material, but here I shall be content with recalling some general points from the early works and leave out the question of land ownership and land rent in the mature works (cf. above, pp. 102, 105 ff.).

To document within a brief compass Marx's vivid grasp of feudal society, we may return to the 1844 "Manuscripts." In two pages regarding the relation to land prior to the capitalist period (first Ms., fols. XVII–XVIII; *MEGA*, I.3:76), everything is present: as to the political aspect, there is "confusion between lordship and land possession"; "feudal land ownership gives its name to its lord as a kingdom to its king"; "it is a narrow type of nationality"; and the situation of the lord in relation to those who cultivate his estate "is thus directly political." As to the personal and sentimental aspect, the relationship has not only a political but "a sentimental side"; there is "the appearance of a more intimate relation than that of material wealth between the possessor and the earth"; "the land is individualised with its lord"; and "it appears as the external [nonorganic] body of its

lord" and, at the limit, "as a person." Then comes the absence of
the distinct economic motivation: "[The lord] does not endeavour to get the greatest possible advantage out of his estate.
On the contrary he consumes what is there and calmly leaves
the cares of procurement to the serfs and farmers." Finally,
Marx seizes on a popular expression of the contrast that will
grace an exemplary footnote on the first page of chapter 4 of
Capital:

> The opposition between on the one hand the power of land-
> ownership based on personal relationships of domination
> and dependence and on the other the impersonal power of
> money is clearly expressed in the two French dictums:
> *"Nulle terre sans seigneur," "L'argent n'a pas de maître"* [No
> land without lord; Money has no master].

At the same time, one finds in this passage, interspersed
among the expressions I have quoted, expressions of a quite different trend. The passage is introduced with these words:
"Feudal property already implied the domination of land as an
alien power over men. The serf was an accessory of the earth." It
is not simply a matter of distinguishing contrary aspects, some
ethically negative, others positive. The personal aspects are
largely "appearances":

> The domination of private property begins altogether with
> [feudal] land possession, it is its basis ... [and finally] ... it
> was necessary that this appearance should be suppressed;
> that property in land, being the root of private property,
> should be engulfed completely in the movement of private
> property and should become a commodity.

This is reductionism; it is the assertion that continuity is more
important than discontinuity in this matter. The assertion is emphatic, hurried, and harsh, because it is weak. (Marx shies away
from "the sentimental tears" of romanticism because he shares
its basic feeling.) It is as if Marx, shrugging his shoulders,
thought: one domination is no better than another; all these
attractive features are only appearances; we know it because we
are in possession of the law of history. At bottom, feudal property in land was not political; it was economic, it was "the root of

private property," and therefore all adornments had to go. The trouble is that the relation thus posited is simply not true. "Private property" here means private property in the modern, bourgeois, capitalist sense; one can hardly speak of property in land in any precise way in feudal times. Actually, the whole question of land ownership and of rent looms very large in political economy and in Marx's work, and the detail of the case proves precisely that, in the modern period, property in land is an aberrant and problematic phenomenon, which Marx himself refused to recognize as such and which is only with the greatest difficulty reduced to a particular form of "private," that is, essentially movable, property.

It may be argued that Marx was unaware of these facts in 1844. Yet he says clearly that property in land was engulfed in the movement of private property; this expression implies a heterogeneity between the two and contradicts their identification. The assertion of continuity, wiping out or belittling the fine insights of Marx, is arbitrary and willful. It covers up a yawning chasm. The truth of the matter is that "private property" is separated from feudal "property," so called, by a revolution in thought and in deed, and Marx knows it pretty well (see the chapter on the expropriation of land in England in the section on primitive accumulation in *Capital*).

I insist on this point because it is of the utmost importance regarding the Marxian and Marxist broad conceptions of history. For reasons that are not far to seek, a discontinuity that is obvious to us, and that was already quite notable for Marx himself, between prebourgeois and bourgeois society is submerged, leading to the facile generalization of essentially bourgeois concepts to the rest of history.

If this is so, if the last and nearest to us of the great historical transitions is obscured in Marx himself, it follows that not much interest can be attached to what can be said, in the same approach, of more remote "historical forms of society." The contemporary discussions about so vague a thing as "the Asiatic mode of production" are little more than Scholastic disputes about how the sun can continue to circle the earth. The task for historians on that level should be, rather, to reach a sound formulation of the modern revolution. That it has not yet been done may come as a shock. Yet the fact must be admitted, I think, as soon as one admits that it is more than a matter of external events and quantitative changes. On the question of the ideological change, all that we have at our disposal are stray recognitions and partial insights due to various scholars, not a global, integrated, and sufficiently articulated picture. Marx's last word in the matter is perhaps found in two pages of the *Grundrisse* (pp. 81–82; trans., pp. 72–73) where he again comes to grips with the problem. The passage is inevitably somewhat involved; it centers on the substitution of material dependence for personal dependence, and it is remarkable for an almost complete lack of prejudice in favor of one or the other forms or in favor of similarity or difference between them. In other words, it comes as near as Marx could, within his general presuppositions, to a scientific, structural comparison of the two ideological universes. It evokes, closer to us, Talcott Parsons's set of alternative variables, which actually belongs here, as Jürgen Habermas justly remarks (1970, p. 61): it is the last and the most precise in a series of sociological perceptions of this change. I would add that its ambition to present an analysis of the universal conditions of social action is justified—and is justified only—insofar as it is through the perception of this change that we have access to such universal conditions. At the same time, its universal orientation hides its real nature, and it captures the whole phenomenon only on a very abstract level—witness our simple distinction, in line with that of Marx, between relations to things and relations between men. It is heartening to find that the same author I just referred to introduces a similar distinction in an effort to reformulate some Marxist or Marxoid problems (Habermas, ibid., p. 62: *Arbeit und Interaktion*, etc.).

To sum up: as soon as we cease to favor our own ideology, the different historical eras and types of society appear discontinuous and heterogeneous. To acknowledge this discontinuity or heterogeneity and then to master it by comparison—without any damage to the historical continuity when it is actually given, as in the case of the medieval-modern transition—is the scholarly task that Marx has left to us, even though it is quite different from what was his primary concern.

Appendix

Value and Labor in
Adam Smith

A Detailed Commentary on
a Few Paragraphs in the First
Book of *The Wealth of Nations*

Part One of this Appendix deals with the beginning of chapter v of *The Wealth of Nations*, which blandly asserts that value consists in labor. In order to reveal the logic underlying this assertion, we must first pluck from chapter vi its initial section, which presents a picture of the "original" situation on which the whole view or theory hinges. Part Two deals with the sections at the beginning of chapter vi, which are more systematic and the main object of our concern and discussion. The references are to the standard text by book, chapter, and, whenever necessary, section, and to Cannan's edition (Smith 1904). To ease the application of my comments, I emphasize some words of the original text (roman type). The marginal indications, §§ a, b, etc., are for convenient reference from the text to the Appendix.

Part One

a CHAP. VI, § 1. [THE STATE OF NATURE, OR THE ARCHETYPAL SITUATION]:

> *In that early and rude state of society which precedes both the accumulation of stock and the appropriation of land, the proportion between the quantities of labour necessary for* acquiring *different objects seems to be the only circumstance which can afford any rule for exchanging them one for another. If among a nation of hunters, for instance, it usually costs twice the labour to kill a beaver which it does to kill a deer, one beaver should* naturally *exchange for or be worth two deer. It is* natural *that what is usually the produce of two days' or two hours' labour should be worth double of what is usually the produce of one day's or one hour's labour.*

Comment: "Acquiring" here means appropriating from nature through labor. In § 4 we read "the quantity of labour commonly

189

employed in acquiring or producing any commodity" as a general formula which will be used also for the civilized state of society. It is clear that "acquiring" and "producing" differ only through a nuance.

On the whole, we have here a definition of value as the quantity of labor employed in the production of the good, as it is, in this case, the "only circumstance" explaining the rate of exchange. But this "natural" or archetypal situation is discussed in terms introduced in the preceding chapter, to which we shall next turn.

Locke had written, "Thus this Law of reason makes the Deer, that *Indian's* who hath killed it; 'tis allowed to be his goods who hath bestowed his labour upon it" (*Two Treatises*, II, § 30). To the deer, Adam Smith added a beaver. Also, "which precedes both ... " recalls Locke's subsequent introduction of money and the appropriation of land. The expressions "natural" and "naturally" make it likely that Smith would have written: "In the state of nature," were it not for Hume's definitive criticism of the notion, and this criticism may also be one of the reasons why Smith did not start the whole discussion with the consideration of the "early and rude state of society" but deferred it to the following chapter (chap. vi), for in fact his argument can be construed as a straight natural law argument: the state of nature tells us that, in principle or in essence, value is labor, or consists of labor, whatever complications or irregularities may be found in the civilized or developed state of society.

On a less immediate or textual level, the parallelism with Locke implies a homology between private property and value, as both are based on labor. Myrdal, searching for the foundations of Ricardo's choice of "labour as the origin of real value," fully recognized this point and the natural law nature of the argument: "Such notions of property and value underlay Adam Smith's proposition that labour is the only real source of value." He spoke of "the property which every man has in his own labour, as it is the original foundation of all other property, so it is the most sacred and inviolable" (Myrdal 1953, p. 72. Adam Smith's passage echoes directly Locke's theory of property. It is from the *Wealth*, book I, chap. x, pt. 2, about the regulation of apprenticeship, and Cannan contrasts this view of property with that of Smith's 1763 *Lectures*. See Smith 1904, p. 123). Myrdal underlines the "attempt of the philosophy of natural law to derive both rights and values from the same ultimate principles" (1953, p. 72).

In fact, Adam Smith begins his discussion of value, or more precisely "value in exchange" (see end of chap. iv) in chapter v, as follows:

b Chap. v. Of the Real and Nominal Price of Commodities . . .
§ 1 (beginning):

> *Every man is rich or poor according to the degree in which he can afford to enjoy the necessaries, conveniences, and amusements of human life. But after the division of labour has once thoroughly taken place, it is but a very small part of these with which a man's own labour can supply him. The far greater part of them he must derive from the labour of other people, and he must be rich or poor according to the quantity of that labour which he can* command, *or which he can afford to* purchase.

Comment: First introduction of "command" and "purchase," which will be a leitmotiv subsequently under the form "purchase or command." Labor can be either "commanded," which expresses a *power* over men (see below), or "purchased," presumably under the form of a commodity.

It is well known that the first sentence reproduces Cantillon's definition of wealth. It is remarkable that it is here referred to an individual subject reminiscent of the state of nature: "But after the division of labour. . . ." The division of labor has been thoroughly discussed in the first three chapters of the book. It enters here as the relevant circumstance that distinguishes the civilized state from the "original" state. We are thus confronted with labor under two forms: (1) as a natural fact ("man's own labour"); (2) as intimately connected with the modification of the natural situation, that is, with the division of labor. The impact of the division of labor for the individual subject is to introduce exchange as a necessary condition, in addition to labor. "Labour + exchange" is the fundamental constellation, and this is characteristic of Adam Smith (Ex.: chap. iv, end of

§ 1: "Every man thus lives by exchanging, or becomes in some measure a merchant ... " and this applies to the laborer himself). The civilized state, or the "commercial society," rests on that pair of concepts, in which labor is more fundamental, but exchange a necessary adjunct.

§ 1 (following):

> *The value of any commodity, therefore, to the person who possesses it, and who means not to use or consume it himself, but to exchange it for other commodities, is equal to the quantity of labour which it enables him to* purchase or command. *Labour, therefore, is the real* measure *of the exchangeable value of all commodities.*

Comment: We go on with the individual subject. It may seem strange that the value of a commodity is defined, not as a social phenomenon, but with reference to an individual subject taken in a particular situation. But for Smith, the situation of exchange is the fundamental situation from which the value of the good emerges. And once the individual is given, he must be made to turn away from the value in use. In the context of an exchange of commodities in general, "to purchase" (a commodity) comes before "to command" (to have the commodity made by a laborer). "Labour ... is the real measure": we note, after others, that Smith is not content with stating that labor is the essence of value; he wants it also to be its measure, a preoccupation that will lead to difficulties. Actually, here the transition is easy, from *quantity* of labor to labor as *measure.*

On the whole, this paragraph asserts forcefully the author's thesis. The state of nature, in which a man is supposed to depend entirely on his own labor for the necessaries etc., of life, is present only by implication. The passage echoes a similar one at the beginning of chapter iv. Yet the implication is decisive, for it introduces *labor* as something antecedent to exchange and more fundamental, in which exchange can thus find its law. Instead of trying to demonstrate his thesis, Adam Smith very ingeniously contrives to make it plausible, and then, as in the following, to make it familiar by repetition. The next paragraph will say very much the same thing as forcefully as possible:

c § 2

> *The real price of everything, what everything really costs to the*
> *man who wants to acquire it, is the toil and trouble of acquiring it.*
> *What everything is really worth to the man who has acquired it,*
> *and who wants to dispose of it or exchange it for something else, is*
> *the toil and trouble which it can save to himself, and which it can*
> impose upon *other people.*

Comment: Again, the first sentence bids us go beyond the social
situation of exchange (buying: what it "costs") to the root of the
matter, that is, the individual in isolation toiling hard to "acquire" a thing. The insistence on "real," "really," marks the
transition to the metaeconomic, ontological ground. Then, in
the second sentence, this ontological ground is substituted in
the actual situation of exchange. Moreover, when "to command" becomes "to impose upon," one senses that Hobbes is
not far.

§ 2 (following):

> *What is bought with money or with goods is* purchased *by labour*
> *as much as what we acquire by the toil of our own body. That money*
> *or those goods indeed save us this toil. They contain the value of a*
> *certain quantity of labour which we exchange for what is supposed at*
> *the time to contain the value of an equal quantity. Labour was the*
> *first price, the* original purchase money *that was paid for all*
> *things. It was not by gold or by silver, but by labour, that all the*
> *wealth of the world was* originally purchased; *and its value, to*
> *those who possess it, and who want to exchange it for some new*
> *productions, is precisely equal to the quantity of labour which it can*
> *enable one* to purchase or command.

Comment: If rhetoric is the art of persuasion, and if repetition is a
powerful rhetorical device, then this passage is a set of rhetorical
variations on a theme of Hume: "Everything in the world is
purchased by labour" ("Of Commerce," in Rotwein 1955, p. 1;
quoted in Bonar 1927, p. 116). Smith plays with great effect with
two meanings or nuances of "to purchase": to acquire (by toil,
etc.) and to buy: "labour was ... the ... purchase-money."
Notice that the stylistic device is used here to bring into close

proximity, almost to identify, the natural or "original" situation and the contemporary one. Everything was originally acquired by labor or toil. This manner of acquisition is paralleled with the modern way of purchasing with money, that is, labor is equated—rhetorically or metaeconomically—with exchange! At the same time, it is asserted that the "original" acquisition has not disappeared but underlies the modern purchase, for obviously goods must be produced before they can be exchanged. The same stylistic device is used elsewhere. Thus chapter viii opens with: "The produce of labour constitutes the natural recompense or wages of labour." Remarkably also, we return in this passage from the individual's viewpoint to a global viewpoint. And here a quite solemn effect is reached: we see mankind from its beginnings toiling to produce wealth, that is, money and goods, to the effect that we may be saved the toil. The upshot is that everything is labor, and labor is everything, so that we labor even when we do not but are content with exchanging. A purist would perhaps remark that near the end, *its* refers literally to "all the wealth of the world," actually only to a part of it.

All in all, we have here two definitions of wealth, or value: one, which is rather left implicit, refers to the "original" situation, and we can complete it by what we have excerpted at the beginning from chapter vi: value consists in the quantity of labor that enters into the production of a good; I shall call it the definition of value *in production*. The second definition is, on the contrary, clearly expressed: the value of a good consists in the quantity of labor that one can get in exchange for that good. It defines value *through exchange*. As it contains labor + exchange, it is clearly superior, for Adam Smith, to the definition *in production* alone; and yet it should not be forgotten that it rests on the latter. At the same time, it is true that the explicit definition alone should count. Perhaps the foregoing slightly distorts Adam Smith's thought by interpreting it in the light of his successors, who did attribute to him two definitions of value. The former one is hardly a definition at all, as it is left implicit. We should not forget that exchange is present even in the original state. One first posits that the beaver is exchanged against two deers, and then only one proceeds to suppose that "the quantity of labor necessary to acquire" a beaver is double that necessary for acquiring a deer. In this case value in production and value through exchange coincide; but Adam Smith knows in advance that they will not always do so, and therefore he retains only the second formula, the only one, according to him, that applies to the civilized state.

If I may introduce a comment within the comment, it will be about the relation to Hume of this remarkable first page of chapter v. We noticed that the hammered-in assertion that value consists in labor was in keeping with a statement of Adam Smith's valued friend David Hume. We also noticed that the picture of the state of nature which in Adam Smith underpins this assertion was—in keeping with Hume's aversion for the notion—called by another name, the "early and rude state of society," and relegated to the subsequent chapter, although it is clearly implied by the repeated reference to the "original" situation in the passage last quoted. It is likely, then, that Hume's authority is one reason why Adam Smith obscured his logic and resorted to trenchant affirmation. We may surmise that, were it not for this circumstance, the continuity with Locke would have appeared still more clearly.

§d The two following paragraphs are remarkable, but I shall not consider them in detail. In the first comes the expected reference to Hobbes and to economic power, and the exchangeable value is finally equated with the power to purchase or command that it conveys to the owner. "Wealth, as Mr. Hobbes says, is power," says Smith. I am not sure that Hobbes does not say something markedly different, at least in *Leviathan*. True, we find in an enumeration (p. 44): "Riches, are Honourable; for they are Power"; but a slightly anterior passage (p. 41) that explains the identification is restrictive and, I should say, quite traditional: "Also Riches joyned with liberality, is Power; because it procureth friends, and servants: Without liberality, not so ... " (quoted by Cannan in a note). What Smith is doing here under the cover of Hobbes is to define a new kind of power, economic power. In that context, "to purchase" encompasses "to command," that is, the subordinating dimension, so that, by successive identifications, "to purchase" has acquired a whole gamut of meanings: to acquire by toil and trouble, with money, by an order based on money. In the next paragraph he raises the difficult question of the quantitative comparison of the different sorts and degrees of labor, and he winds up with a reference to "the higgling and bargaining of the market," which is asserted to carry out this difficult operation, if not in an exact, at least in a sufficient manner. Here, as in Locke's majority rule, once the metaphysical principle is set, we can be sure that the "business of common life" (Smith) will care for its application.

A little further on, Smith comes back to labor as a *measure* of value. In order to measure magnitudes of a given kind, there must be a standard, and he claims to find in labor the standard by which to measure values:

§ 7 (middle, p. 136):

> *Equal quantities of labour, at all times and places, can be said to be of equal value to the labourer. In his ordinary state of health, strength, and spirits; in the ordinary degree of his skill and dexterity, he must always lay down the same portion of his ease, his liberty, and his happiness. The price which he pays must always be the same, whatever may be the quantity of goods which he receives in return for it.*

> *Labour alone, therefore, never varying in its own value, is alone the ultimate and real standard by which the value of all commodities can at all times and places be estimated and compared. It is their real price; money is their nominal price only.*

Comment: Marx has characterized this "confusion": "the measure of value, as an immanent measure which constitutes at the same time the substance of value, is confused with the measure of value in the sense in which money is the measure of values. And Smith searches for a commodity which, having an invariable value, can be used as a standard of value." Or again, "He claims, for the varying value of labour, what is true of labour itself and its measure, labour time [the duration of labor]: in fact the value of commodities is always proportional to the labour time realized in them, whatever the value of the labour" ("Mehrwert," *Werke*, 26.1:48; French trans., 1:173; see also above, note 5 to chapter 6). For us, it is interesting to see why and how Adam Smith came to make this blunder. Why? His concern was to posit labor as the *substance* (as Marx says) of value: a self-sufficient entity is more solidly established if it can be shown to be stable, unvarying, constant through time. The notion of quantities of labor led by association to the notion of measure. Now a measure or standard belongs to the same kind of magnitude as the magnitude measured by it: a length is measured by a standard of length; therefore, to measure value, labor seemed to be (to have) a value. A strange reversal took place, brought about perhaps through the absolute meaning of "value" (wealth, property!). How? It is his recourse, already noted, to the individual subject or agent which this time led Adam Smith astray: he detached "value" completely from the social setting, and, resorting once more, perhaps unwarily, to the isolated man of nature, he asked him about the value of his labor.

Myrdal (p. 74 and n. 26) takes this passage as stating the classics' general assumption of labor as "psychological disutility" and links it with "a metaphysical conception of man's place in nature. 'Man' was always used in the singular." Smith's man of nature is a Christian for whom work is a curse, and, as is well known, psychology was the ordinary expression of eighteenth-century individualism. Actually, Cannan gives (Smith 1904, p. xxxvii) a quotation from Hutcheson that shows Adam Smith to be in line with his master: "A day's digging or ploughing was as uneasy to a man a thousand years ago as it is now." The same passage stresses a constancy in labor and subsistence goods, while the variation of money hides the phenomenon. We touch here a more general connection of the stress on labor: the shift from "monetary analysis" to "real analysis" (Schumpeter 1954, pp. 276 ff.).

In the text immediately following, Smith is actually obliged to reintroduce the economic value or price of labor. To avoid contradiction, he does it with all sorts of precautions, first from the point of view of the person who "employs" the worker, and then by speaking, not of value, but of the "price" (real and nominal) of labor in a "popular sense," returning in the end to the point of view of the laborer: "The labourer is rich or poor, is well or ill rewarded, in proportion to the real price ... of his labour." This time, this "real price" is the true, social price (in goods), and Smith will adopt this view, at least implicitly, in the sequence. The reader is asked to bear in mind these last points in connection with a discussion to come. The muddle is complete: for regarding commodities, their real price is their price in labor, their nominal price their price in money; but regarding labor, its (popularly) real price is its price in goods (hardly determinable as such). And yet the author goes on equating the

two: "The distinction between the real and nominal price of
commodities and labour is not a matter of mere speculation."

Part Two

§ e   CHAP. VI. OF THE COMPONENT PARTS OF THE PRICE OF COM-
MODITIES

General construction: The first part of this chapter, up to § 10,
inclusive, is clearly and emphatically articulated into three sections dealing respectively with: (1) the state of nature, or rather
"that early and rude state of society" (§§ 1–4); (2) the modification introduced by the accumulation of stock (§§ 5–7); (3) the
modification introduced by the appropriation of land (§8), to
which is added a recapitulation (§§ 9–10).

The first section opens with the paragraph relating to deer and
beaver I quoted at the beginning. The conclusion asserts that, in
that primitive state, the quantity of labor contained in the good
(say, one beaver) is equal to the quantity of labor obtained
through exchange (say, two deer). In our terms, value can be
defined in production as well as through exchange. We must
become familiar with the formulation:

> In this state of things, the whole produce of labour belongs to the
> labourer; and the quantity of labour commonly employed in acquir-
> ing or producing any commodity is the only circumstance which
> can regulate the quantity of labour which it ought commonly to
> purchase, command, or exchange for.

Comment: "Acquiring or producing": only a nuance (see above,
p. 190); "commonly" (repeated) emphasizes that the statement
bears on the social average and not on a single, possibly exceptional case (cf. Marx's "socially necessary" labor). We had previously (chap. v) "to purchase or command"; here Adam Smith
adds: "or exchange for." Obviously, he wants his formula to be
exhaustive. I would point to a general aspect of the formula:
clearly, its complication does not result from the case at hand,
which could be put more simply. It results from its orientation to
the more complex cases which are yet to come; it is tailored on
them, not on the simple, natural, or original case. This is seen
also from the use of the word "labourer," for, after all, the
primitive hunter can be called a laborer only by a rather far-

fetched anticipation; and if we call him a laborer, we should add that he is also his own employer. He is a laborer only thanks to a stress on the physical aspect of production at the expense of the human relation aspect of production.

The second section, which deals with the situation created by the accumulation of stock, ends with a conclusion that strictly parallels the preceding one (I emphasize, in roman type, all that is common to the two formulas):

> In this state of things, the whole produce of labour *does not always* belong to the labourer. *He must in most cases share it with the owner of the stock which employs him. Neither is the* quantity of labour commonly employed in acquiring or producing any commodity, the only circumstance which can regulate the quantity of labour which it ought commonly to purchase, command, or exchange for. *An additional quantity, it is evident, must be due for the profits of the stock which advanced the wages and furnished the materials of that labour.*

Comment: "Always," "in most cases": precaution to exclude the case when the laborer is his own employer. This is hardly necessary, but it shows the care Adam Smith takes of covering all possible cases. We see now the reason for the complicated formula, "the quantity of labour ... *employed* ... is not *the only circumstance.*" It is really in this case (and in the third one, below) that this formula is generated, and it is applied backwards, as it were, to the "original" situation.

The third section, dealing with the consequences of the appropriation of land, is very short in the current version. But we know from Cannan (n. 7) that the last two sentences of the paragraph have replaced a much longer development in the first edition, which contained, as expected, the following:

> In this state of things, *neither the* quantity of labour commonly employed in acquiring or producing any commodity, *nor the profits of the stock which advanced the wages and furnished the materials of that labour, are* the only circumstances which can regulate the quantity of labour which it ought commonly to purchase, command, or exchange for; *and the commodity must commonly purchase, command, or exchange for, an additional quantity of labour, in order to enable the person who brings it to market to pay this rent.*

Comment: One detail: near the end, "an additional quantity of labour" throws light on the more elliptical "an additional quantity" in the section above. I quoted this passage from the first edition to show that the parallelism that is found now between the conclusions of the first and second sections then extended to the third. It is not complete in my excerpts: the first part, in sections 1 and 2, which I shall call Part A: "the produce of labour belongs [or: does not belong] to the labourer" is lacking in section 3, but this passage was added, so Cannan tells us, in the second edition (in sections 1 and 2), so that in the first edition the three sections actually closed with the same form of words (Part B): "the quantity of labour commonly employed ... is [or: is not] the only circumstance."

§f Now, the central problem for us arises from the apparent discrepancy between Part A and Part B of the statements, as read most conveniently in section 2 above. From this point of view, differences between the text of the first edition and the definitive text dating from the second edition fall into two kinds: changes made in section 3 are obviously related to the ambiguous place of rent in the *Wealth* as a whole, and as such they are marginal for our present concern. Smith showed from the start his animadversion toward the landlords who, "like all other men, love to reap where they never sowed" (ibid.) and left no doubt that rent was subtracted from the produce of labor: "[The labourer] must give up to the landlord a portion of what his labour either collects or produces" (ibid., in the definitive text). Yet, in the first edition, rent was given as "a third source of value" (Cannan, p. 52, n. 7). Smith must have sensed the incongruity of this statement, not only in the passage, but in connection with another view of rent by which it is not even a proper component of price but its effect (chap. xi, end of introductory part; Cannan, p. 147): to have rent as a dubious component of price is more than enough, without making it a "third source of value"! All this is not absolutely irrelevant for us, but, due to the heterogeneity of rent in relation to wages and profit in this school of thought, it is only marginally relevant. Let us then concentrate on the conclusion to section 2, as quoted above.

We see a discrepancy between Part A and Part B: Part A seems to say that profit is deducted from the produce of labor, Part B that profit is an independent source of value or, at any rate, of price. Part A is reinforced by an unambiguous statement found on the preceding page (§ 5): "The value which the workmen add to the materials, therefore, resolves itself into two parts, of which the one pays their wages, the other the profits of their employer." Now, we know that the discrepancy was not found in the concluding sections in the first edition, which had only Part B, and that the author added Part A in the second edition. It would then seem that he was not aware of any discrepancy. On closer inspection, however, it seems more likely that he was; for, Cannan tells us, Part A is taken over from the the first lines of chapter viii, on wages, and we observe that the same chapter has, only one page further on, another formula that echoes the one just quoted (chap. vi, § 5): "He [the master] shares in the produce of their labour, or in the value which it adds to the materials." It is clear, then, that Adam Smith, while preparing the second edition, wanted to introduce a statement of the kind and that he avoided the more articulate phrase in favor of the one that does not refer explicitly to value.

Moreover, the statement of Part A originates straightforwardly from the "original" state: the whole produce of labor belongs to the laborer (sic), while the statement of Part B, as we observed, originates from the civilized or contemporary scene and is generalized to the "original" state. It appears then that the modus operandi of Adam Smith on this point is the one on which we have already insisted: he brings as close as possible to each other, as if to amalgamate them, a normative view and an empirical view: considered from the state of nature, the only source of value is labor, the produce of which the workman is obliged to share with the capitalist and the landowner; considered from contemporary observation, the actual price of a good (the "natural" price, in chapter vii) falls into wages, profit, and rent. As Marx put it, the first viewpoint is esoteric, the second exoteric; the first unveils the real nature of the process, the second describes the appearances (cf. p. 91, above). For there is no doubt that what Adam Smith transcribes in Part B is an equation like:

$$\text{Wages} + \text{Profit} \ (+ \text{Rent}) = \text{Price (or Value)}.$$

g   Since Ricardo and after Marx, what we do not understand is why Adam Smith transcribes this in language that contradicts

Part A. Coming after Marx, we understand easily that, in this trend of thought, there is no identity between wages and the value created by labor, which can be analyzed into wages and a "surplus value" that accounts—roughly—for profit and rent. In the first approximation (and, be it well noted, only thus) Adam Smith was misled by his previous confusion between labor as the source of value and labor as a value (or "the value of labour"—chapter v and above). On the level of observation the value of labor consists in its wages; and, as all values are in the last analysis quantities of labor, the above equation is rewritten:

$$Q1 + \text{Profit} \ (+ \ \text{Rent}) = Q2 \qquad (1)$$

where $Q1$ is the quantity of labor corresponding to the wages, the "quantity of labour commonly employed in acquiring or producing any commodity," and $Q2$ is the quantity of labor corresponding to the value of the commodity, the quantity "which it ought commonly to ... exchange for." A textual comment is inevitable about the shift in meaning of the expression "the quantity of labour commonly employed in acquiring or producing any commodity" from the first section of this chapter, where it refers to direct acquisition in the "original" state (acquiring a deer) to the present text, where it refers to the wages paid to the worker for the indirect acquisition of the product by the master. (Here again an exchange is interposed.) It is perhaps the point at which the link between ontology and actuality is the most strained. Yet we can understand that Adam Smith has been driven to this formulation because he wanted to bring close together the original and the modern situations while preserving two aspects that were apparently essential for him: exchange, and the actors' roles. We saw in passing how the original situation differentiated itself, so to speak, into the modern one: what had been labor became labor + exchange, and the hunter became two persons, namely, the worker *and* the employer. Part A, we found, expresses the continuity between the original hunter—called for the purpose "laborer"—and the modern laborer: the subject under consideration keeps the whole produce of his labor in the former case, and not in the latter.

We now see that Part B is founded on a similar continuity, this time the partial continuity between the original hunter and the modern employer. What they have in common is a "role" consisting of both investing a certain "quantity of labor"—actual labor in one case, a salary in the other—and of subsequently *exchanging* the produce of that "labor" on the market.

We know that Adam Smith has added Part A in the second edition. It means that he wanted to mark more completely the double continuity in relation to the actors: from the hunter to the worker as producer, from the hunter to the employer as "purchaser" and exchanger of the produce.

As soon as the value of the labor embodied in a commodity is identified with the wages received by the worker who made it, it cannot be maintained that the value of the commodity is identical with the value of the labor embodied in it (Smith's first definition of value), but even then the value of the commodity is equal to the quantity of labor against which it is exchanged (second definition, through exchange). Here is the reason, which Ricardo could not see, why Smith preferred his second definition to the first: it alone allowed for application to the contemporary scene. In other words, what is essential in equation (1) is: " $\ldots = Q2$," and this is the main reason for Smith's unwieldy formula. That such is, in effect, the movement of his thought is shown in § 9, which follows immediately our third section:

> The real value *of all the different parts of* price, *it must be observed,* is measured by the quantity of labour *which they can, each of them, purchase or command. Labour measures the* value *not only of that part of* price *which resolves itself into labour, but of that which resolves itself into rent, and of that which resolves itself into profit.*

Comment: (A note: the relation between "value" and "price" in this passage is very much that between the ontological ground and the actual transactions.) In other words, labor encompasses everything, including profit and rent, once it is taken as a *measure*. This triumph is tautological: it follows from the second definition of value and merely restates the equation in different words, yet the resort to the level of "measure" gives it an air of being definitive.

It looks very much as if the complications of Adam Smith's theory of value had their source in the few paragraphs of chapter vi that we have just studied and in the difficulty he experienced in squaring his ontological theory with the actual transactions he wanted to describe. I conclude that this difficulty explains two features of the theory: (1) the preference for the definition of value through exchange, as the definition of value in production could not cover, in Adam Smith's eyes, the contemporary case; (2) the conception of labor, not only as the substance, but as the technical measure of value, as alone able to encompass the apparently heterogeneous elements of profit and rent and thus to vindicate the ontological thesis.

This brings to an end our textual inquiry. The final question of why Adam Smith did not go further, as did his followers, Ricardo and Marx, in the imposition of the ontological thesis on the empirical datum is reserved for the text.

Notes

Chapter 1. A Comparative Approach to Modern Ideology

1. According to Nur Yalman (1969), the Islamic societies of the Middle East are—or were until recently—equalitarian but not individualistic. I observe that equality did not, presumably, extend to non-Muslims; equalitarianism was not an overall value. Yet I do not intend to brush away the difficulty that Islamic civilization presents, at first sight, to my generalization. I prefer to leave the question open. On the level of ultimate values, it can be argued that this is a case of individualism. Conversely, if we shift the focus from ultimate scriptural values to one particular society belonging to that civilizational complex and to the principles that can be abstracted from that society as it works, we shall probably take it as holistic. But then, by the same token, a European society, say, in the nineteenth century, might well fall into the same class.

My first excuse for not having tested my hypothetical generalization on this case is its difficulty for the nonspecialist, due in part to the wide variations within the complex (cf. Clifford Geertz, *Islam Observed*, 1968). At the present stage I must rest content with three remarks. First, the analysis of modern ideology that I propose does not actually depend on the universality of holism in traditional societies; it is enough that the type exists for the contrast to be drawn and to be applied. The possible existence of a third type would only make the matter more complex, even if significantly so. As I state in the text, the present attempt represents merely the beginning of a comparative study. Second, the case appears much less problematic if one shifts consideration from the single feature, individualism, to the modern complex of features, as mentioned later in the text. Third, the problem can be seen in the different paths taken by two civilizations that developed under the aegis of two religions relatively very close to each other, Christianity and Islam. Certainly the contrast has often attracted attention, but it would perhaps benefit from the wider background sketched here. At any rate, the harder way is open, of a comparison similar in its inspiration to that which I applied to India, beginning with fieldwork and issuing in a study of the modern development, seen this time against the background of Islamic civilization.

2. Actually, I am perhaps only reviving a previous approach. Apropos the Scholastics, Schumpeter mentions (1954, p. 85) the universalist

school of K. Pribram and O. Spann and anticipates the present study: "I do not hold that the categories Universalist-Individualist are useless for purposes other than ours. Important aspects of economic thought, particularly in its ethico-religious aspects, can perhaps be described by means of them" (see also ibid., p. 784 n.). I did not know of this trend of thought until I hit upon the passage in Schumpeter, and to this day my knowledge of it is still incomplete. Yet there is certainly this essential difference: my view is purely descriptive, analytical, and comparative; it is neither dogmatic nor normative. (See below, chap. 7, n. 1.)

3. While summing up the intellectual interaction between India and the West in the nineteenth century, I was led to write: "India integrated everything within an unchanged form, while the West widened a movement which was secure in its principles but which did not admit of any permanent framework" (1969, next-to-last section).

Chapter 2. The Conditions of Emergence of the Economic Category

1. Taking especially Heckscher 1955 as textbook, I saw the issue of mercantilism as unproblematic for the present purpose and concentrated on the basic relation. The reader must be referred to Heckscher for many aspects (the unification of the young State, etc.) that are relevant. Some criticisms of this work, however, might lead to the conclusion that I have been wrong in relying on it (Coleman 1969, pp. 97 ff. and passim). It should be observed in the first place that many of the objections bear on the relation between ideas and the rest of economic reality, which is a question beyond our purview. Thus, Coleman finally allows mercantilism to stand as "a trend in economic thought" (p. 117), which I would understand as "a stage in the development towards economic thought"; he admits that "no systematized body of economic analysis existed" then (p. 111); he also insists that mercantilism makes no sense for one who wants to distinguish economic history and political history (p. 101), but this is not my intention.

On the contrary, Viner's critique is central to my thesis (Viner 1958). He denies that plenty was subordinated to power in the literature of the period, and he claims to show that power and plenty were interdependent ends of equal status. Viner's argument, which is erudite and precise, led Heckscher to revise his text (1955, 2:13, 359) while maintaining his general view: "I do not think that there can be any doubt that these two aims [power and plenty] changed places [one being inferior to the other] in the transition from mercantilism to *laissez-faire*" (Coleman 1969, p. 25). This is for me the fundamental issue, which Viner seems curiously to have evaded. His essay warrants a close study that cannot be undertaken here. To deny the preeminence of power, he states (pp. 289–90) that he has not found a single passage "rejecting wealth as a national objective . . . or subordinating it unconditionally to power." Perhaps this is asking more than is required? For contemporaries, there was no incompatibility, but a general congruence, a "long-run harmony between the two" (p. 286). Yet this fact does not make for perfect symmetry, and a close reading will show that Viner himself implies some dissymmetry in the detail. This dissymmetry Heckscher had probably exaggerated. We could, perhaps, do with Viner's recognition that power and wealth are mixed up, in contradistinction to the subsequent period, but Viner would probably not have allowed the difference. Yet the recognition of a hierarchical relation is important for the description of the general development. One more case of a modern scholar of the first rank—and who was by no means indifferent to the history of ideas (see Viner 1972)—being insensitive to the hierarchy of concepts and to the predominant "ether" of a culture?

Viner himself insisted on the limits of laissez-faire in Adam Smith and assembled an impressive list of matters of State intervention in the *Wealth of Nations* (1958, pp. 213–45: "Adam Smith and Laissez-Faire"). On that level, it could be argued that there is less discontinuity than it seems with the mercantilists, and that, contrary to my initial assumption, the choice of the *Wealth* as marking a discontinuity is too arbitrary. As a matter of fact, the *Wealth* has this: "Political economy, considered as a branch of the science of the statesman or legislator, proposes two distinct objects: ... to enrich both the people and the sovereign." Comparatively, the absence of an explicit reference to State power is noteworthy. (Not to appear to slur over it, it is well known that, in discussing the Act of Navigation, Adam Smith declares that "defence ... is of much more importance than opulence" [1904, 1:429]). The passage quoted comes only as the introduction to Book 4, "Of Systems of Political Oeconomy," and not at the beginning of the work. Moreover, Adam Smith's lectures, anterior to the *Wealth* by thirteen years, were entitled, "Lectures on Justice, Police, Revenue and Arms," which shows economics still "embedded" in politics. Together with the very title of the *Wealth* (not "Political Oeconomy," whatever particular reasons may have led to the choice), all these details demonstrate that the *Wealth* represents a new departure, as its posterity also recognized (perhaps for other reasons)—that it marks a notable step in the emancipation of economics. This is so, even if in some regards the break is not complete, since it is in the nature of such transitions to complete themselves only by successive steps.

2. In one page of his chapter on the wages of labor (*Wealth*, 1:vii; 1904, I:81), Adam Smith makes these two apodictic statements: "Every species of animals naturally multiplies in proportion to the means of their subsistence, and no species can ever multiply beyond it," and "The demand for men, like that for any other commodity, necessarily regulates the production of men."

Chapter 3. Quesnay, or the Economy as a Whole

1. There is more in Marx on the subject, in the 1844 "Manuscripts" and later in "Mehrwert," etc. (for the latter, see Meek 1962, p. 266).

2. It should be clear that what follows in the text is no picture of Quesnay's thought; it insists unilaterally—and very schematically—on one component of it. A complete picture should restore the balance

between traditional and modern aspects and in the first place show the close association between ideal aspects and the empirical, statistical inquiry (see the long, detailed questionnaire in Quesnay 1958, 2:619–67). On the philosophical parentage of Quesnay, see Hasbach 1893. Main general references: Quesnay 1958 and Weulersse 1910. Meek 1962 gives the main texts in English and adds valuable essays on the interpretation of the *Tableau*, the influence, etc.

3. Cf. above, p. 5. Bonar makes the point in relation to Harrington: "The domestic empire . . . is founded on dominion, or proprietorship. . . . He who owns the land is master of the people" (1927, p. 88), and he quotes Harrington's forceful words, "Men are hung upon riches of necessity, and by the teeth; forasmuch as he who wants bread is his servant that will feed him. If a man thus feeds a whole people, they are under his empire" (*Works*, 1737, p. 39). Harrington deduces subordination from subsistence; he gives a modern view of a traditional situation.

4. A more complete and detailed study of Quesnay's configuration of ideas should take into account what he owes to Cantillon. Schumpeter points out that, on the level of analysis, there is little in Quesnay that is not in Cantillon, even if what is "explicit" in Quesnay (cf. above, p. 4) is often only "foreshadowed" in Cantillon (1954, pp. 218 ff.). The idea that agriculture alone is productive was already in Cantillon, and also the idea of a circular flow of the "produce of the earth" which Quesnay elaborated in his *Tableau*.

Chapter 4. Locke's *Two Treatises:* Emancipation from Politics

This chapter reproduces in part, with abridgments and minor changes, a lecture published previously (Dumont 1971a) by the Royal Anthropological Institute, London, whose permission is here gratefully acknowledged.

1. We are now fortunate in having at our disposal the critical edition of Locke's *Two Treatises* prepared by Peter Laslett, who renewed the history of the text and to whose substantial introduction to this edition I shall have recourse (Locke, 1963). I designate as I and II the first and second *Treatises*.

2. To compare Locke to Hobbes on this point: as stated above, Locke denied subordination on the ontological level and reintroduced it on the empirical. At first sight, subordination is stressed in Hobbes, and yet there is a parallelism: in *Leviathan* man is not naturally social, that is to say, subordination is—already—not "natural," but it serves to make it the more drastic and secure as something *artificial*, deliberately willed.

3. Schumpeter declines to see any close continuity between Locke's theory of property based on labor and Adam Smith's labor theory of value (1954, p. 120). The question will be taken up when dealing with Adam Smith (below, pp. 97–98).

4. To base a right on a persons's needs proceeds from an idea of social or distributive justice; to base it on the person's work proceeds from an idea of the individual as a self-contained, metasocial entity. In

both cases we may speak of a claim, but the claim refers, respectively, to a social or an individual principle. Cf. Laslett's note on II, § 28 (Locke 1963).

5. See, in general, Macpherson 1962, chaps. 3 and 5; also p. 153 (short notice, Dumont 1965, pp. 37–38).

6. Locke himself writes somewhat similarly: "The Majority have a Right to act and conclude the rest" (II, § 95; see also § 96), cf. *Oxford Shorter Dictionary*, s.vv.

7. The expression *hedonism* and a good deal of the discussion that follows in the text is called in question or made obsolete by an important article unknown to me at the time of writing and kindly communicated by the author himself in 1973 (Aarsleff 1969). Aarsleff presents there a richly documented argument against several theses I had found noteworthy in the recent literature of the subject. He concludes that there is no discrepancy or gap between the *Two Treatises* and the *Essay* regarding the law of nature, or any sizable evolution between the early Essays and the later works but a progress in completeness, and, finally, that there is no conflict in Locke between divine law, pleasure and pain, and the rationality of morals. If all this is admitted, then it follows that it was useless on my part to mention others' views of such discrepancies and difficulties and, more important, that Locke should perhaps not be considered a deist, as I did, but rather a Christian. On the other hand, my main conclusion, that religion plays an indispensable role in Locke's political theory, will be only reinforced. This is one reason why I decided not to modify my text. Other reasons would take too long to be stated in detail. Roughly: (1) the student is always in a delicate situation when the specialists do not agree between themselves; (2) in contrast to the specialists, the occasional student does not maintain, over time, the level of knowledge and perception he strives to attain, with the help of the specialists, at the time of writing. Therefore, he should be wary of altering his text if he is not able to take up the whole study all over again. Yet the wholesale convergence of views between Polin and Aarsleff is certainly impressive, and I have nothing solid to oppose to Aarsleff but only a scruple or a general doubt: Was Locke really as religious as this interpretation makes him? To this, Aarsleff will rejoin that it is the anti-Lockean propaganda of the nineteenth century that prompts one to see him as irreligious or hypocritical (Aarsleff 1971). Yet a doubt lingers.

8. I am reluctant to sever subjective morality from religion, and should rather consider it as a part of religion in general (cf. 1971a, pp. 32–33). Somewhat more widely, Mauss observed somewhere that we should have difficulty in distinguishing morals from religion if the differentiation had not occurred in our culture.

9. Locke 1954; Gough 1950, p. 16, etc.; Polin 1960, chap. 2, etc. Certainly, Locke's religion poses a question for the anthropologist: when the stress goes from faith to reason, we may ask whether we have not left religion, in the current sense of the word, for philosophy: we are at least confronted with an important stage in the transition from group

religion to individual religion. To replace at the global level (as I proposed in 1971*a*) the consideration of religion by that of the configuration of ultimate values helps us to be aware of the continuity of the process, but it does not help in describing its stages. More widely, the question is that of the nature or place of deism and "natural religion," a problem as vast as it is intricate, which cannot be treated here. I see a clue in Sir Leslie Stephen's statement that their opponents do not argue in a manner essentially different from that of the deists (Stephen 1962): there is a sense in which every writer is a deist. I conclude that the group aspect of religion, which was conscious, has not quite disappeared but has become purely empirical. For, when I decide to submit matters of religion to the judgment of my reason, I certainly do away with conscious reliance upon or communion with the group. Only, it so happens that my way of thinking neither fuses with that of all other members of the universal community of free minds nor is utterly different from that of my neighbors and contemporaries. Similarly, in our own times there is less distance between the atheist and the believer in a given environment than they both imagine, and we should perhaps begin by formulating what they have in common.

10. Kendall also thinks he has detected a sleight-of-hand when what is in the state of nature the duty to punish becomes in society a right to punish (1965, p. 78); on this point Polin is more perceptive: he accounts for the change in terms of the inherent paradox of liberty (Polin 1960, pp. 44, 101).

Chapter 5. Mandeville's *Fable of the Bees*: **Economics and Morality**

This chapter has appeared separately in a slightly different version in *Social Science Information* 14, no. 1 (1975): 35–52.

1. There are signs of a renewal of interest in Mandeville. See, among others, *Mandeville Studies*, edited by Irwin Primer (The Hague: Nijhoff, 1975), (International Archives of the History of Ideas, no. 81).

2. See the remarks of A. O. Lovejoy in Mandeville 1924, 2:451–53. Lovejoy sees in Mandeville a precursor of Veblen and of social psychology.

3. The three stages are taken almost verbatim from F. B. Kaye (Mandeville 1924, 1:lxv n.), who adds as other causes of the evolution of society: division of labor, growth of language, and invention of implements and of money.

4. *Moral Sentiments*, II, ii, 3, intro.; Smith 1963, pp. 145–46. The relation between the *Moral Sentiments* and the *Wealth* was discussed in a literature which is alluded to in the only two authors I could see. My point is not absent from Viner, though he puts another aspect in the foreground (cf. above, p. 104). There is "no reliance on sympathy" in the *Wealth* (Viner 1958, p. 226), and, by the operation of "distance" and otherwise, sentiments—except "justice"—are absent in economic relations (Viner 1972, pp. 80–82). On the contrary, MacFie (1967), who has fine things to say on other points (the rational element in "sympathy,"

etc.), refuses to draw any distinction between the two books and thus implies, if he does not quite state (p. 128), that sympathy is also at the basis of the *Wealth*. Actually, some passages he quotes from *Moral Sentiments* establish, I think, the contrary.

5. The translation in the text is my own. The original reads: " ... que nous servirait-il d'abandonner la communion qui nous a produits et qui nous a élevés si, en la quittant, nous ne faisions que changer de maladie?"

6. Jacob Viner wrote an introduction to a new edition of Mandeville's *Letter to Dion* (reply to Berkeley's criticism; reprinted in Viner 1958, pp. 332–42) that touches on the above argument at many points. The *Letter* presents most clearly two elements of Mandeville's thought: his "rigorism" and the role of the State or government. Viner goes further than Kaye: he holds that Mandeville's rigorism was not sincere, and he points out that rigorism was very much on the decline in the period, the *Fable* being "the only work of prominence in the period in which even lip-service was given ... to ascetic standards of behavior for the general population" (Viner 1972, p. 59). In the *Letter*, Mandeville goes so far in advocating the artificial as against the natural harmony of interests as to write, "They are silly people, who imagine, that the Good of the Whole is consistent with the Good of every individual." Yet the form of this statement is such that it does not contradict a moderate assertion of natural harmony (as above, pp. 69–70).

7. There is no Gordian knot, according to Aarsleff (cf. above, p. 209 n. 7).

Chapter 6. *The Wealth of Nations:* Adam Smith's Theory of Value

1. Other versions of Adam Smith's lectures have come to light, but these were not available to me (Viner, in Rae 1965). I scarcely understand the contrary opinion, according to which Quesnay's influence would have been exaggerated.

2. The necessity for the perilous distinction between productive and unproductive labor is an entailment of the stress on production as a particular relation between man and things. A servant does not produce. To this day the category of "services" is uneasily and illogically appended to the major and (in this trend of thought) clear category of "goods."

3. That the theory taken in its context comes from Locke, that is to say was found in Locke, an author whom Smith did not ignore, does not mean that the idea that labor was the source of wealth or constituted wealth was not widespread. Apart from Mandeville and others (cf. Stephen 1962, 2:245, 253–54), we owe to Marx a valuable reference to Berkeley in *The Querist*, 1750, Question 38, which seems to show that the idea was welcome to thinking persons in the period (Marx, "Mehrwert"; cf. note 5, below: in German, *Werke*, 26.1:348; in the French trans., 4:44).

4. Adam Smith thinks of himself as writing from within a developing

economy, whether in the short run or on the scale of the history of mankind. He also notices in his environment the corresponding drive: "the desire of bettering our condition, a desire which, though generally calm and dispassionate, comes with us from the womb, and never leaves us till we go into the grave," the most common means to that end being "an augmentation of fortune" obtained mostly by saving and accumulating (*Wealth*, II, iii; 1904, I:323–24; see Halévy, I:161 and 335, n. 7).

5. There is some uncertainty here, and I must anticipate the difficulty of giving convenient reference for some works of Marx. I worked primarily from a French translation (by Molitor [Paris: Costes, 1924—], not devoid of blemishes) of Karl Kautsky's version (of 1904?). When possible, I checked on and I give the reference to the edition in Marx and Engels, *Werke*, vol. 26, pts. 1 and 2, for our purposes. But the order of the text is very different in the two editions, and I was not always able to find the concordance. The longer developments are in *Werke*, 26.1:40–60; 26.2:214 ff. and 341 ff.

6. Actually there are places where the link between value and price is maintained. Marx cannot do otherwise, for it is from that connection that the very notion of value arises. At the beginning of the "Critique" (1859), commodities are exchanged according to their *exchange value*. In the address to the First International of 1865, called "Value, Price, and Profit," price and exchange value are identified in at least three places (*Oeuvres*, 1:498, 500, 506), and in the first chapter of *Capital* there is a transition from exchange value, defined in the same manner, to *value* pure and simple (ibid., pp. 563 ff., esp. the last section on p. 565, and p. 568, etc.). Thereafter, if I am not mistaken, *exchange value* occurs only rarely, being replaced by *value* alone. Yet occasionally, as about the production of surplus value (*Capital*, book I, section III, chap. vii, § 2; *Oeuvres*, 1:746), where it is stated that "the capitalist buys at its just value every commodity," including the labor power of the worker, it is clear that value and price are not severed. To throw light on this important transition, a more precise study is needed (cf. Baumol 1974, at end).

7. In Adam Smith this difficulty leads to a contradiction (cf. what Marx says of his "instinct," above, p. 91): rent is or is not a constituent part of price. Land is a "monopoly," actually meaning something like "engrossment"—the expression Smith uses when he protests against legal obstacles to the transfer of land. By the way, my explanation of the contradiction regarding value in chapter vi of the *Wealth* is incomplete because I have not taken into account the link with the question of rent.

Chapter 7. From the Revolutionary Vow to *The German Ideology*

1. See Dumont 1970, pp. 134 ff. In a book published in 1923, the theoretician of "universalism," Othmar Spann, anticipated the present study (see above, p. 205, n. 2). He presented a double catalog of individualistic features and "universalistic" (or holistic) features in Marx's

doctrine (*Der wahre Staat*, 1931, pp. 130–33) and showed the former to predominate in some degree over the latter. Spann said that it took him years to see beyond the economic universalism of Marx's socialism to his fundamental individualism. He came to identify it because he was, on the one hand, deeply committed to "universalism" in the German romantic line, while, on the other hand, he encountered Marxism as his archenemy in politics. Unfortunately, his dogmatism and his hostility seriously hampered Spann's penetration of Marx's thought beyond a certain point. His dry catalog of the two kinds of features is followed by an attempt to destroy "the demon Marx." Spann did not understand that our times are ruled by individualism, nor did he admit it as a value. In his zeal for "universalism" he did not realize that any attempt to subdue its opposite could only issue in a combination of the two as disastrous as any other on that level.

2. For reference, each work of Marx will be designated, not by a date of publication, but by a conventional abridged denomination, as here "Einleitung," "Hegel's Critique," etc. Under each of these headings, the bibliography will indicate the edition(s) and translation(s) used. Similarly, the collected works will be designated as *Werke, MEGA, Oeuvres,* etc. More often than not, translations are mine, and literal even if inelegant; reference to a translation different from that given in the text either follows the reference to the German text or is introduced by "cf."

I should have liked to refer mainly to English translations, but I encountered some difficulties in trying to do so, partly scientific, but mostly practical, as I had worked primarily from French translations and/or the German texts. Given the limited purpose of this study, I did not feel committed to give a complete bibliography of the considerable recent literature on the subject, of which I saw only a part and, for the English works, translations especially, often at a late stage in the work. Only a few titles will be mentioned. I particularly regret that I lacked the benefit of two translations: that of the "Manuscripts" by M. Milligan, published in Moscow, and that of the *Grundrisse* by M. Nicolaus (Penguin).

3. The reconciliation of thought and action is implicit in the whole program. A much earlier letter of Marx (to his father, written in November 1837, at age nineteen) shows it to have been an abiding urge of the young Marx. Moreover, the wish to reconcile thought and action, to insure their coincidence or their unproblematic companionship is by no means special to Marx alone. Such a need is deeply felt in our period among intellectuals and is perhaps one of the main motives of such persons' adherence to Marxism or similar doctrines. Raymond Aron mentions that, between Kant and Hegel, Marx's followers generally prefer the latter, and he refers, among others, to Lucien Goldmann's statement that personal commitment and wholesale perception of the historical process are inseparable (Aron 1967, pp. 180–81). This synthetic aspect, which is problematic for the philosopher, constitutes a strong attraction, especially for our European youth. There is nothing

the young student is more averse to than the sober proposition that thought and action have for a long while ceased to go hand in hand in modern culture and that, as a consequence, whoever wants to keep a clear head must beware of confusing them.

To understand historically and comparatively this deep-seated need, which might seem infantile in our post-Nietzschean era, I should draw attention to a basic difference between philosophy and religion. Both, as Hegel said, give (or strive to give)—as contrasted to science—a global view of man's universe, the one in rational terms, the other in bizarre "representations." What Hegel did not see is that the reason lies in the greater complexity of the religious representation, which includes the dimension of action in a way philosophy does not: it *authorizes, justifies, and includes the action of man* (ritual and nonritual action). I cannot demonstrate the point, which can be endlessly debated unless the level on which it holds is realized. I can only illustrate it by pointing to Kant, who gave to the distinction of the two dimensions its definitive form, and to Hegel himself. Hegel certainly strove to transcend the distinction. That he did not succeed can be seen immediately from two observations: (1) his followers parted into two camps, which shows that the course of action resulting from his philosophy was ambiguous; (2) Marx himself criticized Hegel precisely on that score, and took up the task again, as the "Einleitung" tells us: this time, the dimension of action was truly embedded again in the representation, which Tucker is absolutely right to characterize as myth for this very reason (Tucker 1972, p. 227). That the revolutionary project partly determines the historical or social description—i.e., in nonreligious terms, it distorts it—is sufficiently obvious not to occupy us. It might be possible to derive Marx's communist society from Hegel's State by applying to it an "operator" consisting of the vow with all its implications. At any rate, it is certainly the case that many views of Marx are thus derivable from Hegel, as we shall see occasionally. There is room here for extending the "transformational criticism" to its adepts, and it would be, moreover, a "critical criticism." (See note 4 for the term.) The same dimension of action intervenes also at the level of the basic conceptions and underlying assumptions, where its play is hardly suspected, and it is part of the present task to begin bringing such aspects to light.

In the light of the distinction I propose between religion and philosophy, the widespread contemporary need to reestablish an immediate relation, as close as possible to an identity, between thought and action is easily set in perspective. It expresses the need to return to the easy persuasions of religion; it mirrors the refusal of the modern *Entzauberung* of the world, in particular, the incapacity of many contemporary atheists to live up to a de-god-ed world. We are far from the times of Plutarch: "Rulers are not usually very fond of their Logos, for by increasing their knowledge it might hamper their power to rule and cramp their action" ("To an Uneducated Ruler," *Moralia*, trans. H. N. Fowler).

4. The recent literature insists on Marx's application of the Feuer-

bachian "transformative criticism" or "transformative method." Cf.
Tucker 1972, index, s.v. Criticism; Avineri 1968; McLellan 1969; O'Malley trans. The English reader can now read in translation the "Critique"
and the "Einleitung" as well in O'Malley's excellent edition ("Hegel's
Critique").

5. There is at least one passage in which Marx seems to say that the
relation to the whole (actually, the State) of particular features is their
major determination. It is in his long discussion of entailed landed
property "burdened with primogeniture," that is, the restricted inheri-
tance (majorat) commended by Hegel as insuring political independence (ibid., p. 312; trans., p. 107). It is said there that for such particular institutions (einzelne Staatsmomente) "the political state is the sphere
of their universal determination, their *religious sphere*" (Marx's italics).
The last words announce the introduction of the "transformative criticism." It follows: the (real political) constitution is private property. We
thus see what Marx meant by "The political state is the mirror of truth
for the various moments of the concrete state" (O'Malley's translation),
namely, that the truth of the State is in various social institutions; yet in
this same sentence "the concrete state" is the global society. In other
words, Marx refuses to confuse the global society with the political
State, but at the same time he reduces the global society to its "various
moments": there is no whole, because the whole proposed by Hegel is
false.

6. On this point (p. 354) Marx quotes with approval a few lines from
Hegel's addition to his § 270, whose consideration he had postponed in
"Hegel's Critique" (above, p. 120). "The Jewish Question" thus com-
pletes the "Critique" on the relation between Church and State.

7. "Die Feudalität. Die alte bürgerliche Gesellschaft hatte *unmittelbar*
einer *politischen* Charakter." An example of the use of the expression
civil society to designate economic and social relations, nonpolitical relations (here: possession, the family, the sort and manner of work) outside the modern period.

8. We should be thankful to O'Malley for having highlighted the
frequent use in "Hegel's Critique" not only of Gattungswesen, which he
translates as "species-being," but also of several other expressions built
on Gattungs-: "species-will," "species-form," etc. (see his introduction
to "Hegel's Critique," trans., pp. xli ff., where he also refers to similar
compounds in the "Manuscripts"). Such a ubiquitous form of expression requires investigation in relation to the criticism of Hegel. We shall
pursue it in the "Manuscripts."

There is, much later, an interesting discussion of the species (Gattung) and the individual (der Einzelne, to begin with) in "Mehrwert"
(Werke, 26.2:111; quoted by Rubel in Marx's Oeuvres, 1:1613). Praising
Ricardo's scientifically honest recklessness in advocating production for
production's sake, that is, the "*development of the wealth of human nature
as its own end*" (his italics) against Sismondi's and others' edifying concern for the individual, Marx wrote: "This development of the

capacities of the species Man, although it happens first at the cost of the majority of human individuals [*Menschenindividuen*] and of whole classes of men, finally breaks this antagonism and coincides with the development of the individual [*des einzelnen Individuums*]," and, "In the human as in the animal and vegetable kingdoms the advantages of the species always triumph at the cost of the advantages of the individuals." I do not know whether this evokes Darwin (we are now in 1863), but it does Kant, especially in the last passage.

9. Concerning the positions taken by Marx in his previous work as a journalist, O'Malley mentions "the primacy of the individual ... members of the State over against the institutions" ("Hegel's Critique," trans., p. xxiv). Maximilien Rubel devotes a large part of his introduction to this period in the life of Marx (*Oeuvres*, vol. 2). He stresses forcefully what he calls the ethical conviction of Marx's initial stand (p. xlv, especially) and sees in it the great shaping force that determined the general outline of Marx's thought forever afterward. The fact is so obvious that it is hard to understand that Rubel's thesis is not universally admitted.

10. Translation is not easy. For such crucial passages as this, a critical, cumulative edition is badly needed. The first reading of the manuscript, in *MEGA*, has been corrected in *Werke*. Thus, instead of "activity and spirit," one reads more recently "activity and enjoyment" (*Genuss* instead of *Geist*). It sounds better. Moreover—as no one has bothered to remark—in another, quite similar passage, *MEGA* had already introduced *Genuss* but had failed to generalize it in the passage (notes on J. Mill, *MEGA*, I.3:535–36). At the same time, *Werke* does not reproduce a valuable indication of *MEGA* about a change of words by Marx. Recent translators often verify the printed text by checking it against the manuscript, and they tell us that they have corrected misreadings; but as a rule they do not tell us which.

11. I translate "das Gemeinwesen, gesellschaftliches Wesen ... obgleich ... " as "the common being, social being ... even if...." The identification between *gemein* and *gesellschaftlich* as against "my universal consciousness," which obviously stands for *Gattungswesen* ("generic being"), is worth noticing. The text as a whole (two pages, 116–17, in *MEGA*) uses mainly *Gesellschaft, -lich* ("society, social"), but it has also *Gemeinschaft, -lich* ("community, communal"). Together with a note mentioning that Marx substituted in one place the second term for the first, the text affords a clear distinction: *community* implies that the members are gathered and act together, it is given immediately; in contrast, *society* covers the internalized aspect, so that there is society even when the community is not assembled. Thus, the scholar working in isolation is "social," or, again, the individual is "society as thought and felt."

Tönnies's well-known distinction is here reversed in some manner: the community is not internalized (see below, note 12). *Society* is still the general term; except when it is qualified as civil or bourgeois, it is not an individualistic notion—which means that we are still within individualism.

This detail suggests a systematic study of these terms and of the related vocabulary, which I regret not to be able to offer (but cf. note 8, above). At any rate, the reason for the identification with which this note began is clear. To designate the social nature of man, Marx first takes the term he is wont to use, *Gemeinwesen*, but in his vocabulary the term is insufficient to cover the whole extent of man's sociality. To include its internalized aspect, society as immanent in everyone's consciousness, he must add *gesellschaftliches Wesen*. And this is precisely the place where we would use, after Tönnies, *Gemeinschaft*.

12. The antithesis is between *naturwüchsig*, "of natural growth," and *freiwillig*, "of free will." The latter term comes near Tönnies's *Kürwille*, if the former does not correspond to his *Wesenwille* but purely and simply to the absence of "will," of contract.

13. According to McLellan (*The Young Hegelians*, 1969, p. 133), the passage quoted implies a reference to and a parody of Stirner, to whom, it is true, the longer part of *The German Ideology* is devoted. I take the occasion to acknowledge that the present study is incomplete, since it lacks a close consideration of the polemic with Stirner (if only it were less unreadable!) and of the archindividualist himself. The passage quoted is not a stray passage. It corresponds to the general presentation of the proletarian revolution and the subsequent "society": "Only at this stage [of the appropriation of the totality of productive forces] does the occupation of self [or self-activity, *Selbstbetätigung*] coincide with material life, and this corresponds to the development of the individuals [*Individuen*] into total individuals and to the cancellation of all that had grown spontaneously [*Naturwüchsigkeit*]" (ibid., p. 68). Yes, the emancipated individual actually becomes the only totality, and this is the outcome of the modern artificialist project: "The relationships that were until then [socially] determined" are changed into "relationships of the individuals [*Individuen*] as such" (ibid.).

14. What became of the theme of the future abolition of the division of labor in the last works of Marx? At first sight, the record is contradictory, but it may be that there is no real contradiction. On the one hand, the division of labor is studied in detail in the first book of *Capital*, in the sections on manufacture and on great industry, and no doubt is left there about its dehumanizing, crippling character. Great industry is even shown as already outgrowing it, being compelled to introduce "variation in labour," "varied labour"; the final term will be "the suppression of the *old* division of labour" (my italics) (section 4, chap. XV, § ix; *Oeuvres*, vol. 1, esp. pp. 991–93). In the "Critique of the Program of the German Workers' Party," in 1875, in a well-known passage on the "superior phase of the communist society," Marx says that "the enslaving subordination of the individuals to the division of labour" will have disappeared, "and as a consequence, the opposition between manual and intellectual labour" (*Oeuvres* 1:1420; in English, Letter to Bracke of 5

May 1875, *Selected Works,* 2:15). This passage can be read also as refer-ring to the abolition of the old division of labor and not excluding a new "voluntary" division of labor of some kind.

On the other hand, there is evidence that the end of the division of labor has ceased to be the only preoccupation. The passage last men-tioned is mainly concerned with the principle of distribution of work and reward. Another theme is that of shortening the duration of daily work and of increased leisure as a possibility resulting from the in-creased productivity of labor. It appears in the *Grundrisse* (p. 599), in the first book of *Capital,* section 5, at the end of chapter 17, on the rate of surplus value: "The time available for the free development of the indi-viduals is the greater, the more labour [*manual* labor in the French edition] is generalized among the members of the society" (*Oeuvres,* 1:1023). The crowning piece in this trend of thought is a remarkable fragment in the third book of *Capital,* customarily placed in chapter 48, § 3, and that Rubel puts as a conclusion at the end of the whole work (*Oeuvres,* 2:1485 ff.). There, freedom "begins only from the moment when ceases the labour dictated by necessity," "beyond the sphere of material production." Then begins "the blossoming of the human power that is its own end," and therefore "the shortening of the day's work is the fundamental condition of the liberation." This is a mighty step; not only has human life ceased to be conterminous with produc-tion, but also the relation between necessity and freedom is no longer Hegelian but Kantian, in that there is no alienation in the separation between necessity and freedom; but of course we are in the communist society of the future. At first sight, this is quite another liberation than that resulting from the end of the division of labor. Yet, it may simply be beyond the end of the *old* division of labor, especially that between manual and intellectual labor, which Marx certainly never ceased to consider indispensable.

15. Perhaps something similar happens in a passage of the famous section of *Capital* on the fetishism of commodities (I, I, 1, 4) that is of interest also in relation to other themes. I mean the development in the middle of the section, which introduces Robinson Crusoe and com-pares his work with, among others, that of a union of free men having their means of production in common (and not, it should be noted, having suppressed the division of labor). There is a perfect correspon-dence between Robinson Crusoe's *individually* dividing his labor and the union's *socially* dividing labor among its members. Here is one more example (as in Plato or Rousseau) of a homology in the conception of man on the one hand, of society on the other. But what is remarkable is that the exchange that occurs (implicitly, through redistribution) within the union does not alter anything in the process: Crusoe's labor is simply transferred to a corporation as subject. Thus, the passage on Crusoe closes with the words: "All the essential determinations of value are contained there [in the relations between Crusoe and the things which constitute the wealth he has created for himself]." Here, in a nutshell, is much that I have tried to stress: the relation with things is

a matter of the individual subject, and value is essentially independent from exchange (as Adam Smith was still unable to think).

16. It is said about classical antiquity: "It is the communal private property [*gemeinschaftliches Privateigentum*] of the active citizens" as against their slaves, as "the citizens possess only in their community power over their working slaves" (pp. 22–23; trans., p. 9).

17. In the "Einleitung" Marx had called the instant of the revolutionary assumption of power a "moment of enthusiasm" (*Werke*, 1:388).

Chapter 8. The Encounter with Political Economy and Its Reform

1. A French translator still maintained, recently, that Marx here "only sums up and comments." Marx says, in his opening page: "The ordinary salary is, according to Smith, the lowest that is compatible with *simple humanité*, that is, a beastly existence." Adam Smith: "There are many plain symptoms that the wages of labour are nowhere in this country regulated by the lowest rate which is consistent with common humanity" (*Wealth*, book I, chap. viii). The French translation of the *Wealth* that Marx had used (and continued to use until the "Mehrwert") is not responsible, but only Marx's hasty notemaking. (See the notes, *MEGA* I.3:466. Marx uses inexactly an incidental phrase of Smith from p. 138; the statement quoted above is on p. 148 and was not noted by Marx.)

2. One may perhaps generalize from the initial attitude of Marx and explain a recurrent feature of his life as an economic author that puzzles the biographer. Again and again, in planning or proposing publications, Marx underestimates the amount of work he will need to put in, in terms of length, time, and probable difficulty. I suggest this is understandable from his approach and manner of working: at any single moment, he was in the position of someone who had approached the subject unilaterally, as it were, armed with his a priori metaeconomic stand, and who had, as we know, made extensive collections of extracts interspersed with reflections. These extracts were, in the nature of the case, selective, oriented to his initial stand and not to the subject matter as a whole; and therefore, each time that he again took up his work, for purposes of publication, Marx was compelled by his scientific integrity, which it is impossible to overestimate, to widen his view and investigate the whole matter all over again. This is perhaps why he had such an acute feeling of being incapable of publishing a text at a few months' interval: intellectual hunger was no doubt there, and appalling conditions of work, and progressive exhaustion, but that may not be the whole story. The "haunting" character of economics, taken more and more as a science, is perhaps the other side of the medal of ethical commitment.

3. In two other places in his works Marx quotes or paraphrases Mandeville at length (see *Oeuvres*, 2:399–401 and note). In the first book of *Capital*, when dealing with the accumulation of capital (VII, xxv, 1), "the surest wealth consists in the multitude of the laboring poor," and

in a note in "Mehrwert" (*Werke*, 26.1: 363–64) not only is Mandeville quoted in the end as saying that evil is at the root of all progress and is "the great principle that makes us social beings," but he is also reproduced in the two preceding pages on the productivity of crime, which belongs obviously to the "cunning of reason." Mandeville, whether socialist or not, is certainly a Hegelian of a sort, and one can understand Marx's relish (cf. Tucker, 1972, chap. 3 "The Dialectics of Aggrandizement").

4. This will be done later. The main reference is perhaps that given above to "Mehrwert" (p. 215, n. 8), but already in *Misère de la philosophie* (I, ii), referring back from Proudhon to Ricardo, Marx exclaims: "Ne crions pas tant au cynisme...."

5. One cannot help sensing that something fateful is happening around this place where, among other things, "society is produced by man." I do not pretend to understand the whole development perfectly, but a few things are clear: the permanence of social institutions and activities is seen as a circular process reproducing all its elements and itself. This is the "social character of the whole movement." Now, if the principle is Goethe's "at the beginning was the act," and if the act is "production," then the social nature of man is expressed by saying that society produces man and man society. The latter aspect is implicitly important, for if man produces society, he can of course change it. The former aspect—society produces man—is after all less important: an expression of the social nature of man, somewhat forced for the sake of neat symmetry. This surmise is confirmed from a very similar passage in the notes on James Mill, a passage roughly contemporary, perhaps slightly earlier, which is, I think, somewhat obscured in the translations but which I can quote here only incompletely:

> Men, through the activity of their *being*, create, produce, the human *common being*, the social being, which is ... the being of each and every individuum. Therefore, this *true common being* ... appears through the need and egoism of the individuals, it is produced immediately through the activity of their existence. It does not depend on man that this common being exists or not; but so long as man does not acknowledge himself as man and has not organized the world humanly, this *common being* appears under the form of *alienation*. (*MEGA*, I.3:535–36)

Of course, it has to be so, for man is the only real producer. The process is empirically cyclical but logically linear. Society is, rather, the by-product—albeit important for them—of the "need and egoism" of individual men. Man is a social being empirically, but this is the effect of his primary constitution as individual. Perhaps we get hold here of the true articulation between the rapturous sociological declarations of the "Manuscripts" and the individualist, economic creed that will flourish in *The German Ideology*. And at the same time we grasp, once more, the primacy in Marx of the artificialist, revolutionary postulate over against a true recognition of the social nature of man.

6. One has the impression that the word *whole*, as substantive or adjective, is remarkably frequent in the *Grundrisse* as compared with the early works, as is also the notion of the interdependence (*Zusammenhang*) of the parts, or the metaphor of the organism.

7. I was unaware, when noticing very much the same relation, of reproducing a thought of Marx (1967, last section of section 3).

8. It was probably impossible for anyone to do so in the circumstances, or so we may think, for two reasons: (1) the close links of those ideas with others in Marx's own thought and in the contemporary ideology: in the first place *Gesellschaft*, etc., *Gemeinwesen* with its macro- and micro-sense, etc., and also the Victorian entanglement of the question with that of property and the obsession of primitive communism (cf. my notes in 1970, p. 145, and on Sumner Maine, pp. 112–32); (2) the fact that the distinction was not made later on, till our days, even by people who made related advances, like Tönnies, or who had or could have had the benefit of the latter, like Max Weber or the Durkheimians (see my *Homo Hierarchicus*, 1967, § 3, for some examples).

Works Cited

Works by Marx

MEGA: Karl Marx and Friedrich Engels, *Historische-Kritische Gesamtausgabe.* 10 vols. Moscow, 1927–35.

Oeuvres: Karl Marx, *Oeuvres: Economie.* Edited by Maximilien Rubel. 2 vols. Paris: Bibliothèque de la Pléiade, 1965–68.

Werke: Karl Marx and Friedrich Engels, *Werke.* 39 + 2 vols. Berlin: Dietz, 1957——.

"Einleitung": *Zur Kritik der Hegelschen Rechtsphilosophie: "Einleitung." Werke,* 1:378–91.

The German Ideology: Karl Marx and Friedrich Engels. *Die deutsche Ideologie. Werke,* vol. 3. English translation by R. Pascal, *The German Ideology.* New York: International Publishers, 1947.

Grundrisse: Grundrisse der Kritik der politischen Oekonomie. Berlin: Dietz, 1953. English translation (extracts only), by David McLellan, *Grundrisse.* New York: Harper Torchbooks, 1971.

"Hegel's Critique": *Aus der Kritik der Hegelschen Staatsrecht. Werke,* 1:203–333. English translation, with an introduction, by Joseph O'Malley, *Critique of Hegel's "Philosophy of Right."* Cambridge, Eng.: At the University Press, 1970.

"The Jewish Question": *"Zur Judenfrage." Werke,* 1:347–77.

"Manuscripts": *Oekonomisch-philosophische Manuskripte aus dem Jahre 1844. MEGA,* I.3:29–172; *Werke,* supplementary vol. 1, pp. 467–588. English translation by T. B. Bottomore, "The Economic and Philosophic Manuscripts of 1844," in Erich Fromm, ed., *Marx's Concept of Man.* New York: Frederick Ungar, 1961. French translation by E. Bottigelli, *Manuscrits de 1844.* Paris: Editions sociales, 1969.

"Mehrwert": *Theorien über den Mehrwert. Werke,* 26:1–2. French translation by J. Molitor, *Histoire des doctrines économiques.* 8 vols. Paris: Costes, 1925——.

Works by Other Authors

Aarsleff, Hans. 1969. "The State of Nature and the Nature of Man in Locke." In *John Locke: Problems and Perspectives,* edited by John W. Yolton, pp. 99–136. Cambridge.

———. 1971. "Locke's Reputation in Nineteenth-Century England." *The Monist* 55, no. 3 (July 1971): 392–422.

Aron, Raymond. 1950. *La Sociologie allemande.* 2d ed. Paris.

———. 1967. *Les Etapes de la pensée sociologique.* Paris.

Avineri, Shlomo. 1968. *The Social and Political Thought of Karl Marx.* Cambridge.

Baumol, William J. 1974. "The Transformation of Values: What Marx 'Really' Meant." *Journal of Economic Literature* 12, no. 1: 51–62.

Bonar, James. 1927. *Philosophy and Political Economy in Some of Their Historical Relations.* 3d ed. London.

Bottomore, T. B., trans. 1961. Karl Marx, "Manuscripts." In *Marx's Concept of Man,* edited by Erich Fromm. New York, 1961.

Bréhier, Emile. 1960. *Histoire de la philosophie.* Vol. 2, pt. 1: *Le Dix-septième siècle.* Paris. 1st ed., 1938.

Cannan, Edwin. 1898. *History of the Theories of Production and Distribution in England.* London.

———, ed. 1896. Adam Smith, *Lectures on Justice, Police, Revenue and Arms, 1763.* Oxford.

———, ed. 1904. Adam Smith, *An Inquiry into the Nature and Causes of the Wealth of Nations.* 2 vols. London.

Coleman, D. C., ed. 1969. *Revisions in Mercantilism.* London.

Cottier, G. M. M. 1969. *L'Athéisme du jeune Marx: Ses origines hégéliennes.* Paris.

De Reuck, A. V. S., and Knight, Julie, eds. 1967. *Ciba Foundation Symposium on Caste and Race.* London.

Dilthey, Wilhelm. 1968. *Die Jugendgeschichte Hegels.* Vol. 4 of *Gesammelte Schriften.* Stuttgart.

Dumont, Louis. 1964. "Introductory Note." *Contributions to Indian Sociology* 7:7–17.

———. 1965. "The Modern Conception of the Individual: Notes on Its Genesis and That of Concomitant Institutions." *Contributions to Indian Sociology* 8:13–61.

————. 1967. *Homo Hierarchicus*. Paris. English trans., London and Chicago, 1970.

————. 1969. "Les Britanniques en Inde." In *Histoire scientifique et culturelle de l'humanité, 19ᵉ siècle*, directed by Ch. Morazé, 2:969–1013. Paris.

————. 1970. *Religion, Politics and History in India*. Collected Papers in Indian Sociology. Paris and The Hague.

————. 1971*a*. "Religion, Politics and Society in the Individualistic Universe." *Proceedings of the Royal Anthropological Institute for 1970*, pp. 31–41. London.

————. 1971*b*. "On Putative Hierarchy and Some Allergies to It." *Contributions to Indian Sociology*, n.s. 5:61–81.

————. 1975. "On the Comparative Understanding of Nonmodern Civilizations." *Daedalus*, Spring 1975.

Engels, Friedrich. 1957. "Umrisse zu einer Kritik der Nationalökonomie." In Marx-Engels, *Werke*, 1:499–524. See Marx-Engels, *Werke*.

Fromm, Erich, ed. 1961. *Marx's Concept of Man*. New York.

Geertz, Clifford. 1968. *Islam Observed: Religious Development in Morocco and Indonesia*. New Haven.

Gough, J. W. 1950. *John Locke's Political Philosophy*. Oxford.

Guéroult, Martial. 1930. *L'Evolution et la structure de la doctrine de la science chez Fichte*. 2 vols. Paris.

Gurvitch, Georges. 1963. *La Vocation actuelle de la sociologie*. 2 vols. Paris. 1st ed., 1950.

Habermas, Jürgen. 1970. *Technik und Wissenschaft als Ideologie*. Frankfurt.

Halévy, Elie. 1901–4. *La Formation du radicalisme philosophique*. 3 vols. Paris. English trans., 1 vol., London, 1928.

Hasbach, Wilhelm. 1893. "Les Fondements philosophiques de l'économie politique de Quesnay et de Smith." *Revue de l'économie politique* 7 (September 1893). Cf. *Staats- und Sozialwissenschaftliche Forschungen* 10, no. 2 (1890). Leipzig.

Heckscher, Eli F. 1955. *Mercantilism*. Rev. ed. 2 vols. London. 1st Swedish ed., 1931.

Hegel, G. W. F. 1907. *Hegels theologische Jugendschriften*. Edited by Herman Nohl. Tübingen.

————. 1942. *Philosophy of Right*. Translated by T. M. Knox. Oxford.

————. 1958. *Politische Schriften.* Afterword by J. Habermas. Frankfurt.

————. 1964. *Political Writings.* Translated by T. M. Knox. Oxford.

————. 1971. *Early Theological Writings.* Translated by T. M. Knox. Pennsylvania Paperback.

Hume, David. 1875. *Philosophical Works.* Edited by T. H. Green and T. H. Grose. 4 vols. London.

————. 1878. *A Treatise of Human Nature.* Edited by T. H. Green and T. H. Grose. 2 vols. London.

————. 1955. *Writings in Economics.* Edited by E. Rotwein. Madison.

Hyppolite, Jean. 1955. *Etudes sur Marx et Hegel.* Paris.

Kendall, Willmoore. 1965. *John Locke and the Doctrine of Majority-Rule.* Urbana.

Kuhn, Thomas. 1962. *The Structure of Scientific Revolutions.* 2d ed., Chicago, 1970.

Landes, David S. 1969. *Unbound Prometheus.* Cambridge.

Locke, John. 1954. *Essays on the Law of Nature.* Edited and translated by W. Von Leyden. Oxford.

————. 1963. *Two Treatises of Government.* Edited by Peter Laslett. Rev. ed. Cambridge, Eng.

MacFie, A. L. 1967. *The Individual in Society: Papers on Adam Smith.* University of Glasgow Social and Economic Studies, no. 11. London.

MacIntyre, Alasdair C. 1971. *Against the Self-Images of the Age: Essays on Ideology and Philosophy.* London.

McLellan, David. 1969. *The Young Hegelians and Karl Marx.* London.

————. 1971. *Karl Marx, Early Texts.* Oxford.

————, ed. and trans. 1971. *Karl Marx, Grundrisse* (extracts). New York.

Macpherson, C. B. 1962. *The Political Theory of Possessive Individualism.* London.

Mandeville, Bernard. 1924. *The Fable of the Bees.* Edited by F. B. Kaye. 2 vols. Oxford.

————. 1970. *The Fable of the Bees.* (First part only.) Edited by Phillip Harth. Penguin Books.

Mauss, Marcel. 1930. "Les Civilisations, éléments et formes." In *Civilisation, le mot et l'idée,* pp. 81–108. Centre International de Synthèse. Paris.

————. 1950. *Sociologie et anthropologie.* Introduction by Claude Lévi-Strauss. Paris.

Meek, Ronald L. 1963. *The Economics of Physiocracy: Essays and Translations.* University of Glasgow Social and Economic Series, n.s. 2. London and Cambridge, Mass.

Mill, James. 1808. *Commerce Defended.* 2d ed. London. Reprint, New York, 1965,

Myrdal, Gunnar. 1953. *The Political Element in the Development of Economic Theory.* New York. 1st Swedish ed., 1929.

O'Malley, Joseph, ed. and trans. 1970. Karl Marx, *Critique of Hegel's "Philosophy of Right."* Cambridge Studies in the History and Theory of Politics. Cambridge, Eng.

Parsons, Talcott. 1953. "A Revised Theoretical Approach . . . ." In Reinhard Bendix and Seymour Martin Lipset, eds., *Class, Status, and Power: A Reader in Social Stratification.* Glencoe, Ill.

Pascal, R., ed. and trans. 1947. Karl Marx, *The German Ideology,* Parts I and III.

Polanyi, Karl. 1957a. *The Great Transformation.* Boston. 1st ed., 1944.

————. 1957b. "The Economy as an Instituted Process." In *Trade and Market in the Early Empires,* edited by Karl Polanyi, Conrad M. Arensburg, and Harry W. Pearson. Glencoe, Ill.

Polin, Raymond. 1960. *La Politique morale de John Locke.* Paris.

Quesnay, François. 1958. *François Quesnay et la Physiocratie.* 2 vols. Paris. (Vol. 1, annotated bibliography; Vol. 2, works.)

Rae, John. 1965. *Life of Adam Smith.* With an introductory guide to Rae's life by Jacob Viner. New York. 1st ed., 1895.

Rosenberg, Nathan. 1960. "Some Institutional Aspects of the *Wealth of Nations." Journal of Political Economy* 68 (December 1960): 557–70.

Rotwein, Eugene, ed. 1955. *David Hume: Writings on Economics.* Madison.

Rousseau, Jean-Jacques. 1964. *Oeuvres complètes.* Vol. 3. Paris.

Schumpeter, Joseph A. 1954. *History of Economic Analysis.* Oxford. Reprint, London, 1967.

Scott, W. R. 1937. *Adam Smith as Student and Professor.* Glasgow. (Contains a draft of the *Wealth of Nations.*)

Selby-Bigge, L. A., ed. 1897. *British Moralists.* 2 vols. Oxford.

Smith, Adam. 1896. *Lectures on Justice, Police, Revenue and Arms, 1763.* Edited by Edwin Cannan. Oxford.

————. 1904. *An Inquiry into the Nature and Causes of the Wealth of*

Nations. Edited by Edwin Cannan. 2 vols. London.

―――. 1811–12. *The Theory of Moral Sentiments.* (*Works,* vol. 1.) Reprint, Aalen, 1963.

Spann, Othmar. 1931. *Der wahre Staat.* 3d ed. Jena.

Stephen, Leslie. 1962. *History of English Thought in the Eighteenth Century.* 2 vols. London. 1st ed., 1876.

Strauss, Leo. 1954. *Droit naturel et histoire.* Paris. Originally published in English as *Natural Right and History.* 1949 Charles R. Walgreen Lectures. Chicago, 1950.

Tönnies, Ferdinand. 1971. *On Sociology: Pure, Applied, and Empirical: Selected Writings.* Edited, with an introduction, by Werner J. Cahnman and Rudolf Heberle. Chicago and London.

Tucker, Robert C. 1972. *Philosophy and Myth in Karl Marx.* 2d ed. Cambridge.

Tufts, James Hayden. 1898, 1904. *The Individual in Relation to Society, as Reflected in the British Ethics of the Eighteenth Century.* Part 1 (with Helen B. Thompson): *The Individual in Relation to Law and Institutions.* Chicago, 1898. Part 2: *The Individual in Social and Economic Relations.* Chicago, 1904.

Veblen, Thorstein. 1932. "The Preconceptions of Economic Science." In *The Place of Science in Modern Civilization.* New York. 1st ed., 1919.

Viner, Jacob. 1958. *The Long View and the Short.* Glencoe, Ill. (Includes: "Adam Smith and Laissez-Faire" [1927], pp. 203–45; and "Power versus Plenty in the Seventeenth and Eighteenth Centuries" [1948], pp. 277–305. Also reprinted in Coleman, 1969.)

―――. 1972. *The Role of Providence in the Social Order: An Essay in Intellectual History.* Jayne Lectures for 1966. Philadelphia. (Also available as *Memoirs of the American Philosophical Society* vol. 90.)

Vlachos, Georges. 1962. *La Pensée politique de Kant.* Paris.

Weulersse, Georges. 1910. *Le Mouvement Physiocratique en France.* 2 vols. Reprint, Paris, 1968.

Yalman, Nur. 1969. "De Tocqueville in India: An Essay on the Caste System." Review article. *Man* 4 (March 1969): 123–31. London.

Index

For authors, italic figures signal either quotations or the chapter devoted to the author; for subject matters, italics signal definitions and key passages.